Contents

Acknowledgements

The idea for this book came directly from graduate students in courses entitled 'Language Policy Across the Curriculum' and 'Language Planning in Education' at Master of Education level in Australia and at Master of Educational Administration level in New Zealand. The book responds to the expressed wishes of those students, who were themselves in administrative positions in schools and in school systems, that more material be collated and made available on the development of 'language policies across the curriculum' in pluralist schools. Much of the subject matter of this book is influenced quite directly by my discussions and correspondence with those senior teachers and practising adminstrators in school systems over the years 1984 to 1988. I am especially grateful to those practitioners who have allowed me to quote sections of their tentative or implemented language policies: Heather Bell, John Cockburn, Anthony Ford, Malcolm Glenny, Stuart Harrison, Dave McDonald, and Corallyn Newman.

In bringing the book into its final form I have benefited greatly from the scholarly criticism of the following people: Glynnis Cropp, Graeme Kennedy, Jan McPherson, Bill Tunmer and Noel Watts. Although I have not always heeded their advice to the full, the book is much the better for their criticism. In particular Jan McPherson's help has been invaluable: in writing a significant section for Chapter 9 of the book; and her work as Research Officer collaborating with me on a project for the New Zealand Education Department: 'Language Policy Across the Curriculum'. The New Zealand Education Department's generosity in funding that research also needs acknowledging as does the liaison work of the Department's Research and Statistics Officer, Janet Burns and our project's Advisory Committee.

My colleagues and family have been long-suffering in the final months of 1988 as the deadline for the book's completion came and went. My thanks too to the staff at Multilingual Matters for their help and encouragement and to staff of the School of Education at Bristol University where final touches were made to the manuscript.

David Corson
Massey University, New Zealand

Glossary of terms and abbreviations used

additive bilingual education: a form of schooling in which the student's (majority or minority) mother tongue is maintained while adding competence in another language (see Chapters 6, 7 and 9).

analytic competence: the ability to use language for thinking and for solving problems (see Chapter 5).

codes: different languages or significantly different varieties of the same language (see Chapter 2).

communicative competence: includes knowing the alternatives and the rules for appropriate choice between the many codes, registers and styles of a language. One individual in a complex language community will not be able to produce the full range of varieties that its language displays. Chapter 8 provides a detailed discussion of the sub-competencies that go to make up communicative competence.

context: either the location of a word or other fragment of language amid other words (verbal context), or the total setting in which language use occurs on a given occasion (context of situation).

dialect: a regionally or socially distinctive variety of a language, identified by a particular set of words and grammatical structures, and in its spoken form by a distinctive pronunciation or accent (see Chapter 9).

discourse: language in use, usually a stretch of language larger than a sentence.

domain: a group of institutionalised social situations typically constrained by a common set of behavioural rules.

first phase SL students: those students of a second language who are functionally unable to cope with the language demands of a normal classroom (see Chapter 7).

FL(T): foreign language (teaching).

function: the role language plays in the context of society or the individual. Example: 'language "functions" to communicate ideas, to express attitudes etc. and these are some of its functions' (see Chapter 5).

genre: a purposeful activity of a specific kind in which speakers engage. Even quite casual conversations, like an encounter in a service setting or in a public utility, have an overall linguistic pattern or shape that is relatively distinct and relates to the achievement of some socially determined goal.

interlanguage: a language pattern of rules and responses, integrating aspects of the first and second language, that an SL language learner operates within while learning the second language. While an interlanguage is not an independent 'linguistic system', it does provide a pattern for the learner which the teacher can address and which has some regularity for all language learners moving from and to the same languages (see Chapter 7).

interpretative repertoires: shared abstract representations that provide an agreed 'code' for verbal intercourse between people of similar backgrounds and experiences. They allow mutual understanding and a stable view of the world that makes up group mind for those who are members of the group. They are things that distinguish cultural groups, the things that groups agree about, and the things that make groups homogeneous (see Chapters 3, 5 and 8).

LAC: language across the curriculum.

linguistic competence: two meanings: (i) an innate readiness and capability for language, possessed by all members of our species because of that membership (*viz*. Chomsky in Chapter 5); (ii) the competence to use and interpret structural elements of a language (one of the six components in 'communicative competence': see Chapter 8).

LPAC: language policy across the curriculum.

majority language: the dominant language used in a nation or society.

minority language: a non-dominant language used in a nation or society by one of the three broad types of linguistic minorities (see Chapter 6).

perlocutionary force: the power that language has to cause 'things' to happen by stating them (e.g. promising, blessing).

registers: varieties of language which are more closely associated with the setting or scene in which they are used (eg. courtrooms, history lessons) than with the people who are using them.

repertoire: the range of codes available to an individual or social group.

second phase SL students: post first phase learners of a second language who can meet the language demands of most class activities (see Chapter 7).

SL(T): second language (teaching).

styles: varieties associated with such social and cultural dimensions as age, sex, social class, and the relationships among participants in a language activity. It especially refers to the level of formality adopted (e.g. colloquial, polite, formal etc).

subtractive (transitional) bilingual education: a form of schooling in which the student's (minority) mother tongue is used as a bridge to learning the majority language but without mother tongue maintenance (see Chapters 7 and 9).

third phase SL students: students who function in their second language at levels similar to comparable native speakers, but who experience difficulties in some academic situations (see Chapter 7).

transitional bilingual education: see 'subtractive (transitional) bilingual education'.

utterance: the basic unit of discourse. It is usually shorter and less complete than a sentence.

varieties: regularly occurring ways of speaking which are associated with particular categories of user (dialects) or of use (registers).

1 Language policy across the curriculum (LPAC)

The task of this book is to offer school administrators and teachers a rational approach for dealing with the language problems that confront modern schools in pluralist societies. The book also provides a means for translating an enlarged view of 'language across the curriculum' (LAC) into practice. The chapters which follow show how this enlarged view of LAC can meet the language planning needs of schools in modern pluralist societies. As content for the book I use subject matter taken from original courses in 'Language Policy Across the Curriculum' taught at 'Master of Education' level in Australia and at 'Master of Educational Administration' level in New Zealand, borrowing examples of successfully implemented policies developed by postgraduate students who were themselves practising school administrators or senior staff. The aim of these courses is a simple one: the production of negotiated, appropriate language policies for implementation within the schools from which students come.

'Language policies across the curriculum' are viewed by a growing number of educationists as an integral and necessary part of the administrative and curriculum practices of modern schools, yet relatively few schools anywhere have seriously tackled the problem of introducing them. One reason for this is that until recently schools in many places have not considered themselves very autonomous institutions; they have accepted direction and control in decision-making in important curriculum areas from outside bodies within the wider educational system. Another reason for this is that schools as organisations are only now beginning to recognise the close link between the organisational arrangements that they offer and the style and quality of the curriculum that they provide for children. A third related reason is that in many places the subject area of Education, right up to the present, has kept the sub-fields of 'curriculum studies' and 'educational administration' separate from one another. Students of 'curriculum studies' on the one hand are very acquainted with

1

the LAC literature and with the doctrine itself; LAC had its origins in the minds of people with a 'curriculum studies' perspective on education. In trying to make LAC work, though, students of the curriculum studies approach have often approached their task in schools in a piecemeal way, attempting to manage change without closely involving the school executive and the administrative process.

Students of 'educational administration' on the other hand have often ignored curriculum questions and typically concerned themselves with structural and system issues to do with the technical side of policy and management. Until recently an understanding of LAC has not been systematically communicated to many students of school administration or to principals. Administrators have often incorrectly seen curriculum ideas, such as those conveyed in the doctrine of LAC, as the individual teacher's responsibility. In making policy responses to the problems of a school, administrators have often avoided curriculum issues of substance and importance to concentrate instead on management policy issues. Yet several points about curriculum policy issues are clear: any 'across the curriculum' issue is by definition outside the range of easy control by individual teachers, who are often confined to one class level or subject specialism; by default the task of dealing with 'across the curriculum' issues becomes the responsibility of the school executive. The way to deal with this task that this book advocates is for schools to operate through closely negotiated policies designed to suit the needs of the school, its clients, and its social context. Perhaps the design, oversight and implementation of these policies, especially a language policy across the currriculum, may be the school executive's major curriculum role in future schools.

What is a 'Language Policy Across the Curriculum (LPAC)'?

For the sake of this book's discussion I am defining an LPAC in the following way:

> An LPAC is a brief document compiled collaboratively by the staff of a school (and possibly by other members of the school community) and to which the staff give their assent and commitment. It identifies areas in the school's scope of operations and programme where language problems exist that need the commonly agreed approach that is offered by a policy. An LPAC sets out what the school intends to do about these areas of concern. It provides staff with direction while allowing them discretion. An LPAC is a statement of action that

includes provisions for follow-up, monitoring and revision of the policy itself in the light of changing circumstances.

If the above definition, setting out the aims and scope of an LPAC, is not clear enough, then a perusal of the summary of topics presented in Chapter 10 should make the possible detail of an LPAC a little plainer. I have used the phrase 'language problems' throughout this book but this does not mean 'problems' in any evaluative sense. The neutral sense of the word 'problems' suggests the normal challenges of life that confront us at every moment of living to which we pose some tentative solution as a response. A solution to a problem is something that we test against the real world as a measure of its adequacy. A language policy is very like a solution in this sense or at least it is a bundle of solutions, each one addressing a different problem and the whole addressing the school's language problems. Language problems are challenges that can be met in this problem-solving way by providing the solutions detailed in a policy. In Chapter 4 I say much more about this approach to policy development at the school level.

Goals and objectives of an LPAC

In pragmatic terms, the goal in any school situation is to provide the best solutions to the important problems that the school confronts. The goal of a school's LPAC is to find and agree on solutions to the language problems that the school has. Most schools have a 'philosophy' or a 'charter' to indicate the kinds of outcomes that are thought desirable for students who are proceeding through them, but this is a different set of ideas from an LPAC. A philosophy should be thought through and assembled prior to any form of policy making. Ideally teachers need to be clear about school philosophy before policy making begins. They need to be clear about the 'forms of development' that they consider to be important objectives of the school. In Chapter 5 I provide a list of developmental aims that seem suitable directions for children to be following in modern schools. However an LPAC is a second order business; it is concerned not so much with where the children in a school, department or class are going, but more with how they are going to get there.

This book assumes that the need for primary schools to have a language policy is already established. It also assumes that subject departments within secondary schools need to have a policy about language. What debate that there has been on these specific assumptions has overwhelmingly supported the view that the two needs exist and that they are enduring needs (for example DES, 1975; DES, 1985). Primary schools, their teachers and their administrators need little convincing about the merits of the language policy position. The request from primary schools is always for information on 'what to do' and 'how to do it', rather than for information on 'why do it'. A language policy is consistent with all that primary schools strive to do in the interests of their pupils' development. People in secondary schools often need more convincing of the merits of having a language policy and there is some organisational basis underpinning their scepticism.

Modern secondary schools are usually very large bureaucracies. They are multi-purpose organisations and are inevitably 'loosely coupled' in their management styles, which means that the 'chain of command' can be highly diversified and rather weak. While decision making on curriculum matters in secondary schools is often dominated by external requirements, that are beyond the direct influence of the school and its teachers, there is often a good deal of autonomy of decision making within subject departments. This is so at least within the guidelines of externally controlled curricula that influence the higher levels of schooling and control the concerns of those at more junior levels. These subject departments in secondary schools are often as large in staff and in pupil numbers as medium-sized primary schools. In large organisations like secondary schools policy making on all but the most routine aspects of management may best be carried out at the level of the small departmental organisation. It is at this level where people know their needs and can talk about those needs in more than mere generalities. They can attempt the trial and error approach to policy making that is recommended in Chapter 4 of this book and not risk too much chaos if the trial does not work out as well as expected. For people working in systems of this kind a 'whole school' language policy may seem over-ambitious. For these people there is much in this book that can be taken up and used by policy makers at departmental level in the secondary school. On the other hand, in pluralist societies there are aspects of secondary school language problems that cannot be handled at departmental level. Much of this book aims to address these problems, since they are difficult matters which affect primary and secondary schools alike.

For secondary schools there is probably a need for both kinds of policy: a language policy across the curriculum for a single department and a unifying language policy across the curriculum of the school as a whole. A policy for a department differs from a schoolwide version: in the former attention is concentrated more on matters of pedagogy and evaluation. But at whole school level an LPAC picks up the problems that are too urgent and too value-laden for individual departments to address singly and in a piecemeal fashion. In examining the conventional first language questions that confront secondary schools and relating them to the need for a policy at school level, Marland's chapter 'The Need for a Language Policy' covers the ground very well and the reader is referred to that source. He talks about 'the bargain' that teachers need to make in a policy 'for the mutual benefit of their subjects and their pupils' (1977: 4). Marland sets out the background to the debate, down to the Bullock Report in 1975. I take this discussion further in Chapter 5 of this book and try in part to update those 'language across the curriculum' questions. Marland also argues the need for whole-school policies and sees a language policy as the most important and most valuable of those policies. What his and other earlier discussions about language policy omitted, however, was much consideration of the social and cultural problems that confront schools today. Insofar as they relate always to language issues, these major problems add a new and an urgent perspective to the more narrow debates about language across the curriculum that were the subject matter of the 1970s.

The Diverse Social and Cultural Contexts of Modern Schools

Set out below are brief case studies describing the social contexts and pupil mix of twelve contemporary schools, some identified by name and some by pseudonym in quotation marks. In later chapters of this book I present extracts from language policies that have been developed for many of these schools. Each is a real educational organisation. They are all located in countries where English is the majority language. What will be clear to readers is that, by changing a few details of nationality here and there, these schools and their language problems might exist in almost any contemporary English-speaking country. It has not always been possible to say this about schools in many English-speaking countries. For example even where very pluralist schools have existed, similar to many of those mentioned below, the complexity and uniqueness of the schools' educational problems have often been disguised by social values supporting cultural uniformity, or they have been kept out of the way by prejudices which are only now beginning to fade in modern countries.

This welcome change in social values presents problems of a new kind for the management of modern schools. On the one hand the problems have always existed for many schools in some societies and have always been addressed by them to varying degrees. On the other hand the urgency of the language-related problems affecting those large societies at national level has moved the issue of language policy in the schools of pluralist societies to the top of the educational agenda.

Some contemporary schools in social and cultural context

'Mullamurra' School is an urban primary school in a high density migrant area of a very large capital city. The school's staff have a long tradition of genuine commitment to the language needs of their students and their second language students in particular. The school's population come largely from low-income family backgrounds; it is ethnically diverse and the ethnic families tend to be transient. Large groups of the children received intensive second language instruction on their arrival in the school five years ago and were judged to be proficient for entry into regular classes. Now these children have reached their final years in the school, but many of them are beginning to have major difficulties in handling the content of the curriculum. A special ESL unit for the school is planned, staffed by SL teachers, but the school as a whole is not prepared for this dramatic change which seems to stand as an indictment on the programme that teachers have been offering over the years. The school has no language policy.

Selwyn College is a state co-educational secondary school with more than 1000 pupils, located in a high socio-economic status area of a large city. It is well endowed with curricular and extra-curricular resources and offers a broad academic and non-traditional curriculum. There is a sprinkling of students from minority cultures and new settler backgrounds and these students tend to come from the relatively privileged sectors of their communities. There is little need for an ESL programme in the school since second language speakers of English are integrated into the mainstream curriculum. There are few speakers of the country's minority language although that situation will change as children from bilingual primary and pre-schools begin to enter secondary schools. The spread of ability levels across the school indicates an unusual clustering of high and low ability students with relatively few middle ability pupils.

School 'Rewarewa' is a large all levels area school in a conservative rural setting. Harsh rural economic conditions have reduced employment prospects for farm and forestry labourers in the district and many of their vacant homes have been filled by social welfare beneficiaries who are transient. Social power in the district is in the hands of a few influential families. New children need to conform to local norms of behaviour to gain acceptance and there is strong respect for authority. Some children spend twelve years in the school, beginning at age five, and they take strong pride in the school. Work on the family farm often has priority over school work although school sport has a high profile and boys' sport is accorded a higher status than girls'. A feeling of helplessness associated with their likely unemployment after leaving school is evident among senior pupils. Language is used by most people in the district to state things as they are rather than to speculate about possibilities. Some teachers approach their task as imparters of knowledge; others see one-to-one remedial tuition as a solution to the school's language needs.

'Heatherton' Primary School has a roll of 450 students. It stands on the outskirts of a large city close to an airforce base. Since the school has been operating for over 50 years there is a strong sense of tradition and loyalty among the parents, many of whom attended the school themselves. This promotes a conservative approach to learning and teaching with an emphasis on conventional standards of success. Fewer than 10% of the students are from minority or new settler backgrounds. Overall language skills among the children are average or above: all children perform competently on oral language and reading inventories. The present school scheme is a collection of outdated articles and resource lists rather than a guide to effective approaches and practices for learning. The LPAC currently being evaluated by staff is a part of the rolling review of curriculum areas that the school is undertaking.

Christchurch Girls' High School was founded over a century ago. The school is highly regarded in its community and the number of applicants that it receives for entry always exceeds the places offered. Its priority is to serve the needs of a specific zone of the city, but as many as half the girls attending come from outside the zone. The school is well endowed with resources. It caters for 800 students including 90 boarders. Many of the students attend the school because of parental preference for a single sex school with high academic standing and a reputation for strong discipline. Most pupils are above average in ability; they have well developed extra-curricular skills and interests; and they show a strong commitment to their schooling. As the parents of the children are largely from middle class backgrounds, before arriving in the school the girls are well prepared for success in conventional schooling. Half enrol at university after leaving the school. The school is monocultural in orientation and even its small enrolment of Maori or Polynesian students prefers a conventional grammar school curriculum. A group of its teachers has been working collaboratively towards a language policy suited specifically to the needs of a single-sex girls' school: the policy aims to promote the language growth of girls in conceptual areas and in expressing themselves in public settings

Rotorua Boys' High is a long-established secondary school with a broad social and ethnic mix among its 800 students. Some 40% of its intake are from the minority Maori culture and as a group these children tend to leave school at an earlier age than the rest. English is the language of instruction and is the mother tongue of all but a handful of the school's children, although 10% of the minority group children are enrolled in optional minority language classes. The school has a sprinkling of high and low academic achievers. Surveys suggest that many of the pupils have difficulty in putting their knowledge into written or oral language to the satisfaction of the school. Current impetus for a language policy comes from the eight staff members of the school's Science Department who are developing their own departmental policy in the hope that it will lead to developments elsewhere. Their policy provides a framework for action to address the particular problems and needs of science students while taking into account the skills and qualifications of the staff. The science courses are heavily dependent on practical work in small groups, with a wide variety of reading materials and much written work which is mainly teacher directed. Some progress is being made in pupil-initiated written work.

St John's Otara is a large urban primary parish school. Children from minority group backgrounds make up 96% of the school's roll, but two-thirds of these are from immigrant cultural groups (Samoan, Cook Island, Tongan) rather than from the country's indigenous minority group. Many of the children are ESL candidates immigrating directly from their Pacific Island homes into the district bringing with them a high proficiency in a Polynesian language. Most of the others have attended pre-schools or playcentres before enrolling. An increasing number of teachers with minority culture backgrounds are joining the staff. Classes are multi-level and *Whanau* (Maori: literally 'family') type in arrangement, allowing children to see themselves as both learners and teachers. Like all the country's schools, St John's is charged with the task of helping in the revival of the minority language and with providing a place for other minority languages in its curriculum. Neither group of parents in the community actively encourages this development. They call for more emphasis on the teaching of English. They support cultural maintenance but see cultural studies as their own task, not the task of the school, and provide for it through their own organisations such as Samoan Sunday Schools, the Cook Island Friday Evening Group etc. While there is an ESL class there is no bilingual programme in the school. However language policy developments are moving in the latter direction.

'Chikataw' School is a medium-size primary school in a large city. In the last two years major demographic changes have occurred in the school's community because a new residential complex for low-income families has been sited nearby and because substantial numbers of refugees have settled in the area. The school has doubled in size as a result. The traditional minority groups in the area (mainly the children of Yugoslavian or Maltese migrants) have now been supplemented by newly arrived Indo-Chinese groups whose presence is resented by many older residents. The necessary positive discrimination in favour of Indo-Chinese children in the school has promoted community unrest and as a result a drop in staff morale. The school operates on a split site which lessens the effectiveness of its young ESL teachers and disrupts organisation generally. The methods of SL instruction favoured by the specialist ESL teachers is not understood or supported by their colleagues, while the ESL teachers themselves feel marginal to the school's operation generally. The school has no language policy nor any plans for one.

'Murrumbidgee' School is a small rural junior school whose enrolment includes a large proportion of students of second and third generation Italian descent. There are also Dutch, Portuguese, Greek and Spanish descent children in smaller numbers. The community is a settled one and any new arrivals add to the size of the Italian community, which uses Italian as the language of everyday affairs. There is an Italian language maintenance programme operating in the area which all of the Italian students attend. All staff are very conscious of the need for language support. Newly arrived students are integrated quickly into the school, with bilingual support provided by staff and students. There is a comprehensive and detailed whole-school language policy in which reading plays a major role along with heavy emphasis on oral language work.

'St Jude's' is a Roman Catholic primary school with five staff. Student entry to the school is highly regarded by the parents in this small rural community since the school has a high reputation for discipline, for religious education, and for academic achievement. It has a very conservative curriculum with pedagogical approaches based on traditional church school methods. There is a strong emphasis on tradition and ritual in the school's organisation. Children are expected to sit up and keep quiet. Children are discouraged from challenging authority in knowledge or in Christian values. On the principal's reckoning, staff are unaware of many of the key ideas behind language across the curriculum: that language influences learning; that language teaching is more than skills teaching; that oral language has a role outside testing or evaluating student knowledge; that teachers need to reduce their dominance in class activities; that teachers have biasses in their language use and in their perceptions of students; and that language used in a variety of contexts enhances learning and improves the teaching environment. The school's scheme was created over 15 years ago and has been little influenced by teacher decision making. Under the leadership of its new principal the development of a school language policy is the first move towards collaborative decision making that the school has undertaken.

Otahuhu Primary is an urban school which has on its roll: 13% from the nation's English-speaking majority culture; 38% from its indigenous minority culture; 39% from immigrant families who come from nearby cultures that are related to the indigenous culture; and 10% immigrants from distant cultures. Of those enrolled 46% have a mother tongue other than English, however without exception the children are sent to school by their parents to learn and master English. The indigenous minority in the country are experiencing a cultural and political revival. Their language (whose first language users fell from 90% at the beginning of the twentieth century to 2% at its lowest point) is also reviving and access to learning it in school is quickly becoming a right for all children. In comparison the large immigrant minorities are seeking integration within their new community. At system level there is pressure for all schools to provide a non-racist curriculum and to establish a partnership with the communities they serve and to base this on greater consultation and participation. At government level there is a stress on biculturalism: this spans only the majority and the indigenous minority cultures while leaving the position of the smaller minorities undefined and excludes them on specifically racial lines. The school's staff are all drawn from the majority culture, are monolingual and untrained in SL techniques or approaches. The teachers agree that the school's priority is a language policy and they are working towards the development of a trial document.

'Missouri' School is a medium-sized urban high school in a low-income residential area which has been badly affected by recent unemployment increases and widespread recession. Relationships between the school and its community are not particularly good, especially as they apply to community ethnic minorities whose reputations in the community are not enhanced by the presence of street gangs which are stridently racist and contribute to crime in the area. Until recently minority groups with ESL needs have been taught on a selective withdrawal and options basis, an approach not favoured by many of the staff. There are plans to place all the minority group students beginning in the school in one class to provide them with a more secure social, linguistic and learning environment for much of the school week. For the rest of the time they will be integrated with their peers. Language across the curriculum, as an educational doctrine, has little support among senior staff; it has been widely pilloried as 'a bit of window dressing'. The school has no language policy nor any widely understood policies in any other curriculum area.

Summary of This Book's Contents

The chapters that follow are written for people engaged in language policy making in schools like those described above. In other words, they are written for schools anywhere in pluralist societies. *Chapter 2* introduces the study of language planning in education, discussing it as the source of most of the ideas that are needed for undertaking school level policy making. Working from the assumption that the starting point in addressing any problem is for the problem solver to be in possession of the facts that relate to the problem, *Chapter 3* presents methods and a rationale for 'fact gathering' about a school's language problems. These approaches to fact gathering will also be useful in the later stages of LPAC development, especially when a tentative policy has been designed and is ready for testing against the real world of the school and its context. *Chapter 4* discusses ways and means for constructing policies at school level, seeing that process itself as a collaborative language activity. The chapter concludes by detailing rational stages of policy construction that will allow policy makers to design an LPAC which is as responsive as possible to the language problems of their school. *Chapter 5* deals with those aspects of language development that seem relevant to modern schooling. It looks at teacher roles and approaches and at language across the curriculum itself as an educational doctrine that has much to offer as an organising idea for teachers and schools. *Chapter 6* moves the LAC debate away from an exclusive concentration on mother tongue matters by examining language policies and projects about languages at national levels. Its purpose is to extract from that discussion implications for policy making in schools. *Chapter 7* takes the first language ideas developed in Chapter 5 and applies them to bilingual and second language teaching. It introduces the latest research conclusions in these areas and draws out the implications for teaching practice and school organisation that come from them. *Chapter 8* deals with an area of the language curriculum which often remains separate from the rest, foreign language teaching. It suggests how linking foreign language teaching with cultural studies across the curriculum might lead to improvements. *Chapter* 9 provides an essay which tries to span those social justice issues that relate directly to language and education but which very often seem to be beyond the school's range of influence. *Chapter* 10 provides a summary or checklist of questions, derived from all the previous chapters, that language policy makers at school level might need to address in designing their policies. The summary is set out under headings which offer useful organising ideas for those looking for a format in which to set their school's language policy.

2 Language planning in education

Language planning is the field of study to which matters of language policy relate. Language planning itself fits within 'the sociology of language', although many find the latter a misleading title for an area of inquiry which extends into the language aspects of Psychology, Philosophy, Linguistics and Anthropology as well as into all the areas traditionally associated with Education itself. For Fishman 'sociology of language' is:

> an integrated, interdisciplinary, multi-method, and multi-level approach to the study of natural, sequenced and socially situated language behaviour (1978: 811).

For Trudgill 'sociology of language' falls within that subdivision of the study of language and society that is both sociological and linguistic in intent; it is notionally outside a second subdivision that is uncontroversially called sociolinguistics and which is purely 'linguistic'; and it is also distinct from a third subdivision which is 'social' rather than linguistic in intent (1983: 2–6). The sociology of language includes matters not normally considered in linguistics such as language loyalty, language as source and symbol of group solidarity and language as an instrument of social stratification. The central field of the sociology of language is its concern with the social, political and educational aspects of the relationship between language and society (Edwards, 1976). It touches on the concerns of schools and Education at every point.

Two Directions in the Sociology of Language

Although the sociology of language is fairly recent in its development, gaining impetus only after 1965, it moves in two different and complementary directions (Tollefson, 1981): the 'descriptive' and the 'evaluative'. Both of these approaches relate to the subject of this Chapter, although the direct relevance of the 'evaluative', for language planning at the individual school level, is yet to be shown.

The descriptive approach

Those who follow the 'descriptive' approach try to understand the social organisation of language use and the principles governing changes in language use. They are interested in how language behaviour reflects social structure (i.e. in the social distribution of code availability). They are also interested in how social structure determines speech or language behaviour itself and in how that behaviour defines social structure, thereby affecting social interaction (Grimshaw, 1987a). A good deal of the descriptive work is at the individual level and addresses that very important process for human beings: the acquisition and modification of communicative competence. Communicative competence is central to discussion in the chapters that follow. Being communicatively competent means two main things: knowing how to produce and interpret communication while interacting with others; and knowing the 'rules' for appropriate communication. This involves questions such as the following (after Hymes, 1972; Fishman, 1972): who speaks or writes what language or what language variety to whom, and when and to what end?; what accounts for different rates of change in the social organisation of language use and behaviour towards language?

The descriptive approach deals with more than the mere content of messages passed in language. When we talk about the content of language we can limit 'content' to the knowledge or information transmitted, and the emotions being expressed in the use of language, or the functions of language being served (i.e. to inform, advise, entertain, impress etc). The descriptive approach also seeks facts about the organisation of the 'code' itself: why is one particular language variety used in one setting and another variety in another setting? This can refer to a social or regional variety of a language or to separate languages used in the same country. For example, in New Zealand, the United States, Scandinavia, Australia or Canada sociologists of language are keenly interested in the domains of use of Maori, American Indian, Same, Aboriginal and Inuit tongues and in the phenomenon that we are currently witnessing: the resurgence in the prestige of many of these languages and the sociocultural developments that underlie that resurgence. Using the examples of the indigenous languages mentioned above: how do minority language users decide on when, where and how to use their languages (rather than the majority tongue) and what qualitative effects for their language use do their choices have? Beyond this sociologists of language are interested in the way language is used and can be used by children and adults from different social, ethnic, age and gender backgrounds. Using a majority language example, why are English-speaking monolingual children, who come from low-income backgrounds, less likely to be proficient in using language 'to explain things' in the school setting or to interact with teachers than their more affluent peers often seem to be?

Below I list some examples of the kinds of things that have interested sociologists of language working within the descriptive approach. To open the discussion I have chosen well-known examples of work which have a high interest value:

Ferguson (1959) examined the linguistic phenomenon of 'diglossia': this is a language situation that exists in many countries where there are very different high and low varieties of the same language operating alongside one another but serving different functions. For instance in Greece (until recent decades) the high variety of Greek (*katharevousa*) prevailed in most public spheres while the low variety (*dhimotiki*) was confined mainly to the informal sphere of families and friends. Ferguson found that patterns of social interaction may precisely match the structural divisions within the language codes of the community. In Greece the diglossic situation provided problems for the users of *dhimotiki* in winning an influence in their society unless they became proficient in the *khatarevousa*: the language of power, influence and higher education. In examining diglossic settings like Greece, the choice of the 'high' or 'low' variety provides an index of social solidarity. The same idea can also be extended into bilingual settings where one language is used for informal and community purposes while a second language is used for more official business. Differences in status between the languages will often result.

Rubin (1968) examined Paraguay as an example of this redefined diglossic context that prevails to a degree in many bilingual communities. There appears to be a classic division along high and low diglossic lines in Paraguay between Spanish, which is the language of the country's colonisers, and the original Amerindian language, Guarani. Many Paraguayans, including non-Indians, are bilingual in these two languages. Rubin found that the functions to which the languages are applied are defined according to their level of social importance.

Ervin Tripp (1964) investigated the code shifting of bilingual speakers of American English, namely the Japanese immigrant wives of Americans, whom she compared with monolingual English and Japanese women. She found that a radical change in content of communication occurred when they were speaking in fluent English or in fluent Japanese, even when the language context was controlled. She also found that the women who gave typically American responses in both languages seemed to identify more with American cultural values, while those who gave typically Japanese responses were more oriented towards Japanese culture.

Brown and Gilman (1960) investigated the use of pronouns to express dominance in role relationships. They found that in a social relationship in a traditional society an addresser who was in a position of power often used a pronoun expressing familiarity to address a subordinate. The latter used a polite pronoun in reply. Brown and Gilman show that pronoun use has shifted over time so that in contemporary societies the choice of a pronoun less often symbolises and acknowledges a power relationship and is used more often to represent solidarity. More recently among immigrant groups in Australia Clyne (1984b) reports the problem of a 'generation gap' occurring in this kind of usage.

Labov (Labov et al., 1968) investigated the use of the Black English and Puerto Rican vernaculars in New York City. He found that the use of these varieties of language co-varied systematically and regularly, confirming that these and the myriad other varieties of language that exist as sub-units of major languages are not 'incorrect' forms of the major language but are different social dialects that have their own rules and norms. Later research by ethnographers has shown that major mismatches often exist between the systems of language forms and uses of social and cultural minority students, on the one hand, and of their teachers on the other. Conclusions of great importance for language policy in education were to flow from these findings. Eagleson said it well:

Many children entering our schools come with a language different from that of their teachers. It is the language of their parents and their peers, and it is thoroughly ingrained and continually being reinforced by constant exposure to it. I have found a large number of teachers who do not appreciate the situation confronting them. They regard their pupils as speakers of bad English, and they see their task as a war against error.

When their efforts seem fruitless they come to regard any work in language with their pupils as nigh on hopeless. Worse still, by their attitudes to certain language habits, as well as having lower levels of expectation for their pupils, they frequently promote an antipathy between the school and the child to the detriment of the education of the child (Eagleson, 1976: 25).

It may be that many teachers in the past did not receive from their own education an appreciation of how it is that children and adults acquire different sociolinguistic repertoires. There is a key to this understanding in Erickson's simple discussion of the 'daily round': this is "the entire sequence of social situations the individual engages in during the day". Erickson gives the instance of one individual during the daily round encountering only fellow-ethnics of the same social class while another individual encounters persons of differing ethnicity and class. The two individuals thus routinely experience differing speaking environments and acquire differing sociolinguistic repertoires (1987: 92–93). Extending this discussion to schooling, in making the transition from home and community to school there are bound to be anomalies for all children in the relationships that they perceive in the daily rounds of their several speaking environments. Language and context will interact in unique ways. For many there will be major discontinuities between the daily rounds that they experience outside schools and the new ones that are imposed on them by the school. We now have a good deal of evidence about the severity and range of these mismatches (for example: Romaine, 1984) which suggests that teachers need to adopt a much more cautious approach in their interaction styles, in their pedagogies and in their assessment of pupil performance in language.

The evaluative approach

The evaluative approach to the sociology of language seems at first glance to be of real help to us in the design of language policies across the curriculum. After all, education and schooling are very much concerned with valuing things: with judging and evaluating in order to change and improve. Yet while the work of the evaluative approach is vital for national language policies (see Chapter 6), it is difficult to see more than general points in the work that have application for policies at the level of a school.

While the descriptive approach is concerned with relationships between linguistic structure and social organisation, the evaluative is concerned instead with mechanisms for deliberately altering those relationships: its task is to design prescriptive planning activities. A starting point is the assumption that language planning can bring about changes in the structure and function of language varieties and that we can determine the value of particular changes by setting them against communication needs and against language rights. The evaluative approach transmits its message about language planning in three forms:

(1) discussions of language as a resource that has economic and social value;
(2) conscious statements of future social and linguistic goals;
(3) policy and political action (often) rather than research.

Some of the areas of international activity in the evaluative paradigm are mentioned below. These matters are certainly important for policies at national levels:

(1) *language purification*: as in the work of the French Academy, which represents an extreme example of purification at work in a single language. Less well-known examples are the Spanish Academies, which influence the use of Spanish worldwide, and the Institute of Swahili Research in Kenya which tries to act as a clearing house for Swahili affairs in East Africa.
(2) *language revival*: as in the revival of Erse in Ireland as an act of deliberate government policy following the formation of the Irish Free State; or in the revival of Cornish, Gaelic and Welsh; or in the highly successful experiment in Israel in which the Hebrew Language Academy has modernised and made Hebrew the *lingua franca* of the Israelis; or, in the current resurgence of Maori in New Zealand and minority languages elsewhere.
(3) *language reform*: the classic case is the reform of Turkish beginning in 1922: the high form of the language was simplified to provide a more common tongue and the Arabic script was replaced with the Latin one.
(4) *language standardisation*: where one dialect becomes accepted as the standard for a region, as in the case again of Swahili in East Africa which has a standardised form in Kenya, Tanzania and Uganda, and in the case of the devising of a single Norwegian dialect for use across the country, an act of language planning that came largely from the work of one individual.
(5) *lexical modernisation*: this has been pursued as a deliberate instrument of government policy in Swedish, Czech, Russian and in other Slavonic languages. University College of North Wales,

Bangor, has a responsibility to bring the Welsh lexicon up to date so that it can be used as a language of higher education and technology.

Language Planning

Language planning is another name for the evaluative approach to the sociology of language. Broadly conceived, language planning is concerned with any problem area in which language plays some role: it is 'the organised pursuit of solutions to language problems' (Fishman, 1973: 23–24). Again there are two broad divisions in language planning activities: in 'corpus planning' the structure of a language variety (i.e. its spelling, pronunciation, grammar or vocabulary) is deliberately changed; in 'status planning' the way that the language is used in society is changed and this affects its status (for example in New Zealand the Maori language has recently been given equal recognition as a language for the law courts). These two approaches can overlap considerably, although the second is more concerned with political and economic issues: decisions made reflect the values of those who hold political power (Heath, 1972).

The major dimensions of language planning remain those established by Haugen (1983; 1987) who set out four problem areas that he regarded as the starting point of language planners everywhere:

(1) selection of a norm (deciding what language is to be the norm);
(2) codification of the norm (the assignment of styles and spheres of usage for the language);
(3) implementation of function (spreading the language form that has been selected and codified);
(4) elaboration of function (continued implementation of a norm to meet the linguistic functions of the culture).

Dealing with these kinds of problems is outside the power of policy makers and planners at the school level. If anywhere at all in a given country these areas properly belong to people formulating government policy at the highest level, as in the case of a 'national language policy' (see Chapter 6). Activities of this kind are also highly political, since they are concerned to decide what language can be 'the norm' and the social areas to which its functions should extend. Schooling should be central to all of this. Haugen remarks on the educational complexity that affects language planning in modern pluralist societies: 'the spread of schooling to entire populations in modern times has made the implementation of norms a major educational issue' since some or other élite group no longer has a monopoly in education that is sufficient to allow the implementation of a given norm with reasonable simplicity (1983 p. 272). This point needs to be underlined. It is no longer enough in pluralist societies, where group and individual language rights are recognised, to base education exclusively on the standard language as used by dominant groups in society. Matters of social justice and equity (see Chapter 9) coupled with an explosion of knowledge about linguistic issues and their effects on intellectual development have made the language task of schools much more complex than they seemed to be in the past. Yet, as conventionally conceived, 'language planning' has been well removed from the concerns of classrooms and individual schools.

More relevant to school level language planning are the four steps in carrying out a language plan identified by Rubin (1977) and Horvath (1980):

(1) *fact-gathering*: this step includes determining the needs of the clients, finding out about the sociolinguistic setting and the patterns of usage as well as determining how the language plan relates to other economic and political processes;
(2) *decision-making by policy makers*: in this step, strategies are worked out, material and human resources are assessed and goals are set: in other words, a language policy is drawn up;
(3) *implementation*: in this step, resources are mobilised, problems of sequencing and general coordination are handled;
(4) *evaluation*: in this step, whether or not the plan is working is monitored and modifications are instituted where necessary.

In designing language policies at the school level we are concerned with steps (1) and (2) in this list: fact-gathering and decision-making. Implementation will always follow a well designed policy but like evaluation it is beyond the scope of this book. Chapter 3 is devoted to the various activities of 'fact gathering' that schools might readily pursue before designing language policies. Chapters 4 to 9 deal with the many facets of the 'decision-making' phase of language planning at school level.

3 Fact gathering for language policies across the curriculum

In this book the 'fact-gathering' process means three things: it means coming to grips with the theory (i.e. knowledge) about language and education questions that are relevant to designing language policies across the curriculum; it means thinking seriously about the policy-making process at the school level and coming to see it as an instrument for improving the service to children that an individual school offers; and it means taking steps to understand the unique language situation that prevails in a school and the language needs of its students. The task of 'decision-making' in relation to that 'fact-gathering' is of course the point of the whole exercise: the design of a language policy across the curriculum that is responsive to the assembled facts about the school's population and its social setting[1].

Larger Scale LPAC Research

Where there are many varieties of language that affect the range of language problems which confront a school, more sophisticated kinds of approach to large-scale research may be needed, using the advice and operations of a research consultant of some kind. Perhaps the kind of research that is needed will be so substantial that it will not be possible to postpone language policy development in other areas to await the outcome of that research. It may be that one of the substantive items mentioned in the LPAC itself should be the development of an ongoing research programme addressing significant problems. Clearly, though, the policy will be a much stronger plan for action if it has its roots in some prior research exercise that has been rigorously carried out.

21

In doing large-scale fact gathering, recommendations made for bilingual language planning in education can be extended to large-scale LPAC research, even where bilingualism is not a matter at issue. Fishman and Lovas (1970) for example recommend the following four sets of activities:

(1) A survey of varieties used by speakers including the domains or functions of those varieties;
(2) An estimate of the performance level in each domain;
(3) Some indication of community and staff attitudes toward the varieties and toward their use in various domains;
(4) An indication of community and school staff attitudes towards changing the situation.

Steps (1) and (2) in this list need not refer only to second languages. In many schools in monolingual communities there will be a range of language varieties that are brought into the work of the school in one way or another: varieties used by closely knit social or ethnic groups. Coming from these backgrounds the children may possess two or more 'codes' which they use in their everyday language, perhaps one code reserved for the home, another for the peer group, and a third for the school. This last code may be very close to the standard language. The Patois used by many Black children in Britain, who are of West Indian origin, provides a continuum of codes which the children can range across, switching their code depending on the context (V. Edwards, 1986). There are examples of code switching of this kind to be found to a greater or lesser extent in almost every community where modern schools operate. They offer a different dimension of language variation and it is one which schools in pluralist societies ignore only at risk to the educational prospects of their students.

Steps (3) and (4) in the Fishman and Lovas list of fact gathering tasks move away from descriptive research activities and focus on the prospects for change that are possible and on the normative questions to do with prescribing change. Community attitudes on these questions are a very important basis for policy decisions, especially where those attitudes may be different from those held by staff members or may be in conflict with national or system-level policy guidelines on these questions. While many parents are less willing to see the language of the home being used in the school, others are confused about what might be possible, even about what the issues might be; and others are insistent that there certainly should be a place for the language of their children's cultural or social background in the school's activities. There are no prescriptions that I can make here about large-scale community research on these issues since each school's context of community is so different and will ask for different approaches. Chapter 9 deals with the values questions that affect these issues. While discussion in that chapter offers no broad resolutions that can be taken up and applied by schools, it attempts to describe the boundaries of the problems as they affect contemporary schools. There are small-scale issues that can be addressed and I return to them later in this chapter.

Large scale fact gathering about children's language

The collection and interpretation of language data for educational purposes has become a highly sophisticated and intricate business. The 'teacher as researcher' who approaches these tasks usually has extensive training in some of the many methods of analysis that are possible. Added to this need for training in research methods is another complicating factor: the many approaches to this kind of fieldwork vary in the respect that has been accorded to them over the years as our knowledge about language acquisition and development has grown. As a result the various methods continue to evolve and improve. Some which were appropriate not long ago are no longer suitable. In collecting data, a teacher as researcher might begin by deciding the context of use in which language is to be examined:

—Is it simply the child's use of language within the formal contexts of schooling that is of interest?
—Are there wider contexts that are relevant to the language problem under focus?
—Does the children's home or community language rather than their school language relate directly to the language problem?
—Which speech or writing styles should be studied and in what contexts?

Knowing about the school's community context is very relevant to several of these points. Very often because they have worked for many years with the children of a community the staff in that community's schools assume that they are experts on the local context. The reality may be very different. Teachers who are not members of the local social network, who travel into the community each day and draw their conclusions about it from the filtered impressions that they receive from their students and from the caricatured descriptions that often circulate in the staffrooms of schools, may be highly biassed in their assessments of the school's social context. Often teachers are so affected by their own acute sense of failure with children from certain social backgrounds, or by their apparent success

with others, that they perceive the social backgrounds that those children
come from with a prejudiced or ironic view. It is important to consider the
wider social context anew and in depth when drawing up or evaluating a
language policy. A few guidelines on what to look for may help. In his
study of the community context for the Bradford mother tongue and
English teaching project, Fitzpatrick (1987) examined the following
categories of social factors:

—the material environment in which the community's families lived
—the formal education of parents
—the religious orientation of families
—reading material in the home
—toys in the home
—television viewing habits
—parental attitudes to school and education
—the community language environment
—language attitudes of parents
—language use in the home

Affecting all of these factors, which in turn affect the school and its
programme, is the wider social context of the state or country as a whole.
Discussion of policies at a national level in Chapter 6 extends on this point.
Schools that take their policy making tasks seriously will do their utmost
to gather information in areas such as those above.

This kind of large-scale research has a very serious purpose if firm
policy decisions are to come from its findings, since the rights, prospects
and values of children are at stake. It is important to be aware of the
pitfalls in many of the approaches to collecting large-scale data about
language in its social context. Nicholas (1988) examines the problems in
language diversity surveying as it has been carried out in Britain to date.
His critique covers the annual ILEA Language Census, The Survey of
Linguistic Diversity in London Schools, and The Linguistic Minorities
Project. Edwards and Westgate (1987) and Romaine (1984) also provide
insights into the recurring problems of language survey work. Below are
some of the problems that arise and questions that need considering by
those engaged in fact-gathering for language policies:

—What sampling methods are most suited to the task and what real
  relevance will the samples have to the target population as a whole?
—How can researchers who are socially and culturally similar to the
  planned respondents be used in large scale research?
—Are the results likely to be biased by problems of speech and
  accent?

—Are the results likely to be biassed by different presentations of 'self' by subjects to interviewers of a different gender?

—Are the results likely to be biassed by different presentations of 'self' by subjects to interviewers of different ethnic origins?

—What other problems of in-group and out-group identity might affect the results collected?

—How can researchers ensure the full participation of the communities whose children are under study?

—What arrangements need to be made to choose and to train skilful elicitors?

—How will the research avoid the regular problem of under-reporting by minority informants about their language use?

—What arrangements need to be made to pilot test the methods and materials?

Recent studies also suggest that there are previously unsuspected constraints on language surveys. Punetha *et al.* (1987) examined language and ethnic identity among Asian immigrants in England. They offer this warning to people conducting and interpreting the results of language surveys: forcing respondents to answer questionnaires or to be interviewed in one language rather than another will influence their responses. There is a great need, then, for interviews to be conducted in such a way as to allow repondents to give their views in their own language rather than forcing them to use a language which might distort their responses.

Although widely used in survey work, questionnaires are suspect measures and need to be used with special care. Questionnaires are not very reliable social instruments because the kind of language they elicit is far removed from the interactional and dynamic exchange of opinions that people most often use to shape their ideas and influence the ideas of others. When people say things in answer to questionnaires they are making attitudinal statements for reasons which may change; they are making these statements to audiences whose interests and behaviour call for a set of ideas that may vary depending on context. That is to say, different contexts might produce apparently contradictory 'attitudes'. We know that attitudes are fickle and unreliable things, yet researchers who use questionnaires and the people who interpret their findings still use them to base weighty conclusions upon. Baker (1988: 114) notes five reservations about 'attitudes' (as the outcome of 'attitude questionnaires') and their potential for use as reliable guides:

(1) they are different from and not always congruent with actual behaviour;

(2) they are affected very significantly by context;
(3) they are only one determinant of behaviour (in addition to other things like personality, abilities, rewards, drives, needs etc);
(4) they are different for reality itself and for hypothetical reality;
(5) they are different for 'I' and for 'they'.

Clearly care is needed when we interpret the results of questionnaires as being representative of the attitudes of respondents. On the other hand when using questionnaires there are ways of minimising these weaknesses: for example, we can ask people to say 'what they should do' in a given situation and compare it with 'what they would do'; we can survey the same sample of people using different questions examining the same field of attitudes; we can ask the same questions on two occasions, varying the context and perhaps the interviewer.

When imprecise tools like questionnaires are used, it is important that some of the population or a fraction of the sample be examined using more sensitive methods, so that comparisons can be made. But what are these sensitive methods? The simple answer is that the choice of methods depends on the nature of the problem. In any act of research it is easy to get things the wrong way round by deciding, for example, on an interview survey of some kind without having a clear understanding of the problem that the planned survey is intended to address. Edwards and Westgate cite Romaine's judgment on method selection:

> In deciding to adopt one methodological strategy rather than another, there can be no question of choosing one method which will be universally the 'right' one. Methodology can be evaluated only within the context of some question which one wants to answer (Romaine, 1984: 15).

Large scale research methods

Here is a summary of some of the large-scale but also time-intensive approaches that could be used prior to the development of a policy. These approaches and methods supplement those regular assessment techniques that all schools use at one time or another (techniques yielding information about child language that many now regard as less than complete and perhaps quite misleading). I have included only those methods that may provide some clear guidance to policy makers and administrators about the language problems that their LPAC might address. On the other hand, as already mentioned, the need for this kind of large-scale research could be written into the LPAC as an explicit item for future work:

Ethnography

This approach to research, borrowed from anthropology and now applied with good effect across the social science disciplines, is more than a single method and may include several of the methods mentioned below. Often it is used without the rigour that anthropologists insist upon: in its classic sense ethnography involves immersing oneself in the culture being studied, living with people in the community for a minimum of a year or more, and taking up a position within the social structure of that community as a participant observer. Education, however, borrows its methods from several disciplines: from Psychology we borrow its methodological preference for setting up artificial interactions and observing them; from Sociology we borrow a preference for asking people questions about how they behave in social groups; and from Anthropology we borrow its preference for the direct observation of naturally occurring forms of behaviour. Ethnography comes into the latter category.

One respected approach to ethnography tries to account for the behaviour of people by describing what it is that they know that allows them to behave appropriately in their cultural setting, whether it is in an exotic cultural setting, in the classroom, in a tribal meeting, or at a school staff meeting. Another approach emphasises semiotics (the study of signs and symbols) and the meanings people attribute to events: there is a difference between knowing the behaviour and language of a group of people, on the one hand, and being able to 'do it yourself' on the other. A third approach to ethnography looks not for some 'mysterious empathy' but for 'shared meaning' as the kind of understanding that is a goal of research. All of us at some time or other have been new arrivals in an organisation. In a most practical way we have had to go through the often difficult process of acquiring 'shared meanings' about that culture. We feel rather lost until we do. What this approach to ethnography attempts to do is to identify the processes that the members of out-groups in a given setting must go through to become members of the in-group.

According to those who have used one or other of the approaches to ethnography with good effect in studying children in natural contexts (Heath, 1983; Chilcott, 1987), we get a better perspective on the display of abilities in schools by attending to what children get up to when in community settings. The results of ethnographic research suggest that children may be excluded from real opportunities in school because of factors to do with their social and cultural backgrounds. These factors make it difficult for them to fit into classroom management styles and to meet the regular communicative expectations that are placed upon them by schools. Weighty implications for school policy development can flow from these kinds of ethnographic findings: Schools in some parts of the world have made radical changes to their pedagogy, assessment and curriculum procedures after ethnographic research has been carried out in their local communities. Good ethnography of schooling has the following criteria (Spindler, 1982): it involves prolonged and repetitive observation within the actual context; it disturbs the process of interaction as little as possible; its instruments are generated in the field; hypotheses and questions emerge as the study proceeds; and its major task is to understand what sociocultural knowledge participants bring to the context and generate within it.

Transcript evidence

This is usually based on extensive naturalistic observations of language-in-use using some audio/visual recording instrument. In using transcripts there is always the researcher's problem of checking the meaning that speakers intend in any fragment of communication since very often the language on its own is not enough. We can lessen this problem of validity by questioning respondents later about what they 'meant' or 'understood' at various points in the interaction and by using this to check the researcher's assessment. Other problems include judgments about the representativeness and the frequency of the events on which observations are made: researchers tend to select instances that support some version of reality that the researcher is disposed towards seeing and this biasses results. Another problem is the tricky business of presenting this kind of evidence outside its original context, so that others can evaluate the researcher's conclusions about it for themselves (Edwards & Westgate, 1987). On the other hand the strengths of the transcription method are many: it allows a high level of natural language interaction to be observed; it provides insights into the structuring of classroom discourse, especially the impact of teachers themselves on classroom language and the refinement of knowledge that occurs; it can enlarge teachers' awareness of the language games that they force onto children; it can reveal something of the real flavour of intercultural exchanges; it can reveal those children who are not regular participants in the language activities of the school; and it provides a data base that others can refer to, check back on, and gain new insights from.

Interviews

A more structured variation of the above method is the tape-recorded interview. This has become a standard way of obtaining sociolinguistic data in both the school and in the wider community. The researcher's problem is not so much in setting up a series of interviews, although this needs considerable planning, especially in relation to the problems asterisked earlier in this section. It is the task of interpreting the language data that gives the most problems. Are we entitled to claim that the same interviewees in other situations would use their language in much the same way? If attitudes are so ephemeral, how much moreso is the language used to express those attitudes? This problem can be lessened by 'mixing methods' (see 'triangulation' below) or by replicating or double-checking the results in some way. The more methods that are used to view the same problem area, the more likely it will be that our conclusions will come close to reflecting the real world. In the interview research into adolescent vocabulary use, reported in Corson (1985b, 1989b), double-checks of some kind were used to corroborate the large differences in vocabulary use that appeared among fifteen year olds from different social backgrounds. These double-checks or replication studies took several forms: cross-regional comparisons; cross-national comparisons; and comparisons of the same children responding in writing to the same interview schedule that they had previously met in speech. In schools, comparisons of spoken and written language use are possible and can be used as a check on inferences drawn. Romaine (1984) discusses some of· the many other problems in setting up interview research into language: asking questions to which children can relate; making use of the advantage of being a stranger to the interviewees; compensating for social group and ethnic group differences in interaction styles across settings; changing tasks in order to change the speech style.

Discourse analysis

This approach to research comes in many guises. The one that I discuss here, for sake of example only, is a style of discourse analysis that is used in social psychology (Potter & Wetherell, 1987). Developments have been happening concurrently in a number of different disciplines and the title 'discourse analysis' has been used by some to cover all research concerned with language in its social and cognitive context, by others as a description only for studies of linguistic units larger than the sentence, and by still others to cover technical developments. For some, 'discourse' means all forms of talk and writing; for others, it applies only to the way that talk is meshed together to form coherent units. Most generally it covers all forms of spoken interaction, formal and informal, and written texts of all kinds. So when I talk of 'discourse analysis' I mean the study of any of these forms of discourse, including 'documentary analysis' (see below). One aim of discourse analysis is to obtain a better understanding of social life through the study of oral or written texts. The basic ideas are familiar enough: that language is both a means of constructing social life and also a social construction itself; that it offers or even determines a scaffolding for thought; and that as well as communicating meaning it can be used 'to do things'. This last point suggests how LPAC 'fact gathering' can be helped by discourse analysis. Only a close comparative analysis of language use can reveal differences in the ways that speakers go about using language to do the same tasks. Very often in schools too little account is taken of alternative ways that there might be in a given language community for achieving the same purpose in language (Chapter 9 extends this discussion). Very often too these alternative ways can be misinterpreted by the rather culturally conservative teachers that often staff schools; these ways of using language are sometimes seen by teachers as incompetent, impolite, discourteous, rebellious, challenging, perverted or needlessly unorthodox. Discourse analysis, conducted among the communities that the school serves, can uncover alternative but still legitimate ways of looking at the world and of interpreting knowledge about the world. By applying this information to its operations, the school can become more organic to the community in which it is set.

In analysing student or student–teacher discourse a researcher can begin by trying to reconstruct the interactional and linguistic context: the degree to which those interacting mutually establish and maintain topics of conversation; the degree to which various students of differing ages and backgrounds elaborate on different topics in the conversation. By comparing samples of discourse, showing contexts in which rich passages of student conversational discourse occurred, with samples where low levels of interaction or little topic innovation occurred, researchers can identify the strengths and weaknesses of children. Patterns of interaction style, related to context, can be discovered and these can sometimes be linked with cultural and social differences among the children. For example, children from different cultural backgrounds differ in their styles of interaction with an adult when the context of the interaction is changed from 'examination' to 'interview' and to 'conversation'. Many other factors affect interaction styles and are of concern in the differential treatment of ability: these are surveyed in Chapters 7, 8 and 9.

Discourse analysis can help us to show and explain things that are usually regarded as being 'inside the mind', not just out there in talk: things like attitudes, ideologies, prejudices, frames of reference etc. Earlier I mentioned the imprecision of the questionnaire as a research method. Questionnaires often collect fragments of discourse that fail to tell the whole story. When people say or write things they are making attitudinal statements for reasons which may change and to audiences whose needs demand or allow a different range of ideas. A different context could produce contradictions. Only a close reading of the whole of a discourse, in the context of related discourses, will reveal anything like the full story. As a guide to thinking about doing discourse analysis, the general message is that we should think of an intelligent question to ask about the discourse, then look for patterns in the text (especially patterns of the use of key phrases, contradictions, disclaimers etc) that might have something to do with the answer. The researcher needs to ask: 'why am I reading this passage in this way; what features in the text produce this reading?'. The researcher is looking for the way in which the discourse 'works' in doing whatever it is that it does. None of this can be a mechanical act on the researcher's part. It requires a high level of ingenuity and imagination as well as engagement of the researcher's own 'interpretative repertoires' as a sounding board to amplify the message in the discourse. The best way to become a discourse analyst is to analyse a piece of discourse.

Ethnography of communication

This too is more than a single method; it is a collection of methods, including and especially discourse analysis, that can be used for studying language in a social context. Recently educational researchers have begun to use the term 'ethnography' to refer to any qualitative study, even with its roots in Sociology or Social Psychology. This is partly because the sociologist, the social psychologist and the anthropologist are coming much closer in the ways that they conduct their research and in the theoretical orientation that underlies their work. Integrating perspectives in this way is useful in sociolinguistics (whose alternative name is the 'ethnography of communication'). Both discourse analysis and ethnography proper contribute much to a sociolinguistic approach. Florio-Ruane (1987) and Cazden (1988) advocate similar lines of inquiry illustrating this kind of research: the structure of classroom interaction and variations in classroom discourse; differential treatment and access to school knowledge; and the language links between classroom discourse and student learning. Many of the studies reported in the journal *Language and Education* are versions of the kinds of research projects that teacher researchers can engage in.

Documentary analysis

In schools this kind of research can be used to examine sets of texts written by children and compared with other texts written on the same subject and under similar conditions. There is much value here provided that the researcher does not make unwarranted jumps in extrapolating to wider matters of language from the fairly limited evidence that children's written language can offer. This form of research has the simple aim of assessing children's performance on one of the main activities of contemporary schooling: written language use. Its advantages include: the ready availability of texts of this kind in schools; the ready acceptance by children that a major part of their work in schools is to prepare written texts and 'hand them in' for assessment; the ease in which control of context and task can be assured; the variations in topic and style that can be assessed over several research stages; and the convenience of the evidence, which requires no transcribing and is ready for re-analysis if necessary. Surprisingly schools do little of this kind of documentary analysis as a general check on pupil strengths and weaknesses across the written curriculum. For teachers the main difficulty is the task of managing the collaborative business of deciding the criteria that are to be used in the analysis. Again, the nature of the problem determines the methods of analysis: what is the documentary analysis intended to do?

Comparisons of home and school language

Much of the work linking language, social background and school failure lacks the evidence of systematic comparisons between language used in the home and language used at school. There are only a few researchers who have managed to combine the two (notably Heath, 1983; and Wells, 1979). The slight evidence that we have suggests that the real communicative abilities of children in their classrooms are little understood by teachers. Because of this relative ignorance of the language realities of their pupils, the things that teachers would like to be doing and aim to do in their language and learning work, particularly but not solely with the very young, is very unlike what they are actually doing in their classroom practice. For this reason any form of high quality comparison between the two settings of home and school, that will throw light on differences between home and school in what children can and want to do with their language, is highly desirable. The detailed ethnographic approaches used by Heath or the meticulous linguistic analyses used by Wells are clearly beyond the resources of individual schools or individual teacher researchers. The results of those studies do provide a reference point, though, and a source of ideas for the kind of questions that ingenious school-based researchers might explore in other ways: through systematic interviews with parents discussing their children's language; through tactful discussions of anonymous transcripts of child language with community members; through observations made of child language in use outside the semi-formal constraints of the classroom; or, with older children and as part of the teaching process, through carefully mounted discussions with the children themselves about variations in their language use from place to place. The discussion of 'critical language awareness' in Chapter 9 extends on this last point.

Triangulation

In its original guise, triangulation is a mapreading method for finding out where you are using only a map, compass, protractor and three prominent landmarks. The method asks that you take a bearing with the compass on three landmarks and then plot backbearings (the converse readings in degrees) using the protractor and your map. Where the three lines intersect on the map is your exact position. Apart from the equipment, the essential items in this exercise are the prominent landmarks. I think that the analogy can apply to the landmarks needed in the triangulation approach to educational research. The researcher needs a set of clear reference points which singly do not provide reliable guides but when taken together provide a strong case for knowing 'where you are'. Jick (1979) defines 'triangulation' as the combination of methodologies in the study of the same phenomenon. For example, in checking the effectiveness of a school policy a researcher could first interview teachers, second examine the reports provided by external experts, and third try to observe the policy's operation and its impact on the school lives of children. Any one of these methods on its own (interview, documentary analysis, ethnography) would provide evidence of doubtful value; any two would provide evidence that might be good enough for most purposes; but the three taken together, provided that they supported one another, would yield evidence on which a school could plan and make decisions on matters of great importance. The approach to research in the book *The Lexical Bar* uses a multi-method 'triangulation' approach. Following the Popperian theory of how knowledge grows (Corson, 1985c), those studies used more than just three reference points to get a set of 'intersecting backbearings': the reference points were drawn from all the disciplines that were relevant to the problem area and out of this a theory grew that might have some explanatory power.

Many schools will not be in a position to undertake much large-scale language research before they begin the policy making task. The collection of small-scale data about their children's language will be enough in the early stages for policy planning to proceed. As mentioned, in these cases provisions for more large-scale language research will be built into the policy itself and this data-gathering research can be an on-going feature of the policy's implementation.

Small Scale LPAC Fact Gathering

One attractive result of developing an LPAC is the stimulus that the activity can give to staff interaction and development. Maybin (1985) mentions the exciting work of staff in one school who met on a weekly basis for three years and discussed teachers' and learners' language in the school, using videotapes of one another's lessons and studies of the progress of individual pupils' writing and oral language development. Chapter 4 takes this staff development side of policy construction further. As a method of fact gathering about staff attitudes and current school procedures, Maybin suggests a checklist of questions for use at the school level. This was compiled by school inspectors and circulated in Inner London Education Authority schools:

—Are all staff aware of the language and dialect repertoires of the pupils in the school?

—Do staff recognise that pupils' ability to use language effectively has an important impact on their view of themselves, and therefore on their confidence as learners?

—Do staff accept the validity of all pupils' spoken abilities, and use these as a basis for developing their skills in reading and writing?

—Are staff knowledgeable about what is meant by 'dialect' and do they have a positive approach to dialects other than standard? How is this reflected in the way in which they assess pupils' written work?

—Are staff knowledgeable about the mother tongues which their pupils speak and do they see these as a potential or real strength in the school?

—Does the school acknowledge and support pupils' bilingualism and promote an interest in their language among all pupils?

—Is there a satisfactory system within the school for identifying pupils who need help with English as their second language, for providing this help and for monitoring their progress?

—Are the teaching resources for English as a second language sufficient to meet the needs of the pupils in the school and organised so that pupils have access to them in a range of subject areas?

—Do teachers make positive attempts to draw out the experience of pupils who as yet are not entirely confident in expressing themselves in English?

—Has progress been made in responding to the issue of language diversity through the language policy and practice of the whole school?

A checklist modelled on this one could provide a set of discussion questions for use among staff preliminary to collecting more detailed information about teacher attitudes.

Teacher attitudes and stereotypes

A starting point in confronting teacher attitudes may be to acknowledge that the role that some teachers perceive for themselves blocks much interaction of any kind between themselves and matters much beyond the tight boundaries of their subject disciplines or their teaching programme. If we locate teachers notionally along a continuum between the 'collaborative' and this more 'exclusionary' type of teacher, individual teachers may maintain a fairly steady position on this continuum for a good deal of the time. Those located at the 'collaborative' end are responsive to new ideas; they welcome their colleagues' unobtrusive advice and support; they encourage parents to participate in the classroom or to take a direct role with children in home activities; and they are willing to learn from error and change their practice accordingly. Teachers at the 'exclusionary' end set tight boundaries around the business of the classroom; they are often rigorously fair in judging success and failure on the basis of what they perceive to be objective criteria; they perceive themselves as the professionals and community members as unnecessary distractions to the progress of education. These two extremes are obviously ideal cases, seldom met in the real world, yet the success of any major innovation in a school may well depend on the balance that can be maintained between holders of these two broad sets of professional attitudes. Some suitable, small-scale research examining the location of teachers along this continuum may well clarify what is possible in a language policy and where changes based on professional development programmes are necessary or desirable.

Like anyone else, teachers are prone to the influence of prejudices and stereotypes. Because of the real power that teachers have over the lives of children they are in a unique position to put their stereotypes to work, sometimes with harmful effect. Stereotypes provide much of the content of the 'social categories' that we hold. Based on one analysis (Hewstone & Giles, 1986) four fairly conclusive statements can be made about stereotypes:

—stereotyping stems from illusory correlations between people's group membership and their psychological attributes and traits;
—stereotypes influence the way information is processed about the members of groups (i.e. more favourable information is remembered about in-groups and more unfavourable information is remembered about outgroups);
—stereotypes create expectancies about other people and the holders of stereotypes often search for information and behaviours in others that will confirm those expectancies;
—stereotypes constrain their holders patterns of communication and promote communication which confirms the stereotypes held (i.e. they create self-fulfilling prophecies).

Achievement in schools may seem to depend very much on objective criteria: on the students' ability to express what they know clearly and in an 'accepted' form. After all the educational system is founded on the child being able to display knowledge. This 'display' most often takes the form of spoken or written language. But the influence of stereotypes in setting up categories about the kinds of language that children use may greatly affect teachers' judgments about the acceptability, not just of the language used, not just of the 'display' presented, but also of the 'worth' of the children themselves. Children's language will often be the first contact the teacher has on which an opinion of their potential can be based. The 'quality' of this display, judged by teachers against the yardstick of their own categories about what constitutes 'quality' in language in use, can be used by them as an inaccurate indicator of children's educational potential, especially if there are other indicators that reinforce teacher prejudices (such as children's dislike of schoolwork, lack of parental interest in the school, or evidence of disadvantage in the children's dress or appearance). Expectations can be adjusted accordingly. It is known that the teacher's expectations of children's potential can influence academic success, with children's true potential overlooked or reduced in effect. This view is especially supported by Rosenthal and Jacobson's 1968 study *Pygmalion in the Classroom*. Verma & Bagley (1975) cite the 'considerable amount of research', since the 'Pygmalion effect' was identified, that indicates that the average teacher has different perceptions and expectations of poor and minority group children, which lead to different treatment and depressed performances on the part of such children. The evidence of language is vital in confirming stereotypes and activating prejudices: negative teacher attitudes and behaviours towards the speech of culturally and socially different children undoubtedly affect pupil performance. In one celebrated court case, in Ann Arbor, Michigan, the court as part of its judgment required teachers of culturally different children to take a course of in-service training in sociolinguistics.

Attitudes to non-standard speech held by teachers are important variables that will influence the design of a language policy. Chapter 2 touched on the evidence against the prejudiced views about non-standard language that dogged education in the past. There is no doubt that non-standard varieties of language are just as regular, flexible and logical as the standard form, even though the standard language is more highly valued in schools on the grounds that it is the 'standard'. Yet negative attitudes to children's language held by various groups of people, including teachers, continue to influence their attitudes to the children themselves in ways which have little to do with the children's intellectual potential. A general finding of research is that teachers' perceptions of the so-called 'poor' speech of children produces negative expectations about the children's personalities, social backgrounds and academic abilities (Giles *et al.*, 1987). V. Edwards (1986) reports student teacher evaluations of anonymous children's speech where the academic and interest level of speakers of minority and other non-standard language varieties was viewed less favourably. There is now much evidence to reinforce the view that teacher attitudes to children's non-standard language use are more critical in judging the quality of language use than the children's language itself. Language variety seems to be a central part of the 'cultural capital' that children acquire in their community and which is often unjustly accorded different scales of value by schools. Chapter 9 extends on this discussion and asks some questions related to policies. At the fact gathering stage it is necessary to discover the views of staff and other influential members of the school community so that these can be used as a guide to development.

Soliciting staff opinions about language

Knott (1985) makes various suggestions for collecting teachers' views. His ideas relate directly to secondary schools but some modification of them would be relevant in other settings:

—ask a whole staff (or School Council/Board of Governors) to 'mark' the same piece of children's writing and then analyse the points of difference;

—collect all the writing done by two students over one week in all subjects and ask small departmental groups to discuss what picture of learning the collated writing offers;

—follow an individual pupil or class around a school for one day recording some aspect of language or interaction.

Knott also provides a draft questionnaire for collecting teachers' views:

(1) how do you allow for the importance of language in learning in your subject?

(2) what kind of balance do you think there ought to be between writing, listening, and talking in your subject?

(3) do you see language in your classroom and your particular subject as:
   (a) a means of transmitting knowledge from teacher to pupil: or
   (b) a means of interpretation of new and unfamiliar ideas in terms of what is already known?

(4) do your lessons provide sufficient opportunity for pupils to rework (in talk and/or writing) the information you wish to convey? If 'yes' please explain how in some detail.

(5) how important is the use of worksheets in your subject?

(6) are the worksheets part of a strategy involving the teacher or are they self-contained teaching strategies in themselves?

(7) has group work (up to six pupils) any function/value in your subject? Please explain fully.

(8) in your opinion what sort of difficulties constitute a 'language problem'?

(9) to whom if anyone would you refer a pupil with a language problem?

(10) how important is the marking of errors in spelling, punctuation and expression?

(11) have you any strategies for marking pupils' work?

(12) who should be concerned to develop and extend a pupil's vocabulary?

(13) what special reading demands does your subject make?

(14) is the reading material that is offered to pupils sufficiently clear to them?

(15) do you teach reading in your particular subject? what help do you give in comprehension?

(16) to what extent do you feel the English department should be

responsible for pupils' accuracy of expression?
(17) do you see any value in examining the use of 'language across the curriculum' and developing a common policy for the school? Please be frank.

Staff development

In many schools staff development languishes for want of a spur to action. Fact gathering about preferred development activities may provide that spur. Maybin (1985) offers a grid of activities that could be presented to staff for them to fill in quickly as a guide to the kind of developmental activities that are preferred. On the vertical axis of the grid she lists:

—a workshop run by one or two staff;
—a questionnaire/survey and discussion;
—an outside speaker;
—small groups preparing discussion papers;
—staff discussion of documents, articles etc;
—make and analyse a classroom videotape;
—staff try out particular activities and discuss the results.
—etc.

To gather information on possible subject matter for each of these activities, the grid's horizontal axis lists:

—exploring staff attitudes towards language and dialect;
—involving parents in children's reading and language work;
—supporting bilingual pupils' languages;
—developing a school marking policy;
—discussing classroom talk;
—investigating children's language repertoires.
—etc.

Each of these lists could be extended or varied depending on need. Chapters 5, 7, 8 and 9 provide material that supports thinking in all of these subject areas and suggest many more topics for in-service work as well. A policy group embarking on the fact gathering phase can readily use this small survey approach to gauge possible starting points for staff development in their school.

Current teacher practices

It helps everyone if they know where their own classroom practices stand in relation to the school's norm. Very often teachers have no idea how their colleagues approach their work in the classroom. Sometimes everyone assumes that there are broad practices that are shared by everyone and which noone would disagree with or criticise. More than this, very often teachers have ironic views of their colleagues' professional style and the priorities that they would support in their pedagogies. These views may be based on no better evidence than some item of staffroom conversation or on some random observation of colleagues engaged in teaching. Below is a questionnaire used at departmental level in one Inner London Education Authority secondary school. Again the model could be adapted to suit any kind of school organisation:

'Please answer the following questions frankly after discussing them at a full departmental meeting (i.e. lower and upper school combined):

(1) To what extent are the following language elements important in your subject:
(a) reading;
(b) writing;
(c) talking?

(2) In what teaching situations are the following mostly used:
(a) reading;
(b) writing;
(c) talking?

(3) In the main what sort of writing do you expect from pupils (e.g. copying, notetaking, essay, story, poem, etc)?

(4) In pupils' written work is there a departmental policy for guiding and/or correcting pupils' use of language? If so, what aspects of language in particular?

(5) How does most reading occur in your subject?

(6) What kind of reading materials are used most?

(7) To what extent are the reading ages of pupils taken into account when providing reading materials? Please provide a typical piece of reading normally used in your subject for:
(a) first year;
(b) third year;
(c) fifth year of secondary schooling.

(8) Are there opportunities for talk in your subject? What purpose does the talk serve?

(9) Are there any special language requirements or difficulties in your subject? Are they identifiable? If so, has your department developed any strategies to deal with them?

(10) How far do you see your department responsible for language standards within the school?

(11) If possible, please prepare a brief statement (one page) outlining how your department could contribute to the development of language ability throughout children's years at this school.

Student first language experiences and classroom demands

Valuable information about the school's language programme can be gathered directly from older children. Knott (1985) offers a specimen 'Record of Reading Activities' which pupils can be asked to fill out. A set of records like this, provided by children at different levels over a fixed period surveying the entire curriculum, will be a good guide to children's reading experience and the kinds of demands that are being placed on them across the curriculum. A fragment from Knott's example is shown below:

[Student's Name]

Period →	1	2	3	4	5	6	7	8
Subject →	Drama	French	—PE—		—History—		Music	Math
Monday		READ QUESTIONS FROM BLACKBOARD			READ CHAPTER FROM TEXT BOOK		READ ONE PIECE THREE TIMES	READ ITEMS IN TEXT BOOK

After collating the whole survey policy makers might ask whether or not:

— enough sustained reading is being received by the children across the curriculum;
— the reading provoked any real response;
— there is too much emphasis on worksheets;
— there is enough attention to individual reading skills or development?

Torbe (1980) reports an investigation using the 'fog index' into the reading material given across the curriculum to a first year secondary class. By matching the results of a survey of this kind with tests of the reading age and reading experience of pupils themselves, schools can judge how closely reading development compares with the demands placed on children as readers. The 'fog index' is not perfect but it does provide some guide to a text's difficulty level. It works as follows:

(1) take a number of samples from the text each of 100 words;
(2) count the number of complete sentences in each sample and the number of words in these sentences;
(3) divide the number of words by the number of sentences to obtain the average sentence length;
(4) count the number of words of three or more syllables in the total sample;
(5) divide by the number of 100 word samples to obtain the percentage of long words in the text as a whole;
(6) to obtain the 'fog index' add the average sentence length to the percentage of long words and multiply this total by 0.4. The final figure will give an approximate guide to the year of schooling to which the reading material is suited.

A questionnaire is an alternative way of soliciting pupils' opinions about language issues and language in learning. The risks in using questionnaires already discussed in this chapter become more pronounced in surveying student responses than they were in surveying staff attitudes. When a questionnaire is used with teaching colleagues there is quite a lot of common ground between those doing the survey and those responding; the cultures of the two groups and the 'interpretative repertoires' that they share give good reasons for believing that the findings of questionnaires faithfully represent staff opinion. The more distant the respondents are in culture and world view from the researchers the more likely it is that false interpretations will be placed on the findings, especially if the data supports prejudices and views that are already in the researchers' minds. Children are quite distant from adults in their culture and world view and it is as well to remember this when interpreting their responses to anything, especially questionnaires.

Knott (1985) offers a questionnaire for use with secondary children:

(1) In your lessons each day, do you get work which involves you in:
   (a) *group work*:   a lot quite a lot sometimes hardly ever never
   (b) *talk/discussion*: a lot quite a lot sometimes hardly ever never
   (c) *notetaking*:   a lot quite a lot sometimes hardly ever never
   (d) *revision*:   a lot quite a lot sometimes hardly ever never
   (e) *redrafting*:   a lot quite a lot sometimes hardly ever never
(2) Which subjects in your opinion involve you most in:
   (a) group work;
   (b) notetaking;
   (c) revision;

(d) redrafting?
(3) (i) do you have any preference for any of the above methods of learning? If yes, say which ones.
   (ii) do you know of any other methods of learning?
(4) Why do you prefer your chosen method? Can you think of some reasons?
(5) Do you feel that you achieve less in some subjects because:
  (a) the subject matter is difficult;
  (b) the language in which it is expressed is difficult for you to understand;
  (c) any other reason?
(6) Do you think it would improve your understanding and enjoyment of a subject if the teachers helped you to understand:
  (i) through discussion and exploration;
  (ii) through the language in which the subject matter is expressed;
  (iii) through its specialist vocabulary first?
(7) can you give some reasons why you feel you are not learning or understanding as much as you would like to? List your reasons below without mentioning teachers' names?
  (i)
  (ii)
  (iii)

Knott's analysis of the findings of a small sample of responses to this questionnaire makes interesting reading. A similar analysis conducted with children in any upper primary or secondary school would assemble facts that might offer some basis for planning. Other techniques include: collecting recordings of a range of pupil talk, transcribing parts of these and basing small group teacher discussion upon them; comparing pupil language performances on a specific and carefully defined task; making videotapes of teachers doing whole class or small group teaching and comparing styles and impact; and recording teacher language and overt use of metacognitive skills as a guide to pupil learning through teacher language. Chapter 5 takes all of these matters much further, especially in relation to children's first language development in the eight modes of language use that are described there.

Children's language diversity

Obviously this area of fact gathering has to be approached with care and sensitivity. Perhaps in a pluralist community knowledge under this heading will be so important to a school's operation that its collection is automatically regarded as a large-scale research activity. Methods already discussed in an earlier section may be more suitable and will certainly be more accurate than any simple questionnaire or collection of staff opinions. School record cards are often used as a basis for action in matters of child language diversity. My own experience in using record cards in schools convinces me that in the absence of some carefully controlled and formal process of fact gathering prior to their compilation these documents should be regarded as very suspect: in the absence of confirming evidence school record cards should be treated as unreliable guides for basing anything important upon.

A starting point in surveying children's language diversity is to make sure that parents and children understand what is going on: what sort of information is needed; why is it needed; who is going to have access to it; how long will the information be kept? It is also important that those organising fact gathering in this area are familiar with the fundamental theoretical issues already discussed in this chapter: how is the kind of language that children use affected by different contexts of situation and by serving different functions of language? Teachers need to know a lot about language before they can gather reliable information about language use and this will involve some kind of formal study to gain expertise. Acquiring this kind of theoretical knowledge is part of any fact gathering task. Again Maybin suggests a checklist for carrying out a school language diversity survey and it is presented in modified form below:

(1) What sources are there from which to collect information about your pupils' languages (e.g. pupil interviews, data already available)?
(2) How are you going to discuss with pupils and their parents the reasons for collecting this information?
(3) Who is going to interview the children?
(4) Is there any way in which children themselves can collect information from each other about what languages they speak, when, why and to whom?
(5) How can the results of the survey be seen as a collection of resources that is available for the school to draw on, rather than a list of individual differences?
(6) How can monolingual children be involved?
(7) How can the questionnaire be trialled in advance with a small number of children and revised?
(8) Will some of the population or a fraction of the sample be

examined using more sensitive methods so that comparisons can be made?

The list below provides discussion points which grew out of a single study carried out in one school (Leicester Bilingual Support Group, 1982). In this primary school, teachers asked bilingual children in the school about language behaviour in their families and specifically what language they used across several contexts, ranging from informal family conversations, through peer group interactions, and onto school usage. I have several reservations about this direct approach to the children for information of this kind (see discussion of the Survey of British Dialect Grammar in the final section of Chapter 5) but in this instance it seems to have worked without adverse effects, perhaps because several methods were integrated: with some children the questionnaire was read to them individually and their answers taperecorded; with others it was read to them in groups and they recorded their own answers on paper:

(1) The younger the child the more the mother tongue was used. Do we take account of this in our reception classes?

(2) Once the child is at school the mother tongue is used appreciably less. Should the school encourage more?

(3) Outside the school the younger children use a substantial amount of mother tongue while the older children use it considerably less. Is this an indication of peer group conditioning?

(4) Despite this a knowledge of skipping rhymes, games and name-calling increases with age?

(5) No matter what age the child and no matter how long resident in England, the grandparents always use the mother tongue with the children.

(6) During art and craft activities, older children used more mother tongue than in other school activities. Does the relaxed and informal atmosphere allow for greater freedom of conversation in mother tongue?

(7) Boys used slightly more mother tongue than girls in all situations except for shopping and explaining to a friend. Is this because girls have more responsibility for shopping for the home in familiar local shops?

(8) It was noted in the playground that boys tend to mix in multilingual groups whereas girls' groups are more monolingual. Has the nature of the games being played got any bearing on this?

(9) Many of the children expressed a desire to read their mother tongue, this desire growing as they got older. A possible reason

for this was the need to associate with what their parents were reading and to communicate with relatives abroad. This poses the question as to why these children do not attend mother tongue classes or perhaps they do and we don't know about it? The school could help. Why not teach reading, writing and oral skills in the mother tongue?

(10) There appeared to be certain differences in competence and use of mother tongue amongst different ethnic groups. Punjabi children showed a greater use of mother tongue at playtime and in watching TV where they were able to form their own social groups. However when playing organised games and in name-calling, the opportunity for using the mother tongue was reduced. We assume the reason being that Punjabi is a minority language within the school.

Although this is an admirable discussion of the survey's findings, it still reveals two dangerous tendencies which are always possible in school studies of this kind: conclusions erected on the data in several places are too dogmatic; and rather simple explanations are sometimes offered for child behaviour. The use of an expert consultant of some kind, to help interpret the data, might have lessened these two tendencies; it is possible that an important piece of work like this should have been done through a large-scale survey, conducted by a consultant from the outset. On the other hand surveys of this latter kind are beyond the resources of most contemporary schools and this Leicester school has gone a long way towards compensating for that lack. One outstanding feature of the discussion, reflected in the teachers' genuine concern with the issues and with doing something for their bilingual pupils, is the contrast between this school-level development and the largely monolingual policies for education at a national level in Britain that are discussed in Chapter 6.

The community itself

The task of collecting information about the community itself is more within the range of school-based researchers. Most information of this kind is of the commonsense variety. But because schools rarely assemble this information in a systematic way, it is rarely referred to in systematic discussions of school policies. Increasingly education systems in New Zealand, Canada and Australia urge schools to become more systematically informed about the social and cultural characteristics of their local communities. Questions like the following have particular value when school communities are experiencing high levels of social change, cultural mobility and financial dislocation:

(1) What are the distinctive features of your school's community?
    —residential urban?
    —industrial?
    —mobile?
    —close-knit?
(2) What ethnic minority communities does your school serve?
(3) Who are the leaders in these communities?
(4) What are the communication networks within these communities?
    —church-centred?
    —based on tribal divisions?
    —home based?
    —media contacts within communities?
(5) What procedures are presently used to discover the educational hopes and wishes of the communities?
    —sports gatherings?
    —open days?
    —cultural gatherings?
    —informal social gatherings?
(6) How do you involve the communities in the school's management?
    —curriculum planning and development?
    —staffing decisions?
    —pupil guidance, counselling and discipline?
    —representation on school committees and boards of advice?
(7) What areas of the school programme make use of community members' languages and skills?
    —bilingual assistance?
    —translating and interpreting?
    —inducting new arrivals?
    —across the curriculum?
(8) What facilities are shared with the communities?
(9) What extra-curricular involvement does the school have with the communities?
(10) Is there a person on the staff responsible for home-school liaison?
(11) Are parents and other community members welcome to observe and participate in classroom activities and in student social occasions?

(12) How are parents involved in assisting their children's learning, especially their reading, writing and oral work?
(13) How does the school communicate with parents about their children's language development?

Cultural awareness

Raising the schools awareness of cultural diversity, as it affects the schools, is more an activity for staff development or for general discussion in a school committee meeting. The questions listed in this section and in the next are only introductory. They may lead to more intensive activities, to more searching fact gathering and also spill over in their effect into the curriculum of the school in ways that are addressed in detail in Chapters 5 to 9:

(1) What different cultures are represented within your school?
(2) How is this diversity reflected in the character of the school?
(3) How does the school give value to the special experiences that culturally different children can offer?
(4) How do children and staff learn about important cultural practices of the cultures represented in the school?
(5) What are the provisions for staff, children and community to work together?
(6) What are the different perceptions of educational and social success in the cultures represented in your school?
(7) How does your school presently respond to overt racist behaviour among staff and children (name calling, denigratory comments about other cultures, physical assaults, stereotyping, deliberate mispronunciation of names etc)?

Provisions for community language support

This final fact-gathering activity anticipates work discussed in Chapters 6, 7 and 8 assembling specific policy items that will offer a programme of school action in supporting community languages. The questions below are preliminary ones to provide the data on which initial planning can be based:

(1) What do you know about the languages represented in your school?
—what languages are spoken?
—who speaks these languages?

—how many speak these languages?
—what other languages are spoken in your community?
—what languages do your students understand?
—what languages do your students read and write?
—how can you get this information?

(2) How is the use of community languages promoted in your school?
(a) informally
—cultural activities
—school routines
—enrolments
—reception
—counselling
—others

(b) formally
—ceremonies
—newsletters
—reports
—letters

(3) What provisions are made for the formal learning of community languages?
—language classes
—in-service training
—funding through external study
—space and time allocations
—assessment across the curriculum
—placement of students
—timetabling

(4) Where there are formal language classes, how are they organised?
—multi-level
—emphasis on language awareness
—language acquisition
—language development and maintenance
—bilingualism maintenance or transition
—other

(5) How does your school support community efforts at language maintenance?
—use of buildings
—resource materials, equipment and staffing
—active participation
—publicity
—mutual assistance

Notes to Chapter 3

1. The rest of this book suggests background knowledge that seems important for those engaged in fact-gathering for language policies across the curriculum. By putting forward this catalogue of knowledge, that seems important for people engaged in language policy making, I am also outlining a preliminary and tentative 'curriculum' for those teacher educators in universities and colleges who are interested in introducing courses in 'language policy across the curriculum' at senior undergraduate or at postgraduate levels. These are more modest proposals than those suggested elsewhere for a 'graduate programme in the sociology of language' (Fishman, 1978) and differ in that they have a specifically applied 'education' bias.

4 Policy making at school level

The amount of theoretical work in Education in the area of constructing policies at the school level is small. There is a wealth of information relevant to large scale policies that have their impact across educational systems. Indeed several international journals are devoted entirely to the task of examining large scale policies and reporting theory development in the area of policy studies. Yet very little work has been done to improve our knowledge about policy making and planning at the level of the single institution in education. Part of the problem is that we cannot really have much generalisable knowledge about policy construction at the school level since each institution differs in its needs and arrangements, nowhere more so than in language diversity.

I am advocating here a commonsense definition for 'policy' which is similar to the one offered by Caldwell & Spinks in their studies of policy management at the school level (1986; 1988): a simple policy consists of a statement of purpose (probably derived from the school's philosophy) and one or more broad guidelines as to how that purpose is to be achieved. This taken together with other policies provides a framework for the operation of the school. A policy will allow discretion in its implementation, with the basis for that discretion often stated as part of the policy.

Some differences should be noted between this view of policy and others that are often advanced. An examination of some policy handbooks suggests that what they sometimes refer to as policies are really statements of philosophy or of goals. Other policy handbooks are often simply collections of rules or procedures. The concept offered here mediates between the two: it is a statement of purpose, which is usually derived from what philosophical positions (if any) the institution espouses; and it provides guidelines that are clear enough to make the intent and pattern for action clear, but broad enough to allow those concerned with implementation an opportunity to use their professional judgment from situation to situation. Policies mediate between a school's 'charter' or 'philosophy' and what really happens in a school; policies say 'how we will do what we hope to do'.

A policy then sets out guidelines that provide a framework for action in achieving some purpose on a substantive issue. This suggests that not all issues in schools need a policy but only those of substance and importance. Most curriculum issues in education fall into this category of being substantial and important. We do need policies in modern schools to set out our considered responses to issues that involve beliefs or values or philosophy: things like providing assistance to a wide range of children with special curriculum needs, for the allocation of scarce resources needed by teachers in developing their curriculum programme, for the use of facilities, for integrating the help of parents and the community into the school, and so on. The one policy that reaches across all of these and many other areas is a language policy that sees language as the central instrument in learning and as the most accessible pedagogy available to teachers across the curriculum. An LPAC is not a 'simple' policy however; to appreciate its complexity it may be useful to think of it as a bundle of policies, each one addressing a substantive language-related issue in the school and in its social context.

In designing a school language policy we are engaged in a small-scale act of 'language planning' (see Chapter 2). Language planning at national levels is a highly developed and skilled activity, which in the last decades of the twentieth century is set against a rich background of theory and research. But language planning at the school level is a new activity for which very little background theory is available. In thinking about small-scale language planning of this kind one reasonable approach is to follow the lead already set for language planning at national levels: language planning of this kind is 'the organised pursuit of solutions to language problems' (Kennedy, 1984: 55). Although nearly all of the work in language planning to date has been done at the national or system level, we can derive some broad points about what to do at school levels from that work. Kennedy's focus is almost entirely on large-scale planning; he summarises authoritative views about macro planning in the following way: 'language planning must take full account of the socio-cultural context in which the planning is taking place' and any plan developed 'must be flexible enough to readjust itself to unexpected system linkages discovered during the evaluation phase' (p. 2). This evolutionary approach begins with problem identification and the posing of tentative solutions. Flexibility and tentativeness then are essential components at every point in the process. The approach advocated in this chapter tries to allow flexibility and tentativeness while still providing rigour and purpose.

School Policy, Organisational Theory and the Ethics of School Management

A school policy is a device for guarding against practices that may be insensitive to the needs and interests of children: practices that may not often be deliberate professional malpractice but derive rather from a lack of reflection or from following personal whim, caprice or habits of patronage.

A school that is amoral in its organisational practices is a powerful force for doing harm; it may be massively 'miseducative' in that it gives children clear but unstated examples of human behaviour that are contrary to the explicit messages about human behaviour that the school itself seeks to disseminate through its formal curriculum. As a small example, many schools in the Western world in the 1970s and 1980s moved quickly and compellingly to develop policies on smoking by their staff members in and around the school environment. These policies were responses to major changes in community values about smoking and these changes alerted schools to a serious ethical and organisational problem which created a mismatch between the professed values of schools and the values that they demonstrated to children.

In understanding the range of problems in school organisation that well written and widely supported policies can counter, I find relevance in the work of those educational administration theorists who are critics of the conventional approach to educational administration theory and who offer alternative perspectives on the 'reality' of educational organisations.

There are grave dangers in uncritically applying to policies the rational or conventional approach to understanding educational organisations, which adopts a broad systems perspective: seeing organisations as social systems. The role of the policy maker on this rational account is to generalise, abstract, universalise and so come to understand ultimate social reality and plan for it. Organisations are seen as phenomenal entities engaged in goal-seeking behaviour; they are instruments of social and cultural order. In following this systems approach policy makers set themselves the tasks of identifying structures in their organisation and showing how they work or fail to work in achieving ends. Any pathology in the body of the organisation that policy addresses can be cured in principle by identifying its causes and by then rearranging the organisation's structures, which means making planned alterations in its hierarchical arrangements: tinkering with the structures.

In opposition to the conventional systems approach is the significant movement of theorists who question how much of importance we can really know about educational organisations. This question responds to another more enduring debate which questions what schools ought to be doing; the former debate is of course dependent on the latter at many points, and it informs my own interest in linking educational administration (as means) more closely with curriculum planning (as ends). On this alternative account theories about educational organisations are seen as very limited in what they can tell us. We judge and theorise according to our notions of what is and what ought to be. We interpret our world and from that interpretation construct our own reality. There is always a tension then between conjectures of reality and reality itself; organisations are seen to consist of the accumulation of the realities and meaningful actions of involved individuals: they are areas of belief, not of knowledge, and their problems are not structural, they are ideological. Effective cures for the pathologies of organisations, on this account, are to be found in assessing the intentions of participants and in attempting to change some of those intentions, rather than in attempting first to fiddle with the organisation's hierarchical structures.

This second view about organisations seems closer to what reflective practitioners (in my experience) now believe about schools and school systems. This view about organisations is also broadly consistent with current views in the philosophy of the social sciences.[1] A central point for policy making in educational organisations that comes from this latter view is that there is not much that we can know about the policy needs of organisations without finding out about the values, the inclinations and the motives of the people within them. The relevance of this discussion to school level policy making becomes clearer if we recognise that the chief task of policies is to help us in dealing with values issues: to help us in managing ethical complexity. We can readily appreciate why schools and school systems present situations for decision making that are value laden and complex (Corson, 1985a). The school is far more complex, I believe, in the ethical relationships it harbours than any other institution that humankind has developed. Problems of value complexity are inevitable in a system established on the premise that in order to prepare young people to be 'free' and responsible in a free society we should take away their freedom by having them attend compulsory institutions for 11 or 12 years.

Problems of organisational and ethical complexity often arise in schools because of our need to accommodate to two seemingly opposed inclinations that we hold as professionals: on the one hand we are rightly anxious to treat children fairly and as individuals in schools; on the other hand we are aware that schools are places run on essentially utilitarian lines, where the greatest good of the greatest number is usually and reasonably the only guiding ethical principle that has some relation to reality. Goal confusion can result, frustrating our efforts as administrators to accommodate to either inclination with consistency.

Set against this ethical challenge and the reasonable view that school organisations are belief systems, reflecting each participant's different goals and values, a collaboratively produced set of policy documents, responsive as far as possible to the perceptions of the organisation that each individual has, may represent the only hope of offering a satisfactory plan of action for dealing with complex issues. The alternative may be for educational administrators to see their task as comprising a series of situations that require decisions governed by short term exigencies that can be met by whatever expedient measures are to hand. I prefer the policy approach.

Teachers' Personal Realities, Participation and Commitment

Participation is both an end in itself and a device for producing other ends. When people come together to plan something there is obvious value to them in the feedback, skill development, social interaction and knowledge growth that they receive. More than this, participation usually fosters a commitment in people to the results or product of their participation, provided those results seem reasonable to them. In this way policy making can become a staff development activity that has rewards at several levels.

One way of moving into this activity, with much to recommend it, is for one or two people to compile a brief and well written discussion document which sets out the specific issues, which is sufficiently general not to threaten the interests of its readership, and which canvasses a wide range of tentative directions that could be followed with good educational effect (Goodhand, 1986). The starting point for documents of this kind might be the writings of recognised experts who are working in or have written about the problem area. One aim of discussion documents of this kind should be to promote as much group participation in the follow-up discussion as is possible. A pamphlet prepared by the National Association for the Teaching of English (NATE, 1976) makes useful suggestions about 'who does what' and about 'possible pitfalls'. Another starting point for policy making is when someone is recognised by the group as a whole as coordinating things. This person need not have a senior position in the institution; in fact free participation by others may be hindered when the policy task seems to give new authority to an individual. A coordinator for any task should be a respected person: someone with justifiable influence in the area of concern, not just a person of status. Of course in a small school this may be the principal or a deputy. The ideal coordinator for an LPAC may be a language consultant, either appointed specifically for the purpose of coordinating things or seconded part-time from other duties. As part of their deliberations policy makers will need to consider whether the school is to have a consultant or not, what the limits to the consultant's responsibilities might be, and whether or not oversight and revision of the LPAC can be reasonably left to the consultant?

Because there are many things that can be done to get the policy making process started, sometimes schools place too much stress on these preliminary activities and fail to reach the point of policy making, which is providing solutions to carefully identified problems. Assuming that some individual or small group provides the catalyst for developing a policy, an early task is to float the idea with the staff as a whole and invite participation. These preliminaries will be easier where there is an established policy about policy making (see below). An early need will be a policy planning group which should exclude noone who is interested in participating. I have already mentioned the desirability of a coordinator. Other early steps (in an LPAC) are: to consult the school's board, committee, school council or governors and invite their involvement; establish links with similar policy groups in other schools; and open discussions with key members of the community. The amount of time devoted to any of these things in the early stages of policy making will be influenced by their relevance to the fact gathering activities (see Chapter 3) which precede the identification of the problems that the policy will address.

There are often staff members in schools who lack commitment to some aspect of the school's programme for one reason or another. A new school policy idea, to which those staff members have no clear and direct commitment, may be welcomed in various destabilising ways: by a 'go-slow approach'; by ironicising its purpose (poking fun at it; questioning its real objective; slandering the 'true' aims of its proponents); or by other more direct obstructionist methods. There are many reasons why people behave in these ways in organisations and not all of them derive from simple perversity, personal inadequacy or laziness. For example: people as individuals and as groups have difficulty understanding policies that are handed to them as *faits accomplis* for translation into action within their own settings. As mentioned, there are difficulties for all of us in complex institutions in understanding 'organisational reality'; this problem of understanding the organisation can be made worse when only the dominant (or single policy maker's) view of the organisation is given high credibility since this may be contrary to the way other individuals perceive it. Although the ways that individuals perceive organisational reality are inevitably similar to some extent because of our common membership of a single species and our common linguistic history (Corson, 1986b), individual participants do have radically different views of their organisations and accommodate to them in different ways. Presthus' study (1962) examined the ways in which individuals in organisations accommodate to bureaucratic pressure (of the type that policies regularly bring): some uncritically adopt the values of the organisation's policies and become 'upward mobiles'; some reject the organisation's values (e.g. of what constitutes success and power) and become 'indifferents'; and some cannot make the accommodations necessary to achieve security within the organisation, even while not willing to become indifferent to it, and become 'ambivalent'. There may be other responses. A policy that fails to address the organisational realities of individuals, their values and ends, risks pushing people into a range of undesirable accommodation modes. Participation in the construction of policies can convince people that the aims of the policies themselves are worthy of some measure of loyalty and commitment; genuine efforts at mutual adaptation in the direction of the policy's broad intentions can result. How does this work?

Prudential policies do have a strong role to play in coalescing the interests of people who might not otherwise identify favourable courses of action for themselves. As Fuller (1987) observes: a growing range of studies from radically unrelated paradigms (e.g. social psychology, psychoanalysis, Marxism etc) suggests the incompetence of people in general in judging their own attitudes and interests, including the courses of action that are most likely to produce what they want to happen. The very act of making a policy, then, can attend to the essential 'aimlessness' that most of us feel for a good deal of the time and replace it with a rationally based commitment.

In constructing small-scale policies, then, it is better when the implementers of the policy have had a real hand in policy design in the first place; it is better when personal interests and matters of control are approached as open-ended issues for discussion. Widespread commitment to the resulting policy's ideas and an understanding of their relevance will be more likely. In preparing a curriculum policy, for example, the entire staff need to know that specific tuition in certain skills is to be given by known teachers and at agreed stages; it is also essential that those giving specific tuition know that a context and purpose for the re-application of those skills will be created by their colleagues. Speaking specifically about language policies, Lewis (1981) sets out three requirements: the policy must conform to the expressed attitudes of those involved; it must persuade those who express negative attitudes about the rightness of the policy; and it must seek to remove the causes of disagreement. All of this seems straightforward enough in principle; seeking collaborative agreement of this kind is the essence of good management. But these days we are urged to go further.

Modern schools seeking to reduce the social distance between themselves and the communities from which their students are drawn are trying to extend participation in policy making to parents and others as well. Although in modern democracies parents and community members are increasingly better placed to influence a school's programme, there is often very strong reluctance on the part of parents to participate very much in school governance. In advanced industrial societies parents willingly concede authority to professionals (Murphy, 1980). It will take persistence on the school's part to overcome this reluctance to participate. At the same time it will take strength of purpose not to cater simply for the needs and interests of the politically active in preference to the apathetic (Pascal, 1987), of the rich in preference to the poor, or of the culturally similar in preference to the culturally different (Fargher & Ziersch, 1981). The implementation of a language policy, for example, will need to be explained carefully to parents and to those critics of a school who tend to demand product rather than process from its curriculum. This will pose a serious difficulty in those communities where parents perceive schools as existing expressly to reproduce a particular cultural bias or to maintain a social *status quo*. In New Zealand, for example, the phenomenon of 'white flight' has been noticed in some schools where new 'policies' of biculturalism have been introduced by administrators without the latter communicating and negotiating those policies with the many parents whose backgrounds are narrowly monocultural. Many parents have withdrawn their children from the schools and sent them elsewhere.

A wise policy about policy making will mention ingenious but practical ways in which parents can be involved in the design of policies or at least ways that they can be kept informed about the stages in policy development. If this is to be more than tokenism, the goals and organisational reality of the school will need to be communicated over a long period to the community, beginning in small ways but extending deliberately and purposefully until regular two-way communication becomes commonplace and natural. A well thought out policy may be needed for just this task alone, providing a bridge to other developments.

Schools collaboratively managed and with agreed and working policies are more likely to be places of staff and community commitment. They tend to escape the trap of having their procedures and styles of operation modelled on the dominant points of view only which are inevitably filled with error and narrow in range and compass. In the eyes of the public they are also more 'legitimate' places, a point that relates to the theorising of Habermas (1985) which is at the forefront of social philosophy. Habermas has written extensively about problems of communication and language in general and I am linking his ideas here with policy making at the school level.

School Policy Making as a Language Activity

Habermas' conclusion is that a new form of 'institutionalised discourse' is needed in social institutions in Western democracies if they are to recapture their legitimacy for people in general, their sense of direction, and the motivation of their participants and adherents. Habermas writes of the need for 'an ideal speech situation' in which there are no external constraints preventing participants from assessing evidence and argument, and in which each participant has an equal and open chance of entering into discussion. In this section I look closely but selectively at a complex set of ideas from Habermas that seem to have important applied value for policy making at the level of the school. As well as drawing on Habermas himself (1970; 1985), I also use the work of several interpreters of his ideas (McCarthy, 1984; Bernstein, 1985; Giddens, 1985; Carr & Kemmis, 1986; and Rizvi & Kemmis, 1987).

When a person says something to another, Habermas suggests that the second person is able to make the following [validity] claims:

(1) that what is said is intended to be intelligible, offering a 'meaning'

which can be understood;

(2) that the propositions or factual assertions offered by the speaker as part of the speech are true;

(3) that the speaker is justified in saying what is said, not going outside social rights or norms for that context of speech;

(4) that the speaker is sincere in what is said, not intending to deceive the listener.

In ideal and undistorted communication speakers can defend (by word or deed) all four of the above claims: what is said is meaningful, true, justified and sincere. When all of the participants in a given speech context are able to do this, when all related evidence can be brought into play, and when nothing apart from logically reasoned argument is used in reaching consensus, then the circumstances provide an 'ideal speech situation'.

In describing his 'ideal speech situation' the starting point for Habermas was to discover the ground rules that allow people all over the world to engage in everyday speech acts (what he calls 'universal pragmatics'). His task was to reconstruct the general presuppositions of these consensual speech actions.

A starting point in appreciating what Habermas is up to is to note that when he talks of an 'ideal' form of speech he is not suggesting that any possible speech situation has the characteristics of this 'ideal speech situation'. He admits that the conditions of actual speech are rarely, if ever, those of the 'ideal speech situation'. What he wants to show is that all exchanges of speech tacitly presume that near-ideal conditions apply and that the four types of validity claim mentioned above do obtain. Indeed if communication is going to take place in speech situations and if rational consensus is an aim of the interaction, then these things on their own require us to presume that ideal conditions obtain. What are the conditions that we would like to obtain when we enter into purposeful discourse?

Firstly most of us expect that any speech situation that we enter into will be one from which the true interests of the participants in the discussion can emerge:

all participants must receive an equal distribution of opportunities to select and use speech acts;

all participants must have an equal chance to initiate and maintain discourse;

all participants must have an equal chance to advance their points of view and question ideas, to give reasons for and against claims made in language.

Secondly we expect that argument and debate will proceed without undue external pressures:

all participants must realise that accidental or systematic constraints on discussion will play no part in it;

all participants must be assured of an equal chance to express feelings, attitudes and intentions;

all participants must be assured of an equal chance to oppose, permit, command, instruct, forbid and any of the other things that any other participants are entitled to do.

Thirdly we expect that the 'force of argument' will prevail; that the outcome of discussion will depend on the force of the better argument.

What remains after all these conditions are met is a democratic form of public discussion that provides a forum for an unforced flow of ideas and arguments: domination, manipulation and control are banished. Again remember that Habermas is urging us to recognise an ideal that does not really exist; an ideal that is merely promised and expected in almost every activity of language. In other words the existence of this ideal situation is inherent in the nature of communication itself. We expect that it operates every time we go to speak; in making an utterance we are holding out the possibility that a form of social life exists in which individuals can have free, open and equal communication with one another.

From the ideas of Habermas we can extract a 'critical measure' of the 'quality of interaction' that takes place in social settings and in social institutions. We can extract those things that are so very often lacking in ordinary speech situations, whose absence distorts communication. Bureaucratic communication (as it is often used in schools, especially larger ones) regularly falls short of this ideal since its purpose is usually to command and to control. There is always some strategic purpose behind the communication. It assumes the existence of roles based on legal authority of some kind; it assumes that it is the role of some to receive impersonal messages and to act upon them without debate or question. It assumes that the weight of tradition, of power or of domination is more important in decision making than the need for rational consensus. In all these respects the normal bureaucratic communication of schools runs counter to the kind of collaborative and participative decision making that an ideal speech situation might allow.

Reinterpreting these ideas of Habermas' into the everyday context of managing schools, we find support in them for the methods of policy discussion and construction that are recommended these days in many quarters: for example the system of 'self-reflective meetings' recommended by Carr & Kemmis (1983) or the stages of 'school development' suggested by Prebble & Stewart (1981). There is a limit to how far we can go with Habermas in applying his ideas and this needs to be mentioned: in any real interactional setting there are individuals who are very different in the abilities that they have and in the knowledge that they possess. It follows that complete consensus between individuals who are unequal in these ways is an impossible ideal: conflict and criticism is not just a desirable way of making our knowledge grow, it is also inevitable between human beings since we are inevitably unequal. What we are offered by Habermas is an attractive ideal. One important result of applying his ideas to debate and discussion about the running of schools is that this 'gloves-off' approach allows participants to reach decisions that cannot be easily ignored: staff members come to expect that meetings will produce decisions that will be acted upon. Although it is true that the interests of individuals and groups stand most obviously in the way of rational openness of this kind, it is also true that we protect ourselves against sectional interests only by taking part in dialogue between groups who have different interests (Young, 1987). The resulting dialogue may not guarantee truth, but it will minimise the biases that can distort decision making.

A Policy About Policy Making

Investigations of failed policies have highlighted the importance of having more than an ad hoc system for policy planning. The design of a language policy across the curriculum can be a relatively straightforward task once general procedures for designing policy at the school level are understood and put into operation, and once the kinds of problems that that policy could address are understood. Policy making at the school level, if approached along the lines that I am advocating here, can provide a core activity for staff professional development, giving cohesion and purpose to that development programme. It also responds to the growing movement of interest groups in education who are calling for 'relatively autonomous' schools. Some of the features of schools of this kind, identified by Bolam (1982), are that they are in a position to make their own educational policy, solve their own practical problems, take initiatives, design and evaluate improvements and respond to change.

The starting point may be in having a policy about policy making that sets up, as far as is possible, the framework for an 'ideal speech situation' for determining how decisions are planned or implemented in the school. This 'policy about policy' could include sections on how priorities for discussion and policy making are arrived at; the process of selecting policy working groups; matters of resources and accountability; procedures for reporting back; steps in final decision making; the location of responsibility for decisions; the methods of implementing decisions; and the steps in the evaluation and reform of policies. If this policy is itself collaboratively produced, and regularly revised, then there is a good prospect of staff supporting later policies created in line with its prescriptions: such as a 'language policy across the curriculum'. Policy making is a precise process that can work at the school level if the process itself is well formulated.

Applying the Stages of a Social Epistemology to School Policy Development

Even with a policy about policy making, policy development in schools remains a difficult process. Among all the significant problem areas that schools face there are usually so many factors that relate to the design of a suitable policy that the task of getting started can be a daunting one. The final chapter of this book tries to pull together the range of factors that relate to an LPAC; it provides signposts that schools can work from or a checklist of starting points for a working document. It is impossible to offer generalisations about school policy making for the reason already offered: schools are not susceptible to generalisations in most of the important problem areas that concern them. What we can do by way of generalisation is talk about the stages in policy design that might be generalisable on logical grounds. Working from an evolutionary approach to the growth of knowledge, we can at least prescribe straightforwardly some stages in policy formulation at the school level that can be used as thinking tools by those engaged in this difficult process.

This section presents a rigorous but straightforward approach to school policy making which is modelled on a well known theory about how knowledge of any kind grows (Corson, 1985c; 1988c). The aim of this approach is to identify the stages that might allow policy makers to create a policy that would be as near to perfection as any policy could be. In undertanding the logic of the stages outlined below there are two requirements. The first is to adopt the view (provisionally) that no knowledge is final or absolute: all knowledge is theory or conjecture about the world and is subject to evolutionary change. The second requirement is to see the tenets of a policy as items of knowledge, as tentative theories posed as solutions to a set of problems. I present here a research paradigm for policy development in the real-world context of schools.

Some alternative school policy making models

This section's approach to policy design differs in its stages from four other approaches outlined here for comparisons sake. The first of these also has four stages (Bridges, 1967):

(1) defining the problem;
(2) identifying possible alternatives;
(3) predicting the consequences of each reasonable alternative;
(4) choosing the alternatives to be followed.

The weakness of this approach to policy making is that its vital third stage depends for its logic on an inductive methodology (prediction) which may or may not produce the best plan for action.

The second approach (Caldwell & Spinks, 1986; 1988) deals with 'contentious issues' and asks that three 'options' be considered as solutions to the problem. We are not told in detail why three options should exhaust the possible options or what processes of error elimination might allow two of these options to be discarded and one to survive. Instead three criteria must be satisfied: 'desirability', 'workability' and 'acceptability'. How these criteria might be operationalised is not discussed yet questions are left begging. For example: what do these terms mean in the context of a school; what subordinate criteria can be used as benchmarks and be set against these three overriding criteria?

Ashworth (1988) presents a third approach. His 'PIE-model' has a three-phase cycle: 'planning', 'implementing' and 'evaluating'. It is not clear from the author's description what the starting point for this process should be, although some problem solving method seems to be implied, if we assume that the implementation stage involves a small-scale trial of whatever was produced in the planning stage. I mention this approach since it is discussed in connection with language policy making. I have to admit to being puzzled by it as a plan for action.

Finally many curriculum theorists recommend and practise a process of reflective deliberation for curriculum planning (Bonser & Grundy, 1988). That process is largely consistent with the evolutionary approach to policy design that I advocate below. In the deliberative process there are usually four phases or cycles (of error elimination):

phase I: consists of planning followed by data production and reflective deliberation at the individual staff member level;

phase II: covers the same activities as phase I but they are carried out at small group level;

phase III: also covers the same activities as phase I but they are carried out at whole group level;

phase IV: involves an outside consultant who formulates a statement about the problem's solution and returns it to all the participants for confirmation that it reflects their viewpoints.

In this four phase process the problem terrain is continually traversed, the theories of participants are continually tested against the evidence available (including that most important form of evidence: the subjective views and wishes of the participants themselves) and the final statement provides some basis for action. Like any form of action research, of course, this approach only succeeds when something close to an ideal speech situation can be taken for granted by all participants. A technical weakness in this approach is its reliance on an outside consultant. A more serious weakness for policy making, although not necessarily for curriculum planning, may be the absence of any recognisable problem identification stage in the process. Re-applying this process from curriculum planning to policy construction may encourage policy makers to pose wrong solutions to non-existent problems.

A rationale for the approach to policy making

The possible superiority of the new approach described here depends solely on the fact that it embraces epistemological claims that are widely supported and have survived the test of time: the template for this approach to the growth of knowledge is nothing less than the evolving theory of evolution itself (Corson, 1988c). I have already mentioned one fundamental requirement in coming to terms with this approach: recognition that all aspects of the universe (including knowledge about those aspects) can only be properly understood if we accept that they are in a constant state of evolutionary change. By reapplying Darwin's theory of natural selection to their ideas about the growth of knowledge, theorists like Popper and Dewey accepted this evolutionary first principle as a template for those theories; indeed the 'stages' in their descriptions of the way knowledge grows represent the non-temporal, overlapping stages through which evolution itself is thought to proceed. These are captured clearly in Popper's often-cited formula:

$$P1 \rightarrow TT \rightarrow EE \rightarrow P2$$

where problem 1 (problem identification) leads to tentative theory (solution), which leads to error elimination, which leads to new problem 2. The stages in policy making set out below are based directly on this formula.

A clear understanding of the problem situation[2] is the starting point for policy research. We see immediately why large-scale attempts to impose policies on schools from outside them are likely to fail: those attempts can rarely be based on a clear understanding of the problem situation, which means an understanding of the school's unique and dynamic social context, its student body, its curriculum, its administrative routines and procedures, its staff and other personnel, its changing aims and responsibilities.

Stages in Policy Making

Problem identification (P1)

The first and most important stage in any problem solving process is the identification and statement of the problem. For school administrators or policy groups this activity should be the most demanding stage of policy development since it asks them to make themselves experts in the field of the problem; it asks that they engage in 'fact gathering' about their school in order to isolate its language problems (see Chapter 3); and it also asks that they take into account any theoretical knowledge which might help them understand and state their language problems as completely as possible.

This problem identification stage is all important. A casual response to identifying the problems will produce a policy that may be less than worthless: it may be harmful. The task of identifying the problem is a job for experts; policy makers need to make themselves expert in the field of the problem in any of the ways that expertise is acquired. There is much evidence now from studies into the nature of expertise to confirm this claim about the value in solving a problem of being an expert (Glaser & Chi, 1988). There are some interesting contrasts between experts and novices in their problem solving ability: experts are faster overall in solving problems of all types; they also achieve a four times higher success rate over novices in all types of problem tasks; but experts are markedly slower in identifying the problem and in analysing it qualitatively. The reasons for this are easy to understand: experts have a great deal of highly organised information about the problem; they engage the problem at deep rather than at superficial levels; and in thinking about it they integrate a broad range of information that relates to the problem. Later they are able to use qualitative rather than quantitative reasoning, which means that they can speculate about a suitable solution without the aid of quantitative data (perhaps the collection of this data then becomes necessary only to check the speculation). They also seem to be more aware than novices of errors that they have made; they know more often why they have failed to comprehend and when they need to check solutions. Their ultimate success is largely due to their having a coherent under-standing of the relevant knowledge, rather than the fragmented grasp that novices have. There are plenty of occasions in schools when administrators need specialist expertise; too often they take action before acquiring it.

For example, one increasingly common problem that faces school administrators in pluralist societies is how to provide second language education to new entrant children who have a first language that is other than the majority language of the society. The common response of school administrators has been to immerse the children as fully as possible in the majority language in the hope that they will catch up with the rest as soon as possible. We know now that this simplistic response can be very wrong for a range of reasons explored more fully in Chapters 7, 8 and 9: the place of the mother tongue in children's intellectual development and in their potential for cognitive growth; the relationship between age of acquisition and linguistic level which governs the kind of educational provision that should be made for individual children. Expertise is needed by policy makers in this and many other areas if they are to avoid ruining the chances for educational success of some new entrant children. This kind of expertise is beyond the everyday professional knowledge that educationists currently possess as a result of the conventional forms of training and professional development that they receive.

Having made themselves expert in the field of the problem, a policy group at the school level will need to assemble a set of key points that emerge from their analysis of the problem situation. Each point will represent a fact of some kind or an item of theory or an informed assumption or even a dominant attitude that relates to the school's language situation. In response to these key points the policy group's task can then be stated: what are the real problems that the school should address in its language policy?

Tentative policy (TT)

The second stage in the problem solving approach is the production of tentative language policy guidelines offered as solutions to the problems. These provide policy conjectures about what might be done in the school setting. The applied value to a school of these conjectural guidelines depends on how readily they can be tested against the real world of the school as working responses to its problems. For this to be able to happen the guidelines need to be stated very clearly which means that the language used cannot be vague, high-sounding, or restricted in meaning to some special interest group. The guidelines can only be put through the tests of the next stage if they are widely understood in the same way by all those whom they affect.

These guidelines will suggest some set of actions that need to be taken (e.g. in response to the summary questions provided in Chapter 10) but they will not involve changes that are too drastic; if the prescribed actions prove to be misguided ones it is important that the organisation is not permanently damaged by having given them a trial and error test. There is need to guard against introducing radical changes that are impossible to control from the outset because they run ahead of the knowledge available for trial and error testing. Some of these actions may involve undertaking large scale research of the kind mentioned in Chapter 3 and the nature of this research and its purpose will be mentioned as one or more of the policy guidelines.

Eliminating error from the tentative policy (EE)

In the third stage the policy group tries to eliminate error from their tentative guidelines by evaluating them against the real world of the school. At this stage, small-scale research methods can be used, similar to those suggested in Chapter 3 which were used in the first problem identifying stage (e.g. surveys of community opinion, action research in classrooms, compilation of demographic data, questionnaire's on teacher attitudes, studies of student needs and competencies). These small-scale research methods will differ in their application at this stage because they will be coupled with trial applications of the policy guidelines. This trial and error process will allow adjustments to be made to the guidelines to reform and improve them.

But these small-scale research methods and trial applications are themselves tentative solutions to other problems (i.e. the problems of finding good ways of testing the original tentative solutions): they too are subject to processes of error elimination since they may not tell us what we think they tell us or all that we need to know. For example a survey of community opinion may provide a very unreliable guide in judging the merit of a point in a policy; the survey's results may be overturned by later more compelling evidence, coming perhaps from face-to-face interviews of the same community members. We accept the findings of these trial and error tests provisionally: not on the basis of some convention or other but with the same critical attitude that we apply to other conjectures. We accept the changes that they imply for our policy guidelines in the same way as we accept the verdict of a jury: that verdict can be quashed or revised in the light of later evidence.

The 'official' policy (P2)

The fourth and final stage in policy research at the school level is the statement of the 'official' policy which includes all the guidelines that have survived testing in the third stage. Obviously this policy will still be conjectural (it offers a new problem P2) since none of the stages that have combined to create it depend on claims about knowledge that are authoritative or absolute, since we assume from the outset that there are no claims of this kind. In later chapters there are specimen LPACs which are solutions that have been offered in some schools to problems that policy makers have identified and which have been provisionally tested.

Another good reason for stating the final policy tentatively is that the language context in schools is a dynamic one: language problems come and go as the social setting of the school changes. A school language policy that is responsive to its social context will partly 'self-destruct' at least once a year: it will include guidelines for self-modification that are flexible enough to provide for unexpected developments or changes in staffing, funding, community involvement, first and second language needs, policy changes from within the wider system and beyond, and theory emanating from research into policy making and language issues. In this evolutionary approach there is no conclusion to research; there is always one more test for any theoretical policy statement.

Conclusion

This evolutionary approach to policy making in education needs integration with the other recommendations made in this Chapter:

for the 'problem identification' stage to succeed:
something close to an ideal speech situation needs to be taken for granted by all participants in the policy making process so that the real problems can be identified without inhibitions based on status and bureaucratic influence playing an exclusionary role;

for the 'tentative policy' stage:
there is a need for written policies if people are to be given the chance to criticise them rationally;

for the error elimination stage (at least):
participation by all relevant persons is advisable if the policies are to have some hope of successful implementation;

for the process as a whole: a 'policy about policy making' seems a sensible preliminary step for introducing this democratic form of decision making in schools.

The advantages of all this can be plainly stated:

—a policy group using the above approach is able to offer implementers clear guidelines for action that have been rigorously tested against theory and experience;
—the policy makers are encouraged to focus on problems that have strict relevance to the policy context;
—participants are discouraged from perceiving the policies produced as 'tablets of stone' that will set limits to future change and reform;
—the policy making process in schools becomes a continuing cycle of review and improvement in response to changing circumstances.

Notes to Chapter 4

1. Views which guide contemporary social research are based on claims such as the following: actions and their descriptions are conceptually tied to reasons and motives and these inform each other reflexively (Hughes, 1983; Outhwaite, 1988). Elaborating on this point: action descriptions are always defeasible (in Quinean terms, the evidence available can always support some other theory about the action); the description of social action is problematic for observers and social actors alike; and social action descriptions are always incomplete. It is a short step from these points to the conclusion that we really need another methodology to that presupposed by the positivist conception of a social science which has guided the conventional approach to organisational theory. Recent views of 'science' are important here too. Harré, for example, is not alone in believing that essential elements in theorising about the unobserved operative mechanisms of social science , must be the actor's own theories about the social world (Harré, 1974: see too Potter & Wetherell, 1987; and Bhaskar, 1978). The proposal, then, of a social scientific theory (even as small a one as a tentative school policy) is more like arguing a political or moral case by taking into account views, interests, attitudes and beliefs of the relevant actors (see Chapter 9). As a result in some social sciences an emphasis on method has declined in favour of a renewed stress on the philosophical basis of social study.

2. I have used the phrase 'language problems' already in many contexts and repeat the claim made in Chapter 1 that I am not using the term 'problems' in this book in any evaluative sense. The neutral sense of the word 'problems' suggests the normal challenges of life that confront us, at every moment of living, to which we pose some tentative solution as a response. Human beings, no less than other creatures, are problem-solving animals: our ability to solve problems effectively determines our control over the environment and our survival itself. The knowledge that each one of us acquires comes from many cycles of problem solving, each cycle beginning with a problem to which we pose some tentative solution. A solution to a problem is something that we test against the real world as a measure of its adequacy, eliminating any obvious errors that it contains. A language policy is very like a solution in this latter sense: it comprises a bundle of solutions, each one addressing a different problem and the whole bundle addressing the school's language problems in general. Language problems in schools are challenges that we can meet in this problem-solving way, by proposing a policy as a tentative solution.

5 Language across the curriculum (LAC)

The idea of linking language across the curriculum (LAC) with school language policies received formal recognition in *A Language for Life* (The Bullock Report) and a decade later was underlined in *Education for All* (The Swann Report):

> Each school should have an organised policy for language across the curriculum, establishing every teacher's involvement in language and reading development throughout the years of schooling (DES, 1975: 514)

> Unless there is a school language and learning policy across the curriculum there will be a wastage of effort and often confusion (DES, 1985: 419).

Much has been learned about language issues since *A Language for Life* was compiled. The ideas of LAC itself, which received real impetus in that Report, have also changed considerably and have been heavily influenced by work outside Britain. The greater change, though, has occurred in the context in which modern schools and educational systems operate and it is this kind of change in many countries that reports like *Education for All* are increasingly being asked to address. LAC is no longer narrowly seen as the domain of the mother tongue, nor is it confined solely to the conventional 'four modes of language'.

So much has been written about LAC in recent decades that it is hard for teachers not to know, in broad terms at least, what the doctrine is all about. Perhaps because so much has been said many people have become rather confused about LAC's meaning and indeed about whether it has any meaning that can be translated into practice. Put simply the ideas that LAC espouses place emphasis firmly on learning and less on direct teaching; it tries to put into practice Moffett's view that rendering experience into words is the real business of schools. A commitment to

LAC means asking teachers to move more regularly and more deliberately away from centre stage in the classroom; it means encouraging children to use their own language as their tool for interpreting the content of the curriculum and for mastering it. But LAC does not ask that teachers abrogate their responsibilities; rather it implies greater responsibilities for teachers in planning and individualising instruction. Its widespread introduction may bring to an end what some regard (R. Young, 1987) as the indoctrinatory practices that direct teaching methods usually entail.

On the other hand LAC does not involve greater changes than most teachers already feel are necessary, changes that vary considerably depending on the level of schooling at which they are introduced. The first part of this chapter considers the meaning and place of LAC and the role for the teacher that it implies. By identifying these roles I am implying professional development activities that may be a necessary part of developing an LPAC. Many teachers will find that these roles, spelled out for children at different age levels, are very like their present classroom practices. Others may find in them food for thought in adjusting their teaching practices in relation to an LPAC. Later the chapter looks at the specific LAC areas that a school policy might address. In all of what follows 'language' is seen in its widest possible sense. It includes the following eight modes of human activity:

listening: which is the activity of attending to the oral language of others and giving meaning to it;

speaking: which is the activity of expressing meaning to others by and through oral language;

reading: which is the activity of attending to the written language of others and giving meaning to it;

writing: which is the activity of expressing meaning to others by and through written language;

moving: which includes the activities of using facial expression, gesturing and whole-body movements to express meaning to others;

watching: which is the activity of attending to the movements of others and giving meaning to those movements;

shaping: which is the activity of using visual effects to express meaning to others;

viewing: which is the activity of attending to the visual effects created by others and giving meaning to those effects.

This list includes four modes of language which are not always part of a list of this kind, yet commonsense seems to demand that we see language in this wider way. People from many cultures are talented users of the last four modes while the language user who is confined to the first four may be at a disadvantage in many settings where communication is needed. These eight modes include natural pairs of different kinds. For example:

listening and reading are complementary modes for receiving linguistic meaning;

speaking and writing are complementary modes for expressing linguistic meaning;

moving and speaking are often simultaneous activities that support one another in expressing meaning;

watching and listening are often simultaneous activities that support one another in receiving meaning;

shaping is a tactile complement to moving;

watching and viewing are useful complementary ideas.

This list of pairs can be extended further and this activity on its own may develop useful questions for a staff discussion: how are the various modes related to one another in the work of a class, a form level or across a school; how might the links between these various activities be given more emphasis across the curriculum?

The Meaning and Place of Language Across the Curriculum

A beginning point in putting together a 'language policy across the curriculum' is for policy makers to be aware of the basic tenets that combine in the idea of 'language across the curriculum':

(i)   language develops mainly through its purposeful use;
(ii)   learning often involves talking, writing, shaping and moving;
(iii) learning often occurs through talking, writing, shaping and moving;
(iv) language use contributes to cognitive development.

Many of the thinkers mentioned later in this chapter have been major contributors to the debate that produced the doctrine of 'language across the curriculum'. The psychological thinkers of this century, who have been most interested in children's learning, have regularly approached their subject by considering language issues: Piaget, Vygotsky, Luria & Bruner are all noted antecedents of the doctrine who found rich implications for their work in the area of language. Added to these are those philosophers experienced in teaching children who derived from their experiences views about the links between language and learning: Wittgenstein and Popper both taught in Austrian schools and show the results of that practice in their writings. It is among curriculum theorists where the ideas of these and other thinkers began to come together. Notably Moffett's book, *Teaching the Universe of Discourse*, set the scene for a new direction in curriculum matters as they relate to language and learning.

Moffett's key idea is that our ability to think depends on the many previous dialogues that we have taken part in. LAC emphasises the fact that we often fail to exploit students' language, especially their informal and expressive talk and writing, as a learning resource in the classroom. The four basic tenets of LAC which opened this section have been supported in the research work of many of the theorists cited in this book through their studies examining the observed behaviours of students and teachers. They provide the platform for a worldwide re-examination of the role of the students' own language use in their learning. One of the most advanced in its thinking on these matters, the Ontario Ministry of Education in Canada has adopted the doctrine as a part of its public policy. Below is that policy cited in full (1984).

Language Across the Curriculum

Language plays a central role in learning. No matter what the subject area, students assimilate new concepts largely through language, that is, when they listen to and talk, read, and write about what they are learning and relate this to what they already know. Through speaking and writing, language is linked to the thinking process and is a manifestation of the thinking that is taking place. Thus, by explaining and expressing personal interpretations of new learnings in the various subject fields, students clarify and increase both their knowledge of the concepts in those fields and their understanding of the ways in which language is used in each.

It follows, then, that schools should provide an environment in which students are encouraged to use language to explore concepts, solve problems, organize information, share discoveries, formulate hypotheses, and explain personal ideas. Students need frequent opportunities to interact in small group discussions that focus on the exploration of new concepts. In addition, they should be encouraged to keep journals in which they write thoughts, questions and speculations that reflect on their learning. Principals should provide leadership by encouraging all teachers to participate in developing and practising a school language policy, which is, in effect, a school learning policy. By allowing students to discuss and write in the language they already control, teachers can gain new insights into the difficulties that students are encountering in particular subject areas. In this way teachers can help students to avoid rote learning and to gain clear understandings.

The difficulties that arise in bringing a policy of this kind into operation are many. Part of the difficulty for LAC as mentioned is that its implementation requires major changes in teacher attitudes and in the choice of pedagogy that teachers make. Some rigorous professional development work may be needed and I return to this subject below. Some of the problems for LAC, though, can be eliminated by simply becoming clearer about what it means. Firstly, LAC is not solely or even especially a part of the responsibility of the teacher of English (or the teacher of any other mother tongue). It is the responsibility of every teacher at every level in important ways, since it is a doctrine about promoting learning, after all, and learning is the central concern of education. Secondly, LAC is not much concerned with language as 'product', or with promoting language assessment in some way: its focus is on language as an instrument for learning, not performance in language (although some implications for performance will no doubt follow if the quality of learning through language is to be highlighted). Thirdly, LAC is not concerned with some or other 'linguistic bias'. The enforcement of certain language styles or varieties is not an aim of the doctrine. An important teaching of *A Language for Life* is that teachers should place value upon the language that children bring to schools, and use that as a starting point for education, not as something to be changed or eliminated.

A great difficulty for LAC is suggested in the last paragraph of the Ontario policy above. Because LAC, by definition, cannot easily be the responsibility of any single teacher located at one point in the curriculum or in the age range, then by necessity responsibility for the doctrine shifts in a major way to the school executive: LAC becomes a function to be assumed by educational administrators as perhaps their central curricular concern in schools.

The link between the LAC approaches and their implementation through school policy is provided by the school executive group. They have the task of bringing together national policies on language, current trends in education and LAC itself to show congruence and they need to engage staff members in the exercise of developing a school language policy that responds to that congruency. Graduate educational administration students of mine in 'language policy across the curriculum', who have established language policies in their schools, are unanimous in saying that it is the process of producing the documents themselves that is the most personally and professionally valuable activity. There is a role too in secondary schools for the English department. Knott (1985) makes the point that a powerful English department in a secondary school can play a vital part in raising questions in people's minds about the processes of learning through language, especially to do with the school's reading environment, learning through writing, the power of talk and the need to develop listening skills.

The LAC literature offers many compelling statements that support or justify its approach. A careful selection of significant points can provide the starting point in changing teacher perceptions of their role and promoting wider professional development (for example: Barnes, 1976; Barnes et al., 1986; Britton, 1975; Chilver & Gould, 1983; Corson, 1988a; DES, 1975; Fillion, 1983; French, 1985; Houlton, 1986; Mallett & Newsome, 1977; Marland, 1977; Martin et al., 1979; Maybin, 1985; Moffett, 1968; NATE, 1976; Schools Council, 1979; 1980; Torbe, 1980; Torbe & Medway, 1981). Alongside the tabling of theory can come a restatement of the advice currently being given to teachers by controlling boards and authorities in education. As examples: mathematics advisors in New Zealand for many years have encouraged children, as a learning device, to verbalise the mathematical procedures they are practising; social studies and science teachers in New South Wales have been urged to provide time for children to discuss, debate and dispute issues in the search for learning; the New Zealand syllabus for language in the primary school asks for a language learning component in every part of the school day and urges teachers to make a selection of language objectives in their daily programme to complement the objectives of each of the subjects that they teach. Clearly there is much fertile ground for LAC and for language policy in these and the many other recommendations that are found in the official documents of every country's education system.

LAC's Focus: The Role of Language in Learning

We know that children's differences in language ability, more than any other observable factor, affect their potential for success in schooling. Education is concerned with the activities of 'thinking', 'knowing' and 'learning'. We have strong indications from several disciplines of the way language and thought, language and knowledge, language and the roots of the intellect, are connected. The views of a number of well-known and complementary authorities are useful in presenting the case for this point about the unavoidable centrality given to language in education through its priority in the activities of thinking, knowing and learning.

Bruner bases his developing views on the place of language in education upon wide empirical evidence, much of which he has been instrumental in discovering himself, and upon rich contacts with children in learning situations. In Bruner's discussions 'language' is used in a narrower sense than the wide application (spanning eight activities of language) that I have given it so far in this chapter. This narrower sense for 'language' may be what we mean when we use the word in the phrase 'knowing the language of a culture'. However it takes little ingenuity to extend Bruner's ideas about language to include the symbolic conventions of 'moving', 'watching', 'shaping' and 'viewing' that may be used across a culture for the communication of meaning. In summary Bruner's early conclusions (1966) about the link between thinking and language are these:

(1) Intellectual growth is characterised by increasing independence of response from the immediate nature of the stimulus, an independence made possible by the mediating role of language. For example: if children are asked to talk or write about something, it is easier for them to do so if the subject matter is present in the context; older children are more able to draw on their greater resources of language to compensate for things that are missing in the present context; moreover they are able to use that mediating language as a basis for further acts of language use.

(2) Growth depends upon the development of an internal storage and information processing system which can describe reality. For example: older children, describing something in the present which is absent, are only able to do so easily if they have acquired sets of meanings relating to that something; using their 'storage system' they can attach names to these sets of meanings (the words and phrases of a language) and further, they can make statements about these sets of meanings (using the infinite range of possible sentences made available to them by their grasp of the language's structure). As far as we know the major genetically endowed information storage system that humans have is a language-based one: this means that all the experience-based

memories that we have are to a large extent encoded in some language system.

(3) Intellectual development involves an increasing capacity to display what one has done and what one will do. For example: even though little children's memories may be filled with an immediately past experience (and it is usually immediately past experiences that do fill their memories), little children will be unable to tell you much about those experiences. This is because they lack the language to link up with those memories, to map onto the concepts and to organise their thought into sentences. Also they will have difficulty saying clearly what they plan to do, for much the same reasons.

(4) Systematic interactions between a tutor and a learner facilitate cognitive development. This point speaks for itself: the 'courtesy of conversation' in Bruner's view is part of the 'courtesy of good teaching'; we learn language by using language in the company of experienced language users to receive or to make communication.

In a later paper (1975) Bruner sets out his ideas on language as an instrument of thought. I present these ideas here, interpolated with views from elsewhere. Bruner talks about three different kinds of 'competence' that go together to make up 'language proficiency'.

The first of these is that kind of 'linguistic competence' which is sometimes mentioned by writers in linguistics. Chomsky has long been associated with discussion on this 'faculty'. He contends (1979) that there is a 'universal grammar' that is 'a genetically determined property of the human species'; children do not learn or acquire this competence in any sense; rather they apply it in developing knowledge of language. Perhaps this complex idea can best be grasped by trying to imagine what knowledge of language would be left to us after the knowledge that we have of any single language is taken away; what remains is an innate readiness and capability for language, possessed by all members of our species because of that membership. Since it is something that education cannot affect or influence in any definite way, this kind of competence need not concern us here.

The second kind of competence is 'communicative competence', first introduced as a term in the writings of Hymes (1972). This competence includes the ability to make and understand utterances appropriate to the circumstances in which they are made. Speakers bring to a particular setting certain assumptions and expectations about when and how to speak, and the sorts of things that can be said to particular people in particular situations. Romaine (1984) emphasizes that an individual's communicative competence can be greatly affected by variations in setting. For example, what children in school can do with language in the relative security of their own classrooms may be quite different from what they can or want to do in front of a school assembly. This second kind of competence is of central concern to teachers in infant and primary schools. Junior school teachers in particular have a key responsibility for promoting the development of children's communicative competence as fully as possible across a range of contexts, functions and styles of language. Chapter 8 offers a discussion of the six component sub-competencies that go to make up the possession of 'communicative competence' in a language.

Bruner's third kind of competence is 'analytic competence'. He sees this as a necessary acquisition for engaging in 'formal operational reasoning' of the sort that begins to develop towards the end of the primary years and which is required from adolescents by the intellectual demands of the secondary school. This kind of competence is important not just in discussion about senior secondary schools; the foundations for analytic competence are laid in essential ways at earlier stages of schooling. However, it is children's ability to reach a sophisticated development in their analytic competence that finally determines their educational fate. In short analytic competence for Bruner is the ability to use language for thinking and for solving problems; we are helped in acquiring this kind of competence through exposure to some long-term educational process that integrates rich and complex interactional language activities.

Language, knowledge and learning

As an instrument for thought language helps us to direct attention to items or events; it helps us to maintain that attention; it helps us in classifying things in our experience; it helps us to relate these things to one another, to impose order upon the world; it helps us to recall events by providing a framework to hang our memories around; and it helps us to put old information together in new ways and make inferences. All of these activities are vital for learning across the curriculum. There is a close connection between 'knowledge' and 'learning'. Simply stated, learning is the acquisition of knowledge. The word 'knowledge' usually provides a shorthand way of saying other things: for example we usually mean 'knowledge and understanding' when we say just 'knowledge', since it means very little to have 'knowledge' on its own: 'knowledge' that is not available in some way to help us understand the world or operate within it. Also, in Education, we often use the word 'knowledge' in a broad sense: to include things like 'skills' and 'values'. When children acquire 'knowledge' through education this usually implies that their under-standing of the world has been improved in some way and that this often involves the learning of skills and the development of values or attitudes. In what follows I am using 'knowledge' in that broad sense.

Barnes, Britton & Torbe (1986) are three well-known figures in language and education theory development, even while interested in different aspects of that subject. They are in broad agreement in their views on the links between language, learning and knowledge. Below I present the views of these three theorists in outline. Then I focus on one of them in particular and show how that view of the relation between language and knowledge is very much in tune with an influential view in the philosophy of knowledge.

Torbe describes his stance on knowledge and learning as somewhat contrary to the 'orthodox view', which holds that we can judge that successful knowledge acquisition has taken place when the student has 'got it right'. He believes that those who see learning like that find it difficult to accept a very different model: a model of teaching and learning which values risk-taking, welcomes conjecture and sees error-making as in-evitable and necessary. In brief, he concludes that what all learners have to do is 'discover for themselves', an idea which links very closely with the doctrine of LAC.

Barnes' research, teaching and writings centre on 'talk' as used by teachers and students in schools. From his studies he concludes that certain views on the nature of knowledge seem to be associated with correspond-ing views on the role of language in learning. In particular he contrasts a 'transmission' view of knowledge with an 'interpretation' view: the former is concerned with the acquisition of information; the latter with cognitive and personal development. He sees the assumptions behind most approaches to teaching falling somewhere on a continuum between these two views; with the transmission view concerned mainly with the pupils' performance, and the interpretation view with their struggle to under-stand. These ideas, and his research on problems related to them, have led Barnes to conclude that 'talk' helps learning in any activity that goes beyond the rote and which requires understanding, especially the un-derstanding of processes. For him, like Torbe, all learning takes place through changes in the learner's existing model of the world.

Britton is very interested in expressive writing and the use of interactive activities as an aid in developing quality in written work. He believes that it is part of the very nature of human learning that it proceeds by anticipation: We tackle a problem forearmed with alternative possible solutions. More than this, learners bring with them whatever they already know and interpret it in the light of new evidence. He suggests that it is through language that understanding develops in technical fields, since language brings our commonsense concepts to a point of engagement with the technical concept. These ideas of Britton's are shared by Barnes and Torbe. The ideas also have much in common with prominent views in the philosophy of knowledge, views refined at length and stated persuasively by Popper (1972). For Popper it is only through language that deliberate criticism occurs, and this is necessary for the creation of knowledge. He offers these points to support his case:

(1) A thought, once formulated in language, becomes an object outside ourselves: that is, a thought does not exist for anyone else but the thinker; once put into language, though, it becomes a real world event;

(2) Language is capable of criticism and therefore is part of the world of objective standards: that is, we can try to say when someone is talking nonsense but there is no point in trying to say someone is thinking nonsense, unless we have the evidence of that person's language to go on;

(3) Only thought contents that are expressed in some language can stand in logical relationship to one another, such as equivalence, deducibility or contradiction: that is, we can use the language of one another to find out whether things are so or not, and this creates new knowledge.

A point basic to Popper's view is that the creation of knowledge and any associated learning depend on a rich language framework and the possession of that framework by people. For Popper human thought and human language evolved together: language helps to explain the brain, the mind, human reason and freedom.

Perhaps the link between Popper's and Britton's views could be made plainer: For Britton, when expressive talk is used as a means of education, children bring their commonsense views, as anticipations, into the learning context and are asked to present them in language that is ready for reconciliation with more impersonal and objective public statements. For Popper, all knowledge grows through a process of conjecturing and refuting: we bring our commonsense theories or conjectures, as expect-ations about the world, to our problems and then proceed to eliminate error from those theories. These views seem to me to overlap to a great degree. What Britton describes as a 'learning method' in language work is an instance of what Popper proposes as his entire theory of knowledge: the most efficient way for human knowledge to grow, in Popper's process of conjecturing and refuting, is when our conjectures are made explicit in some language, because then they are available for criticism and im-provement (along the lines suggested in 2 and 3 above). The task is to submit our theories to the most rigorous trial and error tests available, thereby eliminating their error as much as we can. In this way, at a personal level, our own knowledge grows; and more generally, in this way too, humankind's knowledge grows.

There is much more to say about the links between language, knowledge and learning that underpin LAC. A more practical way to say it may be to suggest and exemplify how our knowledge about these matters could affect the everyday practices of teachers. For a discussion of the practical consequences that seem to follow from changes in our knowledge about the links between language, knowledge and learning, the reader is referred to another source which discusses 'the teacher's role in oral language across the curriculum' (Corson 1988a: 41–46; 70–76; 100–109).

Changing Teacher Attitudes: Professional Development and LAC

The pedagogical demands of LAC imply greater difficulties for school leaders than is often appreciated. This fact may partly explain the slowness of LAC's spread in schooling. LAC asks teachers to operate at a level of professional development that many have not reached and perhaps cannot reach without a great deal of support and modelling opportunities. If we accept the conclusion that part of the difficulty for LAC is that implementation requires major changes in teacher attitudes and in the choices of pedagogy that many teachers make, then a prior condition for promoting those changes will be to establish a general level of professional development in the school staff sufficient to make the necessary changes in attitude appear reasonable, realistic and attainable. For some teachers long-standing attitudes about their role have become habits or unexamined prejudices. For example, traditionally when most children enter school they have always been quickly and properly classified as potential or actual readers. But there is rarely a similar concern with their oral language development, with their movement or listening skills. There is little reflection on levels of competence in these areas that might be reached or reachable. Instead teachers often follow the practices used by their earliest teacher training models. For instance, the use of oral language by young children in infant schools often does not go beyond morning talk or 'news' sessions and even these activities are regarded as a warm-up before the 'real learning' of the day begins.

At secondary level the compartmentalised thinking that curriculum subjects still impose on school organisation and development is a major obstacle that needs careful reconciliation in an LPAC. How can teachers come to see that language development in the secondary school is everyone's responsibility; how can subject teachers in senior secondary schools be spared some of the pressures that they feel that make them concentrate on subject content rather than process; and how can the constraints imposed by examination systems be lessened to allow more attention to be given to the fusion of the language process with the learning process? Because of the content-focussed training that they received, often with minimal attention paid to pedagogy, secondary teachers often find the approaches that LAC recommends to be threatening to their own perceptions of their role. Sometimes they bitterly resist their introduction or even their discussion. Professional development for these teachers, who may be present in large numbers in secondary schools, will need to be gradual and carefully scheduled; it will need to build on successful examples of LAC that have been introduced by respected colleagues, either within the school or in neighbouring districts. Involving these teachers in the policy making process itself, as suggested in Chapter 4, may be a very worthwhile professional development activity.

Many teachers simply lack confidence in applying new ideas or even in applying the old ones with much flair and enthusiasm. As Jackson (1988) discovered in the Scottish Writing Project: many teachers do not 'own' their own teaching; much of the curriculum is brought in from commercial sources or imposed by syllabus authorities; and the teachers of older children operate within the strict guidelines of examination protocols whether those strict protocols still exist or not. These constraints affect teacher confidence and can explain their readiness to continue with discredited approaches rather than run the risk of misunderstanding new pedagogies. One answer to this problem for LAC is for teachers to be given greater access to theory, which is professional knowledge about the processes of language and learning, coupled with better information about what children can be expected to do and what they are doing in progressive settings. We know that children can do much more than teachers usually allow them to do and much more than they are doing in some places. But there are usually some schools in a neighbourhood where children are stepping outside conventional approaches to learning and these can often be used as a starting point.

A use of imagination and ingenuity by the teacher, a readiness to experiment in pedagogy and to take risks within limits, can be pricked into life through an equally ingenious and imaginative school programme of professional teacher development. For many teachers, though, more than imagination and good example is needed. According to one well known account, teacher development is a continuum along which teachers proceed, at times progressing and at other times regressing (Beeby, 1966). Although the process is more complex than a model of this kind would indicate, there is value in thinking that most beginning teachers and also many experienced teachers are located at a formal or 'product' stage of development, unable to sustain process methods of teaching. For these teachers the learner is still often regarded as a storage unit to be filled, or an empty vessel, or a 'clean slate' ready for inscribing; classrooms are places of quiet diligence with inter-pupil communication kept to a minimum and even interactions between teachers and pupils minimised, notably with pupils who are 'culturally different' (Cazden, 1987). For these teachers process methods using prolonged and purposeful interactions in language do not easily fit in with expectations of 'good practice' and where they are used there is an accompanying unease, an artificiality, that leads back quickly to the more formal practices that are seen to produce the legitimate 'product'. Clearly teachers like this are not going to be receptive to many of the ideas of LAC. The fact that schools have many teachers located at this level of professional development poses difficulties for implementing sophisticated language policies. It follows that an LPAC should have as part of its focus carefully stated steps for edging staff members towards a 'transition phase of development', a process conducted over a protracted period that will provide ways of actively involving the teachers in their own processes of change. As Maybin concludes (1985) it is the school principal and the school executive who give activity of this kind the status that it needs. A development that goes beyond these early stages could be the appointment of an LAC Coordinator.

A policy for an LAC coordinator

The policy below was developed for use in a conventional secondary school where teacher workloads are important considerations in management. To provide some overall coordination in the LAC area, the policy sets out the goals of the coordinator's position and the range of activities that the appointee will undertake. Other extracts from the full policy are cited elsewhere (Glenny, 1988):

(1) a language consultant, preferably at a senior level, shall be appointed.
(2) this full-time position will involve the coordinator working with other staff, helping them to devise their teaching programmes with an LAC perspective.
(3) the person appointed will have oversight of the LPAC and its revision.
(4) the person will also be responsible for staff development in the practices of LAC and have in-service training blocks of time allotted for that purpose.
(5) the person will act as a consultant for staff on ESL matters.
(6) community liaison on minority language matters and on mother tongue matters will be a focus of this position.
(7) a select committee with a time allowance will actively assist the coordinator in:
—renegotiating the school language policy
—conducting research
—setting language priorities in the school
—evaluating the policy.

A policy for professional development in a secondary school

This section presents a policy for a cycle of professional development giving priority to issues raised in the wider LPAC prepared for the school (Christchurch Girls' High — see Chapter 1). Other extracts from the full policy are cited later in this chapter and elsewhere (Newman, 1988). The extract below acknowledges the need to modify some teaching practices, to support teachers in the process of change, and to provide for increased accountability for professional decisions:

(1) literature related to the topic will be available to all staff before the in-service release day.
(2) staff will be released for the professional development sessions in small groups that cross subject boundaries.

(3) there will be opportunity for discussion of ideas and problems and for observing master teachers with a class.

(4) staff will be encouraged to try out the ideas in their own classrooms with a colleague as observer or assistant if this is desired.

(5) the teacher responsible for the school's reading development will be appointed teacher in charge of this aspect of professional development and will have responsibility for setting up the courses and monitoring the process as it affects the teaching and learning situation. Reports on progress will be presented to the whole staff.

(6) among the topics to be covered will be:
    language principles
    language and thought: language and learning
    using small groups: the nature of discourse
    increasing the range of questioning techniques to create real
        discussion
    showing that students can do more than we allow them to do
    assessment of communicative competence

(7) heads of departments will assist staff to implement the recommended teaching strategies by making adjustments to their budgets for the purchase of any new equipment that is needed and by revising schemes of work.

Assessing Competence and Mother Tongue Testing

An LPAC will address the subject of first language testing, even if it is only to register the fact that no fixed programme of testing will operate in the school. There is a range of opinion on the place of school language testing, especially in secondary schools. Some feel that many of the available tests mainly measure word recognition and sub-skills. Some feel that national testing programmes in the first language are sufficient and that the school has other things to do of greater importance than collecting data about children's language proficiency. Some see careful monitoring of the child's individual progress by a teacher to be more useful than tests, even while more arduous, and that tests do not produce more information about a child than a teacher can discover in a few days observation and discussion. By using tests teachers may avoid meeting their pupils on a level that will allow adequate communication and dialogue; yet these are the things that can provide fuller understanding of an individual child. Tests may do little more than reinforce a negative attitude and assessment using narrow criteria that are not very relevant.

The assessment of communicative competence deserves more than casual attention however. Curriculum theorists are becoming clearer about the place of assessment in controlling the content of the curriculum in school systems: they have discovered that the things that the assessment procedures focus upon are the things that schools deliver to their students. Teachers tend to direct their teaching towards the kinds of outcomes that will receive favourable assessments in whatever the internal or external tests or exams might be. While this is a worrying discovery, it is not really contrary to commonsense. Schools need to take notice of the risks that it involves and plan accordingly to minimise negative effects.

If schools are now being forced to recognise that their assessment procedures dominate their curriculum, then there is a need for them to create systematic stages in that assessment so that children's individual competencies can be identified at various points and be built upon. In any form of communicative assessment, schools need to be aware that factors other than language and intellect often interfere with the quality of the 'language on display' that children are capable of. Romaine (1984) says that it is not so much the knowledge or content that is sometimes at fault but the 'packaging' that children use. In the early years of schooling there are many examples available to us of children's competence being lowly rated on the grounds that they do not use language in the 'right' way (Dannequin, 1987; Cazden, 1987; 1988). A simple example comes from Mehan (1979): in classroom observations he found students who knew correct answers but did not use the right procedures in stating them (i.e. by putting up their hands, using the teacher's language, and speaking in complete sentences). Romaine also mentions children and teachers who 'miss' one another in their communication through not synchronising their questions and answers. Other children go outside the teacher's criteria for success by structuring their narratives in what are seen as unusual ways. Still other children are wrongly assessed, in spite of evidence to the contrary, because of the weight that is given to professionally assessed versions of competence, in preference to lay opinions. I say more about these matters in Chapter 9 while discussing differential ability. The section on language awareness for children at the end of this chapter is also a plea for teachers themselves to acquire language awareness and for them to practise the critical language awareness that Chapter 9 advocates. But a more basic requirement in assessing children's language is for teachers to be sure of the kinds of developmental aims that are appropriate for schools to pursue.

The following checklist of competencies is already in use in schools for overlaying on curriculum proposals. All of these competencies relate directly to mother tongue language competence. In designing assessment schedules, schools could use them as benchmarks or as discussion points in professional development work. The competencies fall into two groups. First there is a set of competencies associated with learning to converse, read, write, calculate. Second there is a set of competencies that depends considerably on the prior acquisition of the first set. This list is borrowed freely from a curriculum document (Schools Board, 1986: 22–23) and is discussed more fully elsewhere (Corson, 1988d). It may be helpful for readers to know that the list was compiled by principals, senior staff and tertiary affiliates (including the author) from all the senior secondary colleges of an Australian State. It therefore represents assembled views from across the curriculum of upper secondary education; it sets out the kinds of developmental outcomes that schooling by its final stages is widely hoped to have achieved.

Prior competencies

acquiring information

This includes listening accurately and critically to oral presentations; using data from computer information systems; identifying the main ideas from print and graphic material as well as from film, television and radio presentations; reading different kinds of fiction and non-fiction; observing and recording practical experiences.

conveying information

This includes talking and writing for particular purposes; using a range of media to tell a story or present factual information; using models to explain ideas; demonstrating the difference between major ideas and less important ones and doing all these for a range of audiences.

applying logical processes

This includes inferring from observations, analysing and interpreting information, calculating number relationships and values, solving practical and theoretical problems, forming hypotheses, anticipating and predicting consequences, identifying assumptions and evaluating requirements.

undertaking practical tasks as an individual

This involves choosing, planning and organising a range of tasks, including those that require a range of physical dexterity and seeing them through to completion without supervision.

undertaking practical tasks as a member of a group

This includes activities similar to those above with emphasis on cooperation, negotiation and leadership.

making judgments and decisions

This includes identifying alternatives, evaluating evidence and ideas, selecting appropriate courses of action.

working creatively

This includes the ability to use ideas and materials inventively-recombining ideas to meet new situations and contexts, extrapolating beyond what has been given explicitly. These creative activities should not be restricted to art, drama and music.

Dependent competencies

act autonomously

by displaying initiative, self-confidence and control, resilience and entrepreneurial skill across a range of human activities.

act responsibly

by considering how actions will affect others as well as oneself, being tolerant or firm when appropriate, and valuing democratic processes.

show care and concern for other people

by being sensitive to the thoughts and feelings of others, respecting different opinions and ways of doing things, being friendly and helpful, being able to express love and affection.

consider questions of beliefs and values

by examining how ideas and actions reflect beliefs, giving careful consideration to personal, individual and group values in all aspects of experience.

We might say with some confidence that graduates leaving school equipped with all of these competencies would have received an education worth having. Clearly some of these developmental aims, as they relate to language competence, are not as relevant at the more junior stages of schooling and at that stage their assessment will be less rigorous. Clearly too most of these competencies cannot be easily assessed using formal tests and it is important to make and understand that point. The place of formal tests in curriculum management is a very circumscribed one, once we take into account these developmental aims that are fundamental to schools.

On the other hand some believe that tests produce very valuable diagnostic information which enables them to help pupils without much unnecessary delay. When pupils are beginning in a new school the screening needed to ease their placement in a curriculum may take several weeks without proper diagnostic tests. Sometimes too the students' mother tongue is not the main language of the school, yet it may need to be used to foster intellectual development or to assist the children's learning of the culture's language (see under 'Bilingualism' in Chapter 7). In these cases a full assessment of the children's first language proficiency will be essential. It is easy to assume proficiency in a language, when a child speaks nothing else but that language, and accordingly to make plans to use the child's knowledge of that language as an aid to learning the majority language. The risks here may be many, especially as they relate to the problem of dialect in the child's first language; perhaps the child's contact with the first language has been through some regional or social dialect of it, rather than through its national or standard form. The child may 'know' the national language at a level that is inadequate for formal education to proceed in it. Chapter 7 takes these matters further and provides suggestions for the assessment of second languages and also for first language proficiency when there may be a need for it.

In mother tongue language testing there are matters that schools will need to develop firm policies about. These matters relate directly to LAC since it may not be possible or wise to separate language testing from other kinds of testing. Almost every form of assessment in schools is a test of language ability so it is no surprise that school success and language proficiency go hand in hand. Where does the school stand in matters of language testing: Is it useful? How frequently should it be carried out and for what reasons? Who should administer tests to students? How is continuity in mother tongue development guaranteed for children moving between schools at the same or at different levels? What use can be made of records from other schools? Whose responsibility is the updating of records? Whose responsibility is it to ensure uniformity and fairness in their use? The whole matter of record-keeping needs some form of coordination in schools since improperly kept records about pupil achievement can easily mislead and adversely affect children's rights: What form will the school's record-keeping take? Who will be responsible for updating and securing the records? What regulations control access to the records?

If the school does choose to use formal language tests, outside advice may be needed, since the range of tests available is wide indeed. It may be that an LPAC coordinator should be nominated to oversee the selection and use of tests, assisted by a sub-committee where necessary. A battery of tests needs to be selected which spans as full a range of language competencies as possible (see Chapter 8) and their application needs to be carefully managed so that teachers are aware of the children's true performances, can take account of the results in their teaching, and are informed about the value and the limitations of any data that are obtained. Rivera (1984b) mentions three responsibilities that those using tests of any kind need to assume: to avoid certainty in making claims about the results of the tests; to avoid mysticism in hiding behind the authority, jargon or statistics of the tests; and to label the tests accurately and use them with considerable care. Tests can be grouped in two categories. Those below are only a sample of tests listed under each category:

GROUP TESTS

Ravens Progressive Matrices
NFER, SRA and SRB AD EH 1–3
Peter's Spelling
Swansea Test of Phonic Skills
Progressive Achievement Test in Reading Vocabulary
Progressive Achievement Test of Reading Comprehension
Progressive Achievement Test of Listening Comprehension
Domain Test of Phonic Skills
Young Group Reading Test
Goodenough — Draw a man

INDIVIDUAL TESTS

Individual Reading Inventory
Daniels and Dyack Diagnostic Tests
Clay's Record of Oral Language

Schonell — used in a diagnostic form
Harrison Stroud Reading Readiness Profile
Corson Measure of Passive Vocabulary
Ravens Coloured Matrices
Get Reading Right
Neale's Test of Reading Ability
Modified Form of Frostig Visual Perception
Modified Form of ITPA
Modified Form of Monroe Test of Auditory Discrimination

In the following pages I present specimen language assessment policies that have been developed for primary and secondary schools. These extracts from wider LPACs provide a bridge between discussion in this section and discussion in the next.

A primary school testing and evaluation policy

The evaluation policy below was developed for use in a conventional primary school (Heatherton — see Chapter 1) as part of a rolling review of curriculum areas and ready for teachers to evaluate in action. It is extracted from a complete LPAC for the school. The underlying assumptions of the original policy stressed a 'whole language' approach to primary classroom work. It presents guidelines for specific and agreed action (Bell, 1988):

(1) Teachers will accept the language achievements and levels of all children and use this knowledge as a considered basis for planning.
(2) Tracking measures will be undertaken regularly and will include such aspects as:
—degree of participation in language areas
—attitude
—skills development
—application of skills in curriculum areas
(3) Samples of children's work in all areas will be available in individual folders.
(4) Regular and systematic analysis and recording of children's progress will be shown in each teacher's 'Analysis Book' and will be used in subsequent planning.
(5) Children will be informed about their own progress as language users.

A secondary science department learning and assessment policy

The policy below was developed by staff of a Science Department for their own use and for possible extension across the school's curriculum (Rotorua Boys' High — see Chapter 1). It is extracted from a complete LPAC for the Department which provides science courses at all secondary levels of schooling for students, including a very large group from the minority culture (Harrison, 1988). Elsewhere in the document strong points are made addressing the rights of the minority students. For example: 'the self esteem of Maori students will be maintained by appropriate use of *Te Reo Maori* (the Maori language) and suitable items from Maori culture in the lessons and environment of classrooms' and 'non-Maori pupils will also be exposed to learning of this kind to benefit their socialisation in an increasingly bicultural country'. The policy was prefaced by a statement stressing the importance of language competence if students are to benefit fully from the range of learning experiences provided by the Science Department. Although presented here under the 'Assessment' section, the policy attends to much of the subject matter of this chapter:

A policy for teacher approaches to learning and assessment

Learning

(1) **Reading**

(1.1) All students will be exposed to suitable reading tasks (including some which demand reading aloud). This will require varied reading resources within any one class. Materials created by staff will be at a high standard of presentation.

(1.2) At all levels teachers will monitor students' strategies in coping with reading tasks. Specific teaching may be required to improve competence. With serious cases science teachers will cooperate with language specialists in identification and remediation of problems.

(1.3) Where students are required to record information from any reading task, they will be discouraged from simply copying large sections of text.

(1.4) When undertaking library research projects, teachers will first check that students possess the necessary research skills.

(1.5) Small collections of books on broad scientific topics at various reading levels will be displayed in each classroom to be used for quiet reading for pleasure when other work is finished. In a multi-level programme the most able will not necessarily be the first finished.

(2) Vocabulary

(2.1) Teachers will use a sympathetic approach in helping children to identify with difficult specialist vocabulary. Help will often be needed in decoding, pronunciation, spelling, root meaning, depth of understanding or memorisation.

(2.2) Common priority vocabulary lists will be drawn up for each level to include words specific to science and common words given specific meaning within science. It is often the latter which give the greater trouble in the classroom.

(2.3) Vocabulary will be learned in contexts displaying the rules for applying words and helped by non-language experiences (e.g. experiments). Junior students especially find difficulty in word learning from texts alone.

(2.4) Students will be given small group activities which encourage the motivated use of specialist vocabulary.

(3) Oral language

(3.1) Teachers will have regard to the interest and familiarity of subject matter for discussion and provide both formal and informal occasions where descriptive and/or explanatory talk will be expected. Respect for speakers and their viewpoints will be expected.

(3.2) Teachers will use 'open' questions wherever possible, thus inviting students to explore and speculate in difficult areas.

(3.3) Students will be encouraged to establish their own ideas and preconceptions in language that they control before comparing those views with expert opinion or with experimental evidence which may challenge their views.

(3.4) Students will be encouraged to view 'errors' as a natural part of learning and useful as active tests of their hypotheses.

(3.5) During practical work students will be given opportunities to use talk to organise themselves, to share their findings and to formulate hypotheses.

(4) Writing

(4.1) All staff will devote class time to the development of students' writing.

(4.2) The less able will not be permitted to avoid writing and the more able will be encouraged to write at length wherever possible.

(4.3) Expression will be improved by defining the purpose clearly and by making the students aware of a real audience for their work (e.g. displays in the lab or library; distributing photocopies of student work; producing small magazines, giving talks or practical demonstrations to other classes; writing for the Head of Department, Principal or parents using feedback sheets etc).

(4.4) Once writing skills are more secure and before facing formal assessments, children will be given practice in writing for anonymous examiners.

(4.5) Various aspects of technical accuracy will be monitored (especially the use of sentences) but concentration should be focussed on only a few points at a time.

(4.6) A high standard of handwriting and presentation will be expected for all final copies. Preplanning, drafting and then editing will be encouraged during creative written work (e.g. experimental reports, problem solving, investigations, essays).

(5) Visual effects in language and learning

(5.1) The output of students for assessment will not be confined to writing and talking. Students will experiment with different media including video, posters, charts, overhead transparencies, cartoons, models or demonstration experiments.

(5.2) Classroom wall displays will be frequently up-dated. Students' work will provide most of the displays.

(5.3) Students will be actively engaged with the activity when viewing video programmes. The recording of information and its critical assessment will be important exercises which may require specific instruction.

(5.4) When teachers are conducting demonstrations for a whole class they will ensure that effects are visually impressive by changing student seating arrangements.

(5.5) When designing worksheets, transparencies or other graphic material staff will attend to the visual effects (e.g. lettering, colour, arrangement, balance between print and picture).

Assessment

(1) Display of knowledge

(1.1) Knowledge possessed will be identified by the students' ability to use explanatory concepts and appropriate vocabulary in various situations. Testing will involve more than mere recognition: questions which invite students to give expanded answers will be used.

(1.2) Assessment will take place throughout a course using a variety of written tasks as well as oral and practical assignments at appropriate times.

(2) Evaluations

(2.1) Accent, pronunciation or language style will not predetermine assessment of the educational potential of any student.

(2.2) Students whose social or cultural background place them at a disadvantage should not be excluded by premature selection devices. Their language development specific to science teaching and learning may take more time.

(2.3) Teachers will make clear and directive comments on students' work and not rely on a grade only to convey an assessment.

(2.4) The reporting of achievement of individual students will not diminish the feeling of self-worth or *mana* (Maori for 'respected influence') of other students and will be communicated in understandable language.

The Development of Reading

A reading programme in a primary school is often the focus of the school's language policy. Schools for older children also need to acknowledge reading development, perhaps by having a firm reading programme broadly similar in outline to those found in primary schools. An alternative is to have specific policies on 'reading for pleasure' and for locating and placing children with functional reading difficulties that need remedial attention.

Skill in the development of reading is a specialist part of a primary teacher's expertise. Just keeping up with the latest research and theory in this complex area is a full-time job for many academic specialists, so it would be out of place here to make many generalisations about the state of the art in reading research. The central controversy that has dogged research for some time has been the debate between the so-called 'top-down' and 'bottom-up' theorists. The 'top-down' position sees reading comprehension as largely assisted by pre-existing schemata that generate predictions in the reader about the upcoming text. In contrast the 'bottom-up' position gives more importance to the decoding of letters, words and stretches of discourse in arriving at a text's meaning. As with so many complex debates, the truth is no doubt somewhere in between these extremes and includes explanatory factors that have not yet been much considered, such as the level of a reader's socioculturally appropriate knowledge and more general language experience. There are many texts which provide specialist guidance in depth. One source, which gives a brief overview but also tries to relate its discussion of reading development to language policies in the primary school, is Ashworth (1988). After stressing the importance of the transition stage in literacy, which itself is preceded by developments in oral language and in an increasing knowledge of the world, Ashworth presents five elements of a reading programme that might offer categories for schools to model their own policy deliberations upon in the area of reading. Below I summarise and expand on these categories from Ashworth:

(1) *Reading classroom authors* refers to children reading material written within the school. Part of the aim here is to ensure a match between the child's language and the language of the text by presenting the child's own accounts, recorded by a second party, for reading. The child starts with familiar meanings. Extensions of this come when other children's accounts are included and when the teacher does some carefully constructed composing of reading material for use by the children.

(2) *Reading aloud* is given special status by Ashworth as a necessary everyday event in the primary school. I would add a rider to his recommendation: It is known from studies of differential ability that there are 'widespread and powerful patterns' in teacher behaviour that need to be counteracted if poorer readers are not to have their disadvantages made worse by teacher correction practices in reading instruction (there is much discussion material that could form a basis for professional development work in this area in Cazden, 1988). It may be that more time should be spent by teachers discussing

children's experiences relevant to the text; also a greater stress on comprehension discussions following silent reading may lessen teacher tendencies towards excessive correction of oral reading errors with poorer readers. For this latter group of children, who may be in the majority in minority culture schools, the teacher's professional skill in choosing appropriate material for reading aloud and also in making the occasions comfortable ones is all important. This kind of attention to organisational detail can make the activity one that is prized even by poorer readers. Components in this teacher skill are sensitivity to the children's needs and interests, awareness of the context and the occasion for reading, and an ear to the recommendations of teaching colleagues.

(3) *Free reading* is a regular part of any reading scheme. With skilled teaching it could be the central part, allowing schools to edge commercial reading schemes and primers a little away from centre stage. 'Free' reading is not an aimless activity though. The role of the teacher in advising children on their choice of reading grows in importance when children are no longer guided by the formal and impersonal directives of a commercial reading scheme. An approach of this kind demands rich library resources, that are constantly up-dated. An LPAC needs clear guidelines setting out the ways in which those resources can be improved and managed. Ashworth devotes a long discussion to the inadequacies of commercial reading schemes which might be consulted by those thinking about investing in them. The key to free reading work in the primary school or elsewhere is found in the motivation and incentive structures that teachers are able to devise: just the act of allowing children to choose books they wish to read and giving them the option to buy the books for a token price can greatly increase the amount of reading done and reading achievement as well (Troike, 1984).

(4) *Help from the teacher* covers things like providing a suitable reading environment, organising reading conferences and working actively with groups of children. Comfortable, inviting, well-organised and well-stocked classroom book corners and school libraries are necessary in a primary school. Positive attitudes to these areas are needed from teachers so that children will come to value them too. An LPAC need not intrude on the teacher's autonomy in matters of pedagogy in reading development. Some things have to be left unstated; policy makers need to assume that methods suited to each child's individual needs will be used and that the use of these will be based on the teacher's professional

judgment, knowledge and schedule. Group deletion (cloze) work, group sequencing work and group prediction work are some of the many activities that can be collected and used across a curriculum. An LPAC addressing professional development might suggest ways for teachers to pool their ideas about reading activities and to use the expert advice that comes from in-service contacts. For example, it seems necessary now to lay less stress on the 'phonics approach' to reading instruction. In-service experts might offer a range of reasons for this widely recommended change in pedagogy: there is the problem of practicality that comes from our growing awareness that there is great variation in the pronunciation of even monolingual speakers of a language, a variation that is compounded by growing numbers of people using second languages; and there is the problem of spelling inconsistency, particularly in English, which leads notoriously to sound/letter mismatching and learning inefficiency. But even our knowledge in these areas is evolving and improving. Because of the way that knowledge grows in an area of inquiry like reading development, the best theoretical knowledge is the most recent.

(5) *Using language to learn* is at the core of LAC itself. Goodman (1987) advocates a use of a 'whole language approach' in classrooms as a way of integrating a view of language, a view of learning and a view of people. The stress here, as in LAC, is on active learning, with children engaged in doing as much as they can themselves, rather than hearing about it second-hand or observing it vicariously. All eight language modes are called upon at various points in the school day, with teachers supporting children positively in their search for meaning and with a classroom environment that is redolent of language forms and functions, rich in printed language and offering activity centres and flexible grouping arrangements that promote interaction.

Reading researchers today realise that reading comprehension is highly affected by the readers' 'knowledge of the world'. There are differences in everyone's life experiences and this affects the knowledge that we bring to any activity, especially to an activity like reading that involves language which in turn maps onto our personal knowledge of the world. The work of Fillmore & Kay (1980) on the protocols that children use to form expectations early in the process of reading a text indicates that reading comprehension always proceeds by integrating the message of the text with 'knowledge of the world'. There is evidence to suggest that this 'knowledge of the world', which is largely culturally determined, correlates with social group background and relates to the kinds of 'language in use' that people from different backgrounds actively display in their oral or written texts (Corson, 1985b). It is not surprising, then, that reading achievement scores, obtained in formal school contexts, and levels of school achievement generally are regularly linked to cultural and social group background since a person coming from a different background may not have the 'knowledge of the world' that is appropriate to understanding the text in the way that the author intended. Reading researchers are now having a lot to say on this matter. There is a fundamental problem for schooling that links into this discussion: how is the school to provide this 'knowledge of the world' while still acknowledging that the alternative 'knowledges of the world' that children's background experiences give them is not thereby necessarily undervalued? I return to this question in the last section of this chapter and address it more critically in Chapter 9.

Reading across the secondary curriculum

At the secondary level a formal reading policy may be even more necessary than at the primary level, where a concern for reading development is inevitably so central in any case. Very often reading development receives a lower priority with older children; there is not likely to be any single staff member responsible for literacy development in a secondary school; and few of the 'at risk' children will receive planned attention. As a result of this widespread 'management gap' that exists across the curriculum of secondary schools, it is likely that children who leave their primary schools with inadequately developed literacy skills will continue at a functionally inadequate level of literacy development throughout their secondary education, perhaps even declining in their actual reading and writing proficiency during adolescence. Poor management practices in secondary schools, then, act in a straightforwardly 'cause and effect' way in producing educational failure. But rather than 'failing in school', these children have been 'failed by their schooling'. As young and older adults, children overlooked in this way may form the majority of the many candidates who present themselves for adult literacy education, even in highly affluent countries (Corson, 1977; 1978a; 1978b). Alternatively their functional illiteracy may remain a burden to them throughout their lives, restricting them in their ease of social intercourse and affecting their views of the world in ways that literate people can only imagine (Corson, 1981).

One secondary school reading policy adopted the following headings in setting out what a reading programme involves at the secondary level. Teachers added detail under each heading (Marland, 1977: 291–299):

vocabulary development;
word recognition;
comprehension and organisation;
reading interests;
study skills;
approaches to reading;
personal development.

The school's policy went on to set out the general procedure to be followed in managing the school reading programme, using these sub-headings:

(a) area of concern;
(b) general procedure;
(c) reading test;
(d) reading procedures across the curriculum;
   —text testing techniques;
   —pupil testing techniques;
   —study techniques.

The policy concluded by establishing the criteria by which the reading development policy's success would be judged. More specific than these broad policy recommendations, here are some 'reading for pleasure' developments trialled with success in Inner London Education Authority secondary schools:

(i)   ensuring that all pupils use the school's library at least once a week for quiet reading and borrowing;
(ii) placing small collections of books in class boxes so that quiet reading becomes the norm for children when other work is finished;
(iii) increasing the time given to reading across the curriculum and to reporting back on the results of that reading;
(iv) accepting that private voluntary reading for pleasure provides one good indicator of general competence in language matters;
(v)   creating book-clubs and school bookshops.

Rather than adopting policy ideas from elsewhere, many schools prefer to address their own problems in their own ways, since secondhand policies often carry less meaning and significance than those that staff themselves have had a hand in compiling. When we routinely adopt secondhand policies sometimes they are implemented only perfunctorily and this is another reason for frequently updating a policy: new staff members will see more meaning in something that they have had a hand in creating. As a plan for attacking the reading sections of an LPAC at secondary level, the following questions could be asked:

(1) how is the school to demonstrate its complete commitment to universal literacy among its pupils?

(2) how will reading be taught at all levels so that the children's level of reading mastery is continually extended?

(3) how can pupils be prepared in their early secondary years for the reading demands of later years?

(4) what opportunities can be built into the curriculum and what is the role of the various subject departments in providing:
—for private reading?
—for reading aloud?
—for reading for pleasure?
—for extension reading?

(5) what is the most recent knowledge available about the teaching of reading and how can that knowledge be applied across the curriculum?

(6) what resources for reading are there in the school and how can these be brought up to satisfactory levels?

(7) is the central library widely used?

(8) is there a class library system?

(9) are the functions of central and class libraries understood by children and staff?

(10) how are books recommended to the children?

(11) is there a school bookshop?

(12) are books displayed?

(13) can the children read for pleasure or must they always write a review?

(14) do the teachers read outside school?

(15) are the teachers seen reading in school?

(16) can children take books home?

(17) are parents involved?

(18) are there opportunities to share responses to books?

(19) is a varied reading diet being offered: story, poem, novel, play, children's own writing?

(20) how are the poor readers to be identified and how are they to receive assistance that will lead to a planned upgrading of their skills?

A policy on reading for a girls' secondary school

The extract below presents a policy on reading prepared for a single-sex school which has few problems at the level of functional literacy (Christchurch Girls' High — see Chapter 1). The reading policy is prefaced by comment on the place of reading for understanding in the modern context and the personal benefits that can come from reading for pleasure (Newman, 1988). Teachers are urged to encourage the reading habit by:

(1) ensuring that in every subject students have the format of textbooks, including the function of the graphics, explained to them so that they can use them to their best advantage.

(2) ensuring that the students have been properly instructed in the use of the reference works in the library in the subject.

(3) monitoring textbooks and photocopied material for technical vocabulary that needs explaining and for the appopriateness of the reading level.

(4) explaining the approaches used by specialist authors in organising their information in paragraphs and using established writers as models for the students' own writing in the subject.

(5) talking about books and magazine articles that are subject related and encouraging students to talk about the books they have read.

(6) liaising with the teacher in charge of reading development in order to ascertain if there are any students who need special encouragement or help with reading tasks.

(7) conferring with the teacher-librarian to ensure that the buying policy of the library reflects the needs of the subject.

(8) allowing substantial periods of time in class for reading so that students can discuss difficulties as they arise and so the more able can read ahead at their own pace.

(9) reading aloud occasionally to provide a model to the class and opportunity for discussion.

The Development of Writing

The goals in teaching writing in the primary school can be simply stated: to create autonomous writers and to give them increasing competence in using language to express, record and communicate meaning for different purposes and in different styles. Vygotsky's views on the development of language are very relevant to this discussion. Ashworth gives an overview of primary school writing development. He invokes Vygotsky's views about the skills needed for learning to write: the obvious roots like speech and listening; and the less obvious roots that lie in drawing and gesture, in storytelling and pretend play. We begin to see how important the conventional 'free' curriculum of infant schools and kindergartens is for creating the framework on which writing can be developed.

All of these incidental things are very necessary in the development of writing. But there is a transition stage that is not incidental; it has to be purposefully provided by schools. This transition stage allows the child to move away from seeing writing as 'speech written down' to having an understanding of the nature of the written word. This means using some of the background information provided by speech but not others. For example, the intonation patterns of speech can play little part in writing. Also when we interact with others this provides the chief stimulus for talk, but interaction is not usually available when we write, so young writers need to have a developing command over their internal dialogue. Again learning the role and structure of a written sentence, which is much more formal than that appropriate in speech, and the various types of sentence is a key achievement for the child. But this is only one step in appreciating the need for cohesion in theme between larger units in a piece of writing. This need for cohesion is less of a constraint in speech, except in the most formal of contexts. There are also subtle differences between the purposes for which we write and the purposes for which we speak.

On the other hand we know that writing is often approached in schools in a manner which disregards the need for spontaneity and expression that is a part of any natural language activity. In a Scottish research study of primary school writing (Raban, 1988), children were found to be writing lengthy but trivial assignments, which invited extensive teacher feedback on the errors made, but teachers in their turn made little effort to remark on content or enrich it. From these not uncommon approaches by teachers to their pupils' writing, children learn that the main point of writing in school is to achieve neatness and tidiness. Part of the problem may be that many teachers seem to lack a model of writing to guide their efforts. Being able to pick up mistakes in children's writing is easy; knowing their cause is more difficult yet this knowledge is far more useful in the pedagogical process. The Scottish Committee on Language Arts in the Primary School (SCOLA, 1986) provides a model of writing as a way of encouraging teachers to respond to children's writing in positive and helpful ways.

Chandler *et al.*, (1989) summarise criticisms of teachers' marking: it is found sometimes to be 'inconsistent', 'inappropriate', 'overly negative' and too often focussed on form rather than on content. The same study strikes an optimistic note, however, by concluding that the marking behaviour of teachers in training is moving broadly in the directions that are currently advocated.

The 'process writing' approach (Graves, 1983) emphasises writing as a meaningful communicative activity, which needs to have a real purpose, a genuine audience, and an accessible support system of advice and editing. Graves (1978) found that most of the writing that children undertook in his studies was copying out information or reproducing teacher texts. As in the Scottish studies, the feedback on their work that children received tended to be based on superficial attributes of their writing like correctness in grammar, punctuation and spelling. Although there is an important place for giving attention to these things, there are other more important things that need to be addressed as well in evaluating children's writing: the quality of their engagement with their own world; the richness of the ideas that they express; the suitability of the language that they use to convey their thoughts. These things are best approached through discussion sessions with their peers, with the teacher or with some other interested adult.

In correcting surface forms it is the manner of the correcting that is most important, since there is much evidence that the routine approaches to correcting adopted by most teachers are not very effective. As in other areas of learning in schools (and I am re-applying here the 'learning from errors' theory of knowledge that is discussed above) the teacher's task in correcting written work is to think carefully about what approach to correction will be most likely to allow the child to learn from the error that has been made. The approach which suits one child may not suit another. By adopting a rigorously uniform approach to correction, teachers may be discriminating against those children whose capacity to learn from their mistakes may be expressed in different ways. Some children, for example, may need to know that their written work is going to be seen by others (as part of a poster display, a real letter, a class book etc) before they will pay careful attention to its formal correctness. Others may be motivated in different ways. The key ingredient in correcting children's work efficiently is student motivation. What teachers need to provide are contexts in which children really want to have their work corrected; this means creating classroom contexts where the children will be disappointed if their work is not corrected.

The teacher's role in most of this, as in other areas of professional autonomy, cannot be laid out in a school language policy. Teacher behaviour depends on professional judgment which recognises a right to autonomy of action on the teacher's part. There are things, however, in the primary and secondary school to do with writing development that can be covered in a policy and these are mentioned in sections below.

Handwriting and marking policy in the primary school

This is so clearly an 'across the curriculum' responsibility that it needs little comment here. The possession of a legible and individual style of handwriting is the aim for any school graduate. The beginning point is for the young child to learn some or other formal style, based on a model adopted across the school, practising it until a high level proficiency in reproducing that style is reached. By the later years of primary or junior schooling, children should be developing their own preferences in letter shape, slope and size. The role of the teacher changes from an instructor in a conventional style to a mentor in matters of legibility. The school's task becomes one of setting minimum standards in presentation and ensuring that they are reached. Policy questions could include:

(1) is agreement on the style of presentation of written work necessary?
(2) do teachers accept any agreed pattern of presentation in their teaching or in their own written work?
(3) is handwriting to be taught? by whom? how?
(4) is there need for a fixed style of letter-shape (e.g. cursive, script etc) across the school?
(5) at what stage in the school's programme will formal handwriting classes end or begin?
(6) is there a handwriting expert on the staff who could assume a consultancy role?
(7) as an extension activity or option, can the techniques and scope of calligraphy be made available on a regular basis?
(8) what research about the assessment of children's writing can be introduced into the school to improve marking techniques?

A primary school written language policy

This written language policy was developed for use in an integrated church primary school (St Jude's — see Chapter 1) following an extensive programme of discussion in staff meetings held to address the school's special range of language problems. The original policy was prefaced by a statement of the four key tenets of LAC. The policy presents guidelines for specific and agreed action (Cockburn, 1988):

(1) oral language will be used as a precursor to writing to generate necessary understanding, purpose and motivation.
(2) we shall encourage writing as a communicative process in the following ways:
—dramatisation
—letter-writing
—presenting or displaying
—personal intent
(3) we shall give children the freedom to write daily.
(4) monitoring of student work for correction and extension of ideas and skills will be done on a collaborative basis.
(5) within 'process writing' the teacher will become a helper, a facilitator and a writer in a purposeful, productive and non-threatening environment.
(6) we shall give everyone the opportunity to publish their work.
(7) teachers will keep records of the conferencing undertaken with students showing levels of literacy competence achieved and activities introduced.

Writing and marking across the secondary curriculum

One study of children's writing at school identified 'the audience' as the single most influential factor that the child doing the writing has in mind. The study set up different categories of audience as follows:

(1) self
(2) peer group
(3) teacher: (i) as examiner; (ii) as trusted adult
(4) wider known audience (e.g. other classes in school; parents or friends)
(5) wider unknown audience

The category least likely to promote learning was 3(i) yet this category accounted for 90% of school writing examined in the study (Torbe, 1980).

The matter of providing an audience in the secondary school for children's writing relates directly to the place of examinations at more senior levels of education. The staff of a secondary school, examining the implications of LAC for their own policies, may first need to uncover and debate their attitudes to examining and examinations, both external and internal, and the constraints that these place on what is possible and desirable in students' written language opportunities. Britton's ideas on this question are very relevant: It is true that the student may need to learn how to write on occasions for the unidentified examiner, or for the general audience, but not all life's use of language is like that. Staff might debate Britton's view that the more sophisticated uses of language, such as those required in examinations, are nourished by their expressive roots, both in talk and in writing; they might ask if there is an unhealthy obsession in secondary schools with writing information for an examiner; they might ponder Britton's conclusion that this situation is starving the linguistic potential of most students who stay voluntarily at school and that because of it the school might have ceased to seem relevant to those who leave early. Indeed the capacity to write clear informational prose may itself become impaired if the diet is never varied.

A starting point in overcoming the dietary deficiency is for teachers routinely to establish the kind of writing required in any exercise that they assign to children and try to ensure that pupils are equipped to produce writing of that kind. If there are types of writing that are regularly missing across the curriculum then there are clear grounds for action. Some of the fact gathering exercises mentioned in Chapter 3 provide other useful methods for uncovering the status quo. There are basically three functions of writing (Britton et al., 1975):

expressive: which is a personal language used in descriptions or in imaginative accounts; it forms the basis of other kinds of writing and may be very like speech itself; in the early years of secondary education this is the most frequently used function;

transactional: which is a language of direct instrumental intent used to communicate facts and information, to summarise, to offer objective description, to argue, give opinions and persuade, to translate from other sign systems (e.g. statistics, maps, diagrams) and to make notes; planned opportunities for its gradual development need to be inserted into the curriculum in the first three years of secondary schooling since higher levels of academic assessment require high proficiency in using this function;

poetic: which is a highly ordered and patterned language used at an advanced stage in play writing, novels, short stories, poetry etc; its use is often enhanced by carefully planned teaching contexts where motivation to write is linked with affective experiences of one kind or another.

As with reading, at the secondary level a widely agreed writing policy may be more necessary than at primary levels since there is likely to be no single staff member responsible for writing development and few children will receive planned attention. There is also a need for a marking policy that is consistent across the school. As a basis for a policy the following questions could be asked:

(1) how can skill development in using the three functions of writing be guaranteed across the curriculum?
  (i)   starting with early exclusive concentration on writing in detached informational modes;
  (ii) adding to (i) some forms of expressive and poetic writing deliberately as across the curriculum strategies;
  (iii) adding to (ii) regular demands for practical uses of writing to record, to report, to theorise, to direct, to inform, to mediate and to fantasise.
(2) how can real audiences for each child's writing in the three functions be provided across the curriculum?
(3) how can the approval and interest of parents in the children's writing be encouraged and sustained?
(4) what kinds of errors in children's work are to be marked as children progress through the school?
(5) is assessment of writing to be evaluative, summative or both?
(6) is agreement possible on the kinds of comments (positive or negative) that are to be appended to children's written work?
(7) are conferences between individual teachers and children routinely provided to give feedback on writing?

A secondary school writing policy

The writing policy below was developed for use in a conventional secondary school (Selwyn College — see Chapter 1) following an extensive survey of staff opinion (see Chapter 3). The original policy was prefaced by a rationale stressing the significance of writing in helping students to personalise their learning, pointing to its importance as a necessary skill in adult life, and mentioning the three different types of writing that usually go on in secondary schools (see above). The policy is a judicious blend of position statements and plans for specific action (Glenny, 1988):

Approaches to writing

(1) writing should be integrated with and arise from other language activities (e.g. speaking, listening, reading, demonstrating).

(2) teachers must clearly establish with students the type of writing expected before the task is begun and should ensure that students are ready to perform the task.

(3) teachers of all subjects should devote time to the development of writing: maintaining a balance between the three modes and offering a variety of writing tasks are important even at senior school level. It is important too that the less able students not avoid writing tasks.

(4) given the concern expressed in a staff survey of opinion on writing, a seminar devoted to techniques for developing trans- actional writing will be held early in the new school year as part of the staff professional develop ment programme.

(5) students' motivation, interest and self-esteem are enhanced by writing activities that give them the opportunity to think about and comment on their learning. Students should therefore be encouraged to spend part of their time doing their own personal writing: this is private writing that can be used as a basis for dialogue between student and teacher:
—journals
—brainstorming immediate thoughts
—letters
—descriptions or stories
—identifying with people mentioned in the learning.

Audience

Writing develops better if students are able to write for a real audience, whose response they value. Teachers should try to provide audiences for language work in every subject: other teachers, other students and parents.

(1) teachers should talk with students about their written work to

provide them with feedback or give them written comments where a conference is not possible.

(2) student audiences should be created as far as possible by:
—displaying written work in the classrooms
—regular displays around the school
—reading written work to a class
—duplicating written work for an audience
—producing magazines of student work.

(3) ways need to be explored for encouraging parents to look regularly at their children's books. Next year a parent/teacher meeting will be devoted to this topic to find ways in which all parents' interest in their children's writing can be encouraged and sustained.

Marking

Students in general want to write correctly.

(1) while it is one of the main aims of the English Department to teach students to write with technical accuracy, this needs to be reinforced by the efforts and support of all other teachers. Marking of written work should include correction of punctuation and grammar.

(2) spelling should be corrected where the words are part of the specific word list of a subject and where they are high frequency words which appear in general spelling lists. It may be appropriate to correct all spelling errors in some students' written work. Too much correction in weaker students' work may be discouraging so with these students only certain aspects should be corrected at any one time, making it plain to students that certain kinds of errors are targetted.

(3) comments on students' work should be specific, constructive and clear. They should also be reinforced in a conference with the student.

Neatness and handwriting

Neatness, careful presentation and clear handwriting should be insisted upon by all staff.

(1) all teachers should spend time encouraging a legible style of

handwriting. Where there is a major difficulty the R-team are available to provide help.

(2) school will produce a written guide for teachers on how to help students with handwriting problems.

(3) all work written by teachers for students should also conform to these standards.

Role of departments

(1) Departments should include in their schemes at each level a statement as to how writing in each of the three modes will be catered for.

(2) writing statements will also list ways in which audiences will be created for children's writing efforts.

(3) each Department will establish a clear marking policy before next year, taking into account this policy.

Watching and Moving: Improvisation and Role Play

In the early stages of schooling opportunities for improvisation are frequent. They flow into the classroom from children's natural play and the imaginative teacher can build on these to enrich learning across the curriculum. As children progress through school the opportunities become fewer, yet the value of improvisation work remains. In an LPAC formal drama is probably out of place. The aims of formal drama are more specific than the aims of LAC: there is detail to be mastered, moves to be learned, scripts to memorised. While all these things are important activities that should find a place in the syllabus of every child's school year, more general and unique opportunities for wider learning derive from improvisation work and role play (Corson, 1988a). The general aims in this area are to develop an ability to communicate through movement and to receive meaning through the movements of others by becoming aware of the use of gesture, whole body movements, facial expressions, posture and grouping.

An improvisation is a play without a script. In preparing for improvisation work, children can work in groups, allotting characters in their discussion, and deciding how they can best reveal their insights into the story they intend to represent in the improvisation. Improvisation as a pedagogy for learning within subjects provides the direct experiences necessary for further learning and vicarious representations of events which cannot be brought into the classroom in any other way. Its subject matter can be drawn from any of the curriculum knowledge areas.

Role play's links with the development of communicative competence are obvious ones. Role play is an aid to honesty, since the children engaged in a role play situation, which they accept as real, become emotionally as well as rationally involved. Insight and learning become possible for the group involved, while an audience witnessing the role play is equipped with a three dimensional basis for viewing the issue presented and for informing later discussion. It is an excellent vehicle for dealing with the more remote or exotic topics of the middle years of schooling. In role play children can be presented with a real-life problem in outline, perhaps drawn from an everyday crisis faced by people in another culture. A role play exercise, prepared in discussion groups, will bring out the human issues which affect decision-making, and confront children with problems which can then be related to their own world.

In some schools there may be few teachers who will feel confident about using improvisation, role play and social drama. These things are not always catered for in the training of teachers. If the school recognises the importance of these activities and staff want to see provision made for them in their LPAC then there may be a need for staff development, for using an outside consultant to advise staff members or for one teacher who is proficient in these areas to take on a leadership role.

Shaping and Viewing: The Media and other Creative Arts

Administrators unfamiliar with educational developments in these areas are sometimes overly optimistic in their efforts to integrate them into the curriculum. Successful integration is more than a matter of making some space in the school timetable for teaching them as syllabus items and then recruiting suitable experts. The central place of shaping and viewing, as complementary modes of language that reinforce and enhance development in the other modes, needs to be recognised by teachers, especially now that 'the media' is so dominant an influence in everyone's life. What may be needed to promote a successful integration of this area into the curriculum is nothing less than a wholesale retraining and resocialisation of teachers, a process of in-service education that would have its focus in ways and means of using shaping and viewing activities to promote learning across the curriculum and across the age ranges.

Critical awareness and genuine appreciation in these areas may only arise for children when teachers themselves come to recognise the critical gaps in their own life experiences that need to be filled. Film and television, for example, present a 'predigested' orderly flow of imagery which allows a highly passive viewer to grasp their messages very easily (Heinich, 1982). Teachers, no less than anyone else, have been seduced into accepting the ease with which film and television work in conveying their array of messages. As a common result of our socialisation as modern human beings we seem to have become unwilling to critically examine the stages in the sequences of communication that film and television present. Students may need a syllabus that includes tasks to make them aware and critical of the various sequencing strategies that film and television use: they need to reconstruct programs in verbal form to see what is taken for granted when only the audio/visual mode is used; they need to ask whether socio-cultural background affects viewers' dispositions to decode the meanings conveyed in visual effects. The discussion of 'critical language awareness' in Chapter 9 is relevant here.

The task is a challenging one for those developing a language policy: how can teachers be equipped with an appreciation of the place of visual effects in the language and learning work of their classrooms; how can viewing and producing videotapes, newspapers, films, television pro-grammes, photographs, paintings, comics, cartoons, signs, charts, collages, models, dioramas etc. enhance learning across the curriculum; and how can children be made more critically aware of the explicit and subtle effects of these modes of communication?

Oral Language Across the Curriculum

The central place of oral language in schooling comes from the importance of dialogue in promoting understanding and learning. In schools quality oral language work is always carried out in a context that has a meaning for the child, a meaning which is not dominated by some artificial goal like the assessment of the child's speech product. As part of this, because natural talk is always a collaborative venture, oral language work needs to be a social activity, with motivated talkers and listeners engaged in some purposeful task that is of interest to them. Talk always operates best and grows in quality when it is undertaken in an atmosphere of freedom, when things that really matter to participants provide topics for the dialogue that is proceeding. Discussion of the 'ideal speech situation' in Chapter 4 is also relevant to this section. Consider the validity claims that are said to obtain when one person says something to another in this ideal situation:

(1) that what is said is intended to be intelligible, offering a 'meaning' which can be understood;
(2) that the propositions or factual assertions offered by the speaker as part of the speech are true;
(3) that the speaker is justified in saying what is said, not going outside social rights or norms for that context of speech;
(4) that the speaker is sincere in what is said, not intending to deceive the listener.

The task of the school in creating talk situations is to provide contexts for discourse where these validity claims might prevail. In doing this there are two main tasks for the teacher: to locate suitable kinds of subject matter that are appropriate to the aims of the curriculum; and to motivate children who are moving into talk situations by creating contexts conducive to interaction about that subject matter. These points refer to matters that are more specific than an LPAC need be and I deal with them more fully elsewhere (1988a). On the other hand an LPAC can be specific in setting out its programme for oral language across the curriculum. As yet conventional schooling has made few advances and improvements in the range and quality of oral language work across the curriculum and a brief discussion of the reasons for this is not out of place here.

If the case for oral language is such a compelling one, why does it remain so understressed in the world's schools? The reasons for this are complex ones. They do need to be addressed if changes in direction are to be advocated and followed. There are many obvious factors operating against a use of dialogue in education, such as problems of class size, teachers' feelings of inadequacy in oral activities, the apparent inappropriateness of oral language subject matter, and the relative absence of effective pre-service training in this area. Teacher education institutions and those administrations engaged in selecting beginning teachers bear much of the responsibility for the present underdeveloped state of oral language work. However, even the practices of these organisations simply reflect deeper reasons. It is necessary to turn to the sociology of knowledge and the curriculum in order to suggest these deeper explanations.

Much of the work of schools is directed towards preparing children to succeed in higher levels of schooling. Curricula become increasingly more academic the closer children come to the end of schooling. Very often that endpoint is marked by an academically oriented series of examinations or other assessments that focus on the academic curriculum followed. Academic curricula pay high regard to what M. Young (1971) calls 'high status' knowledge. They tend to be abstract, highly literate, individualistic and unrelated to non-school knowledge. Young also suggests the contrasting conditions under which non-academic curricula will be organized: oral presentation, group activity and assessment, concreteness of the knowledge involved and its relatedness to non-school knowledge. It is easy to see from these attributes which style of curriculum is more readily adapted to a use of oral language work and why formal schooling, as presently structured, lays less and less emphasis on oral language work the closer students get to their final years in school. It is also clear, though, that the curricula of first and middle schools lend themselves very readily to a wide use of oral language work since they are regularly non-academic in content and can display the organisational features that Young identifies. That they do not make a wide use of oral language work seems a result of teachers' dispositions and habits, picked up in their own schooling and training, not a result of lack of opportunity. Furthermore the positive influence of talk on effective learning probably increases for adolescents in the senior school. What I am advocating here, then, to teachers at every level, is not the artificial incorporation of oral language as yet another subject of the curriculum but its use as an indispensable learning tool: a pedagogy across the curriculum.

At all levels of schooling, teachers need to see oral language work more as a contribution to effective learning, not as something to be assessed in performance. They need to place value on the oral contributions of children in order to provide motivation in the talking context. They need to move away from centre stage more often and become listeners. As mentioned above, in the early stages of the elementary school, apart from listening to children, teachers need to give them something real to talk about, to make time for conversation and dialogue, and to develop an atmosphere of trust and respect that encourages talk. Teachers of very young children often do this as a matter of course, since for much of children's first school experience, oral language is the curriculum. As children age and the curriculum of the school becomes more formal, deliberate strategies are available.

Whatever the subject area, there is room for talk through which pupils can solve their own practical problems or come to terms with complicated ideas. Group discussion is the most favoured approach, focusing on manipulable materials with younger children and on issues and questions using work cards with older children. Improvisation work (plays without scripts), prepared by children in group discussion, is an approach to learning within subjects. It can provide vicarious representations of events and activities that cannot be brought into the classroom in any other way. Similarly, role play work fosters insight and learning in all those subjects where 'values' are principal considerations. Role play equips children with a three-dimensional basis for 'getting inside' the issue, as participants or audience, and for informing later discussion. Telling and retelling stories is a significant element in everyday communication. It has a place across the curriculum, and, like role play, improvisation or group discussion can be a precursor to written work. There are variations in the use of these pedagogies that are appropriate at different levels, depending on the needs of the curriculum or whether it is communicative competence or analytic competence that the teacher wishes to promote. Oral work not only leads to new learning; as a technique of revision it also reinforces the initial learning and prevents it from slipping away. Oral work can be used as an evaluation of pupil progress when teachers intervene in group talk and become consultants. It can precede any subject matter to reveal students' levels, interests and expectations, putting teachers in touch with the reality and culture of their pupils (Freire, 1972).

In establishing the functions of oral language that the school hopes to develop, there are several lists for staff members to discuss and choose from. Halliday (1975) outlines seven functions of language. Robinson (1978) suggests fourteen and Wilkinson (1975) offers sixteen functions. Maybin (1988) reproduces the following list of 'general purposes' that are being used as a basis for assessing pupil proficiency in oral language use. I am citing Maybin as the source for these 'purposes' rather than their original source since Maybin provides a critique of their use in formal oral language assessment which offers appropriate warnings about using this list too rigidly as a basis for assessing oral language:

> describing and specifying;
> informing/expounding;
> instructing/directing;

reporting; narrating;
arguing/persuading;
structured discussion/collaboration;
speculating/advancing hypotheses.

The range of styles of oral language that the school can give children experience in using might begin with the children's casual speech itself. Some children who are in the early years of schooling might not have had much opportunity to use their own casual speech across a broad range of functions and contexts. The task for the teacher with these and other children is to provide natural talking situations that serve the purposes of the school and the child. Later other styles can be introduced deliberately: careful speech of the kind that is sometimes needed in communicating a difficult message or instruction, or in speaking on the telephone to a stranger, or in speaking to a person whose first language is different from one's own; reading aloud; reading word lists or lists of names; using the formal language of ceremonies and public speaking; engaging in the conventional 'language of politeness' with strangers, which may vary considerably from place to place. For older children colloquial exchanges or a use of dialects that are not their own might be possible, even a move into complex argots and jargons.

The kinds of experiences that a school can provide to further the development of oral language are only limited by the imagination of teachers themselves. There may be value, though, in being specific in an LPAC so that key experiences provided for the many are not overlooked for the few. For example: how do field-work and excursions fit into the school's oral language programme across the curriculum; what roles do adults other than teachers play in the language work of the school; what opportunities are available to provide children with models of language in use and with examples of language variety; how does the school plan the social contexts of its classrooms and grounds to take account of the way in which human beings develop a command of language; and how are the many experiences across the curriculum adapted to give the children something real and purposeful to talk about?

Cazden (1988) suggests four cognitive benefits that can come from discourse with peers and gives the research evidence for each. These are central to the theme of this chapter since the point of LAC is the link it provides between language and learning:

discourse acts as a catalyst to learning and problem solving;
discourse is the enactment of complementary roles;
discourse creates a relationship with an audience;

discourse acts as exploratory talk rather than as 'final draft'.

The pedagogies that can be used depend upon student age level and the teacher's skill. A policy at primary and secondary levels needs to mention the kinds of oral language methods that are desirable ones for teachers to use while working with individuals, with groups, with whole classes or in arranging activities for children working with other children: where does small group discussion fit into the school's work; where does role play or improvisation fit; where do drama, pair-work, public speaking and debates fit; where does the telling and retelling of stories fit or the reading of poetry?

Listening as a part of oral language work

In ensuring that talk is seen by all as a social activity that involves give-and-take, it is important that an emphasis be placed on listening skills somewhere in the curriculum. Successful listeners need to adapt their approach to listening to suit the situation in which they are placed and this knowledge can be communicated deliberately to children, especially when teachers use natural language situations as their starting point. Children can be brought to appreciate that there are times when careful listening is appropriate and necessary; that there are other times when we can be more selective in our listening; and that there are still other times when it is very appropriate to enjoy the pleasures of reverie. Music making and music listening activities provided at all ages are very suitable for this kind of 'listening training' since music of different kinds invites a broad range of listening styles, while the discipline of participating in group music making activities asks for the concentrated attention demanded by careful listening.

Developing 'critical listening' skills can be another matter, because it demands rather more involvement than the more everyday forms of listening. The need to adopt the stance of a critical listener is very relevant to children's engagement with the modern media, where the listener's role is a passive one and where there are no opportunities to check and question messages received. The discussion of 'critical language aware-ness' in Chapter 9 extends this point. But people also need to be critical listeners when they engage in serious talk if they are to be real participants in that talk. This form of critical listening is an important skill whose possession confers great benefit on the owner because it is the way in which we acquire most of our knowledge about the world: through the trial and error interactions of extended sessions of dialogue, conducted either with others or with ourselves while reading or reflecting, we eliminate error from our theories about the world and thereby give ourselves new knowledge with which to interpret that world. In dialogue good listeners actively engage in filtering what is heard; they sort out information about the speaker's knowledge, prejudices and attitudes; and set it against their own experiences, views and plans for action. All this is a complex exercise but it is one which most people learn to master without much more assistance than that offered by the trial and error learning experiences that come from the regular listening encounters provided by dialogue. Some children, though, may experience few opportunities in their lives outside schools to engage in critical listening of this kind. Teachers may sometimes need to identify distinct listening skills and develop them purposefully as syllabus items. At most times the arrangement of suitable talk contexts which attend to some important aspect of the curriculum may be all that is needed for critical listening skills to be developed. Provided that genuine motivation is present in those talk contexts, in the shape of some agreed endpoint for the discussions, then over time this kind of activity should be enough to develop critical listeners, since we learn to listen and talk by listening and talking to some purpose.

A primary school oral language policy

The oral language policy below was developed for use in an integrated church primary school (St Jude's — see Chapter 1) already discussed earlier in this chapter (Cockburn, 1988):

(1) oral language will be emphasised in every learning situation. These situations will generate a variety of speaking modes: formal, informal and social.
(2) pedagogy and organisational strategies will create a wide and changing variety of class groupings: class/teacher; group/teacher; child/child; individual/teacher.
(3) we shall work from the child's present understanding and experiences: moving from the concrete to the abstract.
(4) we shall promote understanding through oral language by using the following activities:
  —drama
  —mime
  —art
  —direct experiences (visits)
  —vicarious experiences (video, books, film, visitors)

—cultural and sporting exchanges
—debating
—discussion groups
—music
—presenting (drama/poetry/speech/book festivals)
(5) the following thought processes will be encouraged throughout the school:
—describing and specifying
—informing and expounding
—instructing and directing
—reporting and narrating
—arguing and persuading
—speculating and advancing hypotheses
(6) we shall value diversity of opinion and diversity in language use. Children will feel free and secure when talking. We shall develop an atmosphere of trust, tolerance and respect by:
—taking time to listen
—letting children interact to relate their experiences and show their understanding
—making dialogue opportunities real and purposeful
(7) teachers will regard all planned and unplanned encounters with children as an opportunity to develop the language skills of listening and talking and as opportunities to develop cognitive growth through language.
(8) teachers will keep running records of students' communicative competence and the situations that were helpful in developing their competence.
(9) skill in listening will be promoted by:
—drama
—interviewing visitors/students/teachers
—music and music making
—summarising, discussing and applying concepts and ideas across the curriculum
—keeping records of successful activities and pupil development.

A secondary school listening and speaking policy

The listening and speaking policy below was developed for use in a conventional secondary school (Selwyn College — see Chapter 1) already discussed earlier in this chapter (Glenny, 1988):

Approaches to talking and listening

(1) the challenge to teachers is to create contexts in which meaningful talk can occur: students need something real and purposeful to talk about, in a natural situation and one which serves the purposes of the curriculum.

(2) students need to be given opportunities to practise words and rehearse ideas many times in speech to make them their own. It is crucial then that a classroom atmosphere encourages spoken language and values student contributions.

(3) teacher questioning should include open questions that invite exploration and speculation.

(4) spoken language is the basis of all other language activities: out of oral activities comes practice in reading and writing.

Listening

(1) creative listening is a difficult but important skill which cannot be assumed in a secondary school but rather must be taught.

(2) listening is a language skill involved in all subjects: all subject teachers have the responsibility to develop it.

(3) listening problems, inattention and discipline problems arise when students are not sure of the task in hand. Teachers can help by:
—signalling a clear start to lessons
—establishing links with previous work
—describing what will happen in the lesson
—giving clear instructions
—checking the level of understanding constantly
—checking at the end of the lesson that students are able to say what they learned
—ending the lesson clearly

(4) active listening can be taught by making it purposeful. A number of tasks can be devised to involve students in active listening:
— completing a table, graph or diagram
— correcting statements
—finding mistakes
—marking or numbering a sequence
—gap filling
—dictating a diagram or graph

(5) developing 'critical' listening skills, especially with regard to

media such as television, also needs to be taught actively in the senior school.

Promoting talk

(1) all subject teachers should provide students with the opportunity to express themselves in speech. Small group and pair work creates an appropriate method for encouraging constructive language development.

(2) small groups can be used as a learning tool to help students to:
—clarify ideas
—share ideas and information
—help one another follow what is happening

(3) lesson planning should include situations where students can explore a topic in their own expressive language. Demands are made then on their spoken language and students are encouraged to speak appropriately in different situations.

(4) techniques such as barrier games, information gap activities, and ranking/sequencing activities are structured means for promoting meaningful talk in pairs and groups.

(5) other useful techniques to extend speaking ability used in the school include:
—role play and improvisation
—drama
—public speaking and debate
—poetry reading
—the telling and retelling of stories.

A policy on oral language for a girls' secondary school

The extract below presents a policy on oral language that links to one of the key language issues that staff identify in this single-sex school: the specific language needs of adolescent girls (Christchurch Girls' High — see Chapter 1). This oral language statement (Newman, 1988) also relates to questions of language awareness that are presented in the next section and to gender issues raised in Chapter 9:

Believing that purposeful talk is a tool for learning, teachers will use a variety of classroom strategies which will allow their students to talk about the new ideas they are encountering in the course of their work.

These strategies include:

(1) introducing new concepts when they are needed by relating them to their function and to words that are already in the active vocabulary of the students and if possible by reference to their morphology and derivation.

(2) using a variety of questioning techniques to encourage students to ask questions in reply, to speculate, to hypothesise, to identify, to categorise, to sequence and to build upon each other's ideas.

(3) teaching the strategies of social discourse and modelling the techniques of critical listening, sharing the topic, and building on others' contributions in classroom interactions.

(4) providing more opportunities for small group discussion than class discussion so that most of the class are actively involved in the learning process.

(5) providing opportunities for students to talk about their findings to audiences that are larger than a small group in order to build confidence and self-esteem in the learner.

(6) using role-play and improvisation when appropriate to encourage students to engage in learning on the affective as well as the cognitive level.

(7) using practical work, including research, as a means of providing meaningful cooperative tasks in which students can practice oral skills including planning and sharing for a common purpose.

(8) providing time after the talk for students to record their ideas or their findings.

Extending Language Awareness

In this chapter so far I have concentrated on those aspects of 'language in use' that children need to possess and to develop as aids in inhabiting, discovering and understanding the world. Specifically this has meant a concentration on what language can be used to do, the skills for doing it and the role of language in learning. Halliday talks of three simultaneous kinds of learning in relation to language: we learn language, we learn through language, and we learn about language. Each is dependent on the other. This final section is concerned with the last of these kinds of learning. It responds to a question that many ask about the curriculum of schools: what are the things that children need to know 'about language itself' that schools can reasonably help them to acquire?

Below I list nine areas of language knowledge that schools might include somewhere, with purpose and in depth, in their programmes across the curriculum. Ideally every teacher should have a plan of action for developing 'language awareness', a plan which does not artificially separate language awareness from language practice. Few of these areas fall neatly within the subject matter of any single discipline; as a result a deliberate policy decision at the school level may be necessary if individual language knowledge areas are not to be overlooked in the education of individual children. Rather than addressing questions about 'knowing how', the nine areas below raise questions about language of the 'knowing of' and 'knowing that' variety:

(1)   Knowledge of the structuring patterns of their own language

Hawkins (1988)[1] mentions some of the themes that this knowledge area includes and the following come from his list: the sounds of our language; the alphabet of our own language contrasted with other alphabets; words as labels; joining words together; doing things with words; talking about the past and the future; word order and meaning. Many of these things come under the heading of 'grammar'. There is an important place for them in the programme of any school, although we need not conceive of 'grammar teaching' as a throw-back to the discarded traditions of the past. Britain's 'Kingman Report' stresses the point that

> teaching language must involve talking about language, since learning without that activity is slow, inefficient and inequitable (in that it favours those whose ability enables them to generalise without tuition) (DES, 1988: 13).

There is much to criticise in the Kingman Report (see later in this section) but it is useful for my purpose here in that it provides a table which carefully sets out information on 'the forms of the English language' (p.19) (see Figure 1). A language policy for a school could acknowledge the place that these forms have in the school's programme and ensure that children during their time at school, depending on their age levels, made formal and regular contact with curricular material addressing them. The rider can be added that if pupils are to acquire these terms for describing language this should be achieved mainly through an exploration of the language that they themselves use, not through routine exercises that are produced and worked through, away from a natural language context. The Report provides illustrative notes on Figure 1. It maintains that a person who is knowledgable about these forms of language can reflect disinterestedly and with clarity on a range of issues, observations and problems that arise in everyday language use. In summary these notes are:

Knowledge about the aspects of 'speech' in Box 1 aids reflection on:
    pronunciation
    stress and emphasis
    rhythm and rhyme
    tone
    spelling patterns
Knowledge about the aspects of 'writing' in Box 2 helps reflection on:
    letter shape and form
    the alphabet
    using dictionaries and reference books
    spelling patterns
    punctuation conventions
Knowledge about the aspects of 'word forms' in Box 3 helps reflection
on:
    regular patterns in word morphology
    inflections
    derivations
    dictionary skills
    synonymy
    compound words
    metaphors
    puns and word games
Knowledge about the aspects of 'structures' in Box 4 helps reflection
on:
    the sentence
    the verb
    number
    word order
    modal verbs
    use of prepositions
    sentence form and sentence function
Knowledge about the aspects of 'discourse' in Box 5 helps reflection
on:
    paragraph form and function
    referential meaning
    ambiguity
    conjuncts
    boundary markers
    collocation

The forms of the English language

The following boxes exemplify the range of forms found in English. If forms are combined in regular patterns, following the rules and conventions of English, they yield meaningful language.

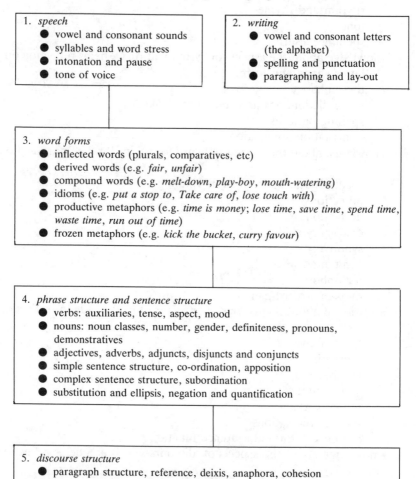

1. *speech*
   - vowel and consonant sounds
   - syllables and word stress
   - intonation and pause
   - tone of voice

2. *writing*
   - vowel and consonant letters (the alphabet)
   - spelling and punctuation
   - paragraphing and lay-out

3. *word forms*
   - inflected words (plurals, comparatives, etc)
   - derived words (e.g. *fair, unfair*)
   - compound words (e.g. *melt-down, play-boy, mouth-watering*)
   - idioms (e.g. *put a stop to, Take care of, lose touch with*)
   - productive metaphors (e.g. *time is money; lose time, save time, spend time, waste time, run out of time*)
   - frozen metaphors (e.g. *kick the bucket, curry favour*)

4. *phrase structure and sentence structure*
   - verbs: auxiliaries, tense, aspect, mood
   - nouns: noun classes, number, gender, definiteness, pronouns, demonstratives
   - adjectives, adverbs, adjuncts, disjuncts and conjuncts
   - simple sentence structure, co-ordination, apposition
   - complex sentence structure, subordination
   - substitution and ellipsis, negation and quantification

5. *discourse structure*
   - paragraph structure, reference, deixis, anaphora, cohesion
   - theme, focus, emphasis, given and new information structure
   - boundary markers (in speech and writing)
   - lexical collocation (i.e. drawn from the same vocabulary area)

FIGURE   1. *From The Kingman Report (DES, 1988)*

Clearly few of these 'forms' are appropriate topics for younger children to approach formally, even though there is evidence that a nine year old has a highly developed implicit knowledge of much that is outlined above (Lyons, 1988). Some aspects of the topics (i.e. Boxes 1, 2 and 3.) could be covered in an introductory way at junior levels, especially if skilled teachers were able to raise them incidentally as the children's natural language use allowed. More thorough treatment of these topics is possible in senior primary and at secondary levels. At these more senior levels schools could also add the more advanced topics in Boxes 4 and 5.

A priority in teaching about these topics is not so much that children should be able to talk explicitly about the abstract concepts involved, although that might be desirable among older children. The real priority is that schools can verify that children are successfully using these forms in their own language. On the other hand, if a school's language policy does include provisions that children should be able to recognise these forms and talk about them in a meaningful way, then there are some further points to be made which seem to be generally agreed to by language awareness theorists.

In discussing the abstract terminology that provides the traditional subject matter for 'grammar', children need to understand and appreciate the distinction or the relationship that a term refers to before they are asked to acquire the abstract name for that distinction. If teachers keep this principle in mind (the abstract meaning first, then the word which names it) when designing language awareness courses in this first knowledge area, then the pedagogy that they adopt will inevitably involve discovery by the child rather than prescription by the teacher. At the same time most of the grammatical terminology used in Figure 1 has withstood the test of time and seems to refer to distinctions and relationships that all of us can share in. It follows that children can probably discover these regularities in language for themselves provided that the appropriate learning context is created for that discovery. There is much evidence to suggest that children can be brought to examine and articulate their own theories about how language works and can be encouraged through skilled teaching to eliminate error from those theories about language.

(2) Knowledge that other languages in their structures and in the meanings that they encode may be very different from their own

The subject matter of Chapter 8, which looks at foreign language learning and cultural studies, extends discussion about this area of knowledge. For many reasons a good way into this topic may be through a purposeful examination of the social and cultural forces that shaped the history of English (Corson, 1985b). Like many languages, English has a colourful background touching on many other languages. It has its major lexical roots in languages that are so important to our culture and history that an examination of the etymology of English and its word relationships can provide a fascinating and vital study for any speaker of the language. From an historical analysis of this kind children can grasp a fundamental fact about language which can be liberating for the mind and for the person: the conventions for the use of language and discourse grow out of historical events and social struggles that are still continuing and which we all share in and can contribute to.

Studies of this kind, introduced at upper primary and lower secondary levels, can also provide the necessary basis for foreign language learning and cultural studies (see Chapter 8). In the latter a major task is to help children to see that we understand and interpret our world largely through abstract 'interpretative repertoires' (Potter & Whetherell, 1987) or conceptual frameworks. These abstractions 'survive' in people's minds because they embed distinctions and relationships that are important in our culture. When we engage in serious learning about other cultures we do so while acquiring a knowledge of the different interpretative repertoires that those cultures have. These shared representations that are possessed by the members of one culture provide an agreed 'code' for verbal intercourse; they allow mutual understanding between members of that culture; and they provide a stable view of the world, a view that constitutes group mind for those who are members of the cultural in-group. They are the things that distinguish cultural groups, the things that groups agree about, and the things that make groups homogeneous. There is much more, then, to acquiring another language than learning its vocabulary and its grammar.

(3) Knowledge of varieties of their own language that exist in their own society

People living in monolingual societies sometimes find it difficult to appreciate that there are regular, systematic and wide variations in language use, in language attitudes and in language behaviour among groups of people within their societies. These variations are often not so much due to issues of nationality or ethnicity; they are the result of social divisions, different patterns of behaviour, differences in power, and differences in language experience. There is a tendency for human beings to see the world of language as something stable and natural; as something which is not generated and controlled by social forces, by struggles and by historical events. In order to explain away differences in language use, people sometimes pillory variations in the language use of others'; they describe differences as poor or sloppy speech, arising from the speaker's ignorance, laziness or even perversity (see (7) below). The facts though are rather different: we all make errors in our language use at some time or other, especially when speaking informally, but the 'errors' that people often perceive in the language of others (who are usually from slightly different social groups) are not really errors: they are evidence for the existence of a different social variety of the language, a variety which preserves its features as systematically and regularly as any other language variety.

Children can best appreciate the points made above by real world experience of varieties of language in use in their own society. But schools cannot easily provide this experience with the sensitivity that is needed, even though the burden of coping with this problem is usually allotted to teachers. Clearly the task for schools is a complex one and I do not agree with some of the solutions that are offered in this area (see the discussion of 'critical language awareness' in Chapter 9). There is much more to the issues than can be solved by a facile use of the linguistic diversity of the community as a resource to be brought into the classroom and to be built upon in the curriculum. A warning about this can be found in V. Edwards' work (1986) when she studies the use of West Indian Patois by adolescent speakers of English in Britain. She finds that that variety is used widely by Black children but that their competence in using it is related to the social networks that they themselves belong to and is affected by the context of situation in which they are interacting. Well-intentioned but insensitive attempts to bring different varieties into the school, to promote language awareness in this area of knowledge, might reinforce the prejudices of some people, might alienate speakers of the variety itself, and might allow the root causes of local racism to be overlooked by concentrating on 'language' as the imagined source of the problem.

One ingenious response to the problem is suggested by the work of the 'Survey of British Dialect Grammar' (Cheshire et al., 1988). This project begins with the view that there is very little information on dialect grammar for teachers to consult that could be brought into the classroom setting. Its aim is to establish a network of teachers and their pupils who might help in collecting this information by taking part in collaborative classroom projects. The method of data collection is a questionnaire, but the project minimises those problems of sensitivity that were discussed above by asking teachers to recognise the children themselves as the experts in matters of local language variation. Any teacher taking part agrees to undertake work with children on issues such as standard and non-standard English, language variation and language change, drawing on lesson suggestions and resources provided by the project. In all discussions the teacher takes the role of the non-expert. In this way the children's consciousness about language issues is raised. Gradually information can be gathered to the benefit of all concerned. There is a strong clue in this project to the kinds of pedagogical approaches that can be reasonably introduced in communities where language variation can provide language problems for schools (which is almost every community).

Because this is a controversial area there is more reason for schools to have a sensitive and well thought out policy that deals with it. It is an area that even official reports on language attempt to avoid. For example, the Kingman Report in Britain (DES, 1988) places a proper stress on 'historical and geographical variation' but curiously ignores social and cultural variation, perhaps in the vain hope that these latter varieties of English will disappear if they are ignored. But this is not likely to happen because sociocultural variations within a language are signalling matters that are of great importance to their users; varieties within a language serve valuable group identity functions for their speakers. It follows, in non-totalitarian societies where the repression of minority identities is not routinely practised, that sociocultural varieties of language should be entitled to respect and recognition. On the other hand they can never be the central 'language' of the school: there is an overriding need for schools to extend access and mastery of the common language of the culture to all its members so that they will not be socially or economically disadvantaged relative to their peers. The tensions for schools that these apparently conflicting needs set up are discussed more fully below and in Chapter 9.

(4)   Knowledge that there are other varieties of their own language that are used in other societies

As far as it affects classroom practice, this area is more straightforward. Knowledge in this area can also be deliberately used as a point of entry to the more controversial topics of language awareness such as (3) above. Children and adults do enjoy looking at the ways that people in other lands use the same language that they speak. There are still risks here though. Teachers may not always be sensitive to the fact that attitudes established by children in relation to the language usages of distant peoples can also provide a model for their developing attitudes towards different users of language in their own society. Children can enjoy observing and exploring differences in English usage by British, Australasian, Asian, African and North American speakers of the language and they can take delight in the differences; but if they also see the differences as faintly ridiculous versions of their own language then great harm can result. If children cannot be encouraged to respect the variations in language usage of distant peoples, then our hope of them respecting and understanding language variation among social and cultural groups in their own community is probably a vain one.

(5) Knowledge of the existence of other languages that are used in their own society

Language minorities of one kind or another exist in most modern countries. Broadly speaking there are three main types of minorities in modern societies: indigenous peoples; 'established' minorities; and 'new' minorities (see Chapter 6). In helping them to understand the communities in which they live, schools have not always encouraged children to recognise ethnic groups as contributors to the breadth and richness of the local culture. Until very recently in many countries, policies of cultural assimilation were the norm and schools concentrated their efforts on identifying important aspects of the majority culture and encouraging all children to identify with that culture. These policies are now beginning to fade; the insensitivity and the discrimination that they involved is now more widely recognised. Cultural diversity is gradually becoming more a cause for celebration in many countries and is actively promoted through national policies on languages and through educational policies. As part of this development, new attitudes to minority and community languages in education are evident in many places, even though rather reactionary attempts are sometimes made to keep them out of schools and even out of the debate about language and education (see for example Britain's Swann Report (DES, 1985), Kingman Report (DES, 1988) and Bourne and Cameron's discussion (1988)).

Discussion of the 'Survey of British Dialect Grammar' under 3 above, reaches easily into this area as well. Chapter 6 extends this topic by considering minority languages and their place in majority and minority culture schools as matters of concern for a nation's language policy.

Discussion under 'Critical Language Awareness' in Chapter 9 is relevant here too.

(6) Knowledge of the lexical history of their own language, its etymology, its semantic fields, and the relationships between its words

My experience in language awareness work in this area began with quasi-experimental work undertaken in the teaching of English spelling based on etymology and word relationships (Corson, 1972). But the results that can come from developing children's knowledge in this area are much wider than just in spelling. Much of the English lexicon itself seems not to be a 'motivated' vocabulary for many speakers of the language when compared with many other speakers. Many specialist words in the language, of the kind needed for successful communication at higher levels of schooling, seem to fall within the relatively 'unmotivated' section of the lexicon (Corson, 1985b). There are probable links between this 'lexical bar' and rates of educational failure for many children who come from some social groups. Access to certain English semantic fields, which extend over the conventional knowledge categories of the secondary curriculum, may be affected by this phenomenon. Reversing this situation is not a simple matter since we may be addressing a key mediating factor in educational failure generally at the senior levels of schooling which might call into question the very aims, methods and policies that we adopt in compulsory education.

The school's task is complex: on the one hand to create conditions in which any educationally necessary vocabulary and its meanings can become a motivated and well regarded feature of children's active language use; and on the other to encourage children to recognise that there are very different ways of using words to represent experiences and that these ways depend upon the point of view of the speaker and on his or her intention in relation to the audience. Doing all of this is clearly an 'across the curriculum' task; it is not possible just to choose words to be taught to children since there are so many words, so many meanings to be expressed, and so little time. Nor is it just a matter of setting up opportunities for children to encounter words since these are easy to create: the words and meanings to be learned appear naturally in discourse attending to those areas that use them; the importance of the areas themselves makes the words worth knowing. Because of this the words and meanings to be acquired 'select themselves' when children closely engage with relevant aspects of the culture that are encountered across the curriculum. The difficulty seems to lie in making the vocabulary 'motivated' for all children: removing the strangeness that some types of words possess for some children and reducing what may be unnecessary levels of abstraction and difficulty that attach to many word meanings.

Some recommend and practice the teaching of Latin as one specific vehicle for transferring this knowledge. An introductory study of Latin, approached not for the sake of learning Latin but for the benefit that a study of this kind brings to an understanding of the difficult lexicon of English (which is mostly derived from Latin) is a curriculum approach that has been tried with success in many places. These 'innovators' propose the teaching of elementary Latin as a foundation study for the transfer value that it brings to learning the English language at advanced levels. If the Cambridge Latin Course, for example, is placed in the hands of skilled teachers the Latin becomes accessible to highly motivated students and might provide this kind of bridge (SCDC, 1982). Proposals of this kind, though, can be misinterpreted by the many these days who do not recognise the connection between the two languages, who feel that Latin has had its day or who feel that an uncritical presentation of a Latin-based programme will reinforce harmful ideologies that lie behind the meanings of many Latinate words. Certainly, as has been found with immersion teachers of Welsh, the teachers of successful Latin programmes may be more committed to their subject than the average junior school teacher and this fact alone might explain the remarkable success that Latin-based programmes have had in many places. Others recommend the middle course mentioned under 2 above and present courses of study into the structure of English words with a focus on the etymology and morphology of the language (for example: Spooner, 1988).

The best approach to this problem is probably the one that suits the needs and resources of the individual school and its language problems. Whatever this approach might be it could be spelled out as an item in a school's language policy. Alternatively the processes of vocabulary acquisition can be a policy aim implemented within departmental teaching in a secondary school; if a department has its own policy a major feature could be discussion of the ways in which the subject-specific semantic fields are to be introduced to students. Before 15 years the acquisition of complex lexical meanings is best achieved by children engaging in a variety of motivated conversations which put those meanings to use. I need not add that this means giving planned attention to oral language activities of the kind already discussed in this chapter.

In helping to decide the approach, it might be worth recounting here three advantages which Latin teaching in former times used to offer to students in this area of knowledge, advantages which are not widely available elsewhere in contemporary school curricula. I make no specific recommendation but ask this question: how might a school or department's language policy, without Latin, provide the following three features?

(i) metacognitive skills: the rich exposure to the etymology of our language that is offered in translating into and out of Latin has always been regarded as an interesting if minor bonus that accompanied the subject. Yet this process of analysing words into their bases and affixes might be very relevant to establishing certain conscious and unconscious metacognitive skills that are necessary for higher level intellectual functioning (see point (8) below). This learning activity involves discovering patterns that facilitate thinking processes. These patterns may act as cues for retrieving words in the mental lexicon. Acquiring these patterns may be an achievement of considerable intellectual sophistication, one that is rarely provided for outside the institution of formal education.

(ii) conceptual development: most specialist words have meanings that are low in imageability, difficult to grasp and subtly changeable across contexts. The learning of specialist concepts is made possible by wide and regular encounters with them used in motivated discourse. In this kind of language exchange we set meanings against other meanings which contrast with them or complement them. Foreign language study can offer rich transfer benefits for a first language, especially if the cultural contrasts in meaning preserved in the two languages are significant ones. Latin is doubly significant in this way because the cultural contrasts extend across both time and space. Sharwood Smith (1977) describes this process as it applies to Latin translation: the outlook on the world and the unexamined assumptions of members of a modern society necessarily become explicit when ideas have to be expressed in language which would have meaning for a reader in a pre-Christian, pre-industrial society; there is an inevitable explication of the concepts involved. Gramsci (1948) suggests similar reasons for the study of Latin: it not only invites students to engage prior intellectual traditions and supercede them in their thinking; it can also accustom them to reason, to think abstractly and schematically, and to distinguish the concept from a specific instance of its application. For Gramsci, too, the constant comparison between Latin and the language one speaks involves the distinction and identification of concepts; it suggests the whole of formal logic, from the contradiction between opposites to the analysis of distincts.

(iii)   access to the concrete roots of abstract words: English words of Latinate origin are likely to become more morphologically motivated for a language user who is familiar with their roots (i.e. the word's meaning becomes more transparent because of its analysis into component parts which themselves have some meaning). Without this motivation specialist words can remain 'hard' words whose meanings are needlessly perceived as alien and bizarre. The concrete roots of abstract words very often provide a strong clue to the abstract meanings allotted to them within a modern language. This offers an organising idea or a mnemonic which can give more ready access to both meaning and use of the word. Either way familiarity and confidence in using the words increases.

(7)   Knowledge of values issues in judging 'appropriateness' in language use

Following the Bullock Report, schools have often tried to encourage children to see that varieties of language other than the dominant variety do have a rightful place in language use, but that this place is a lesser one than the majority language's place. There have been good intentions behind this practice and its danger has been overlooked: doing this serves to marginalise the language of minority groups, and thereby schools take sides with the discriminatory language situation that affects minorities and other oppressed groups. If schools uncritically present dominant and other varieties as differing in conditions of appropriateness, then this devalues the other varieties since inevitably children will see them as having a lesser role in those places where prestige really matters. Yet if we accept that schools need to extend mastery of the dominant language to all children if they are not to be disadvantaged socially and educationally, what is to be done? There is another way of passing on knowledge about these value questions. The discussion under 'Critical Language Awareness' in Chapter 9 extends these key issues.

(8) Knowledge of conscious metacognitive skills that are valuable in certain styles of language use and for certain purposes

What I am talking about under this heading is 'knowledge about knowledge about language': skills in self-monitoring and self-correction. Although there are clear links with the 'forms' of language that were discussed under (1) above, I am not referring here specifically to that kind of knowledge. Metacognition includes those learning strategies and other matters of metalinguistic awareness that allow us to control our knowledge of language so that we can use language better to suit our purposes. This is one important facet of 'analytic competence'. As Bruner (1987) concludes, it is also an aspect that can be taught successfully as a skill. This is a very important conclusion for education to have reached since metacognitive activity is very unevenly distributed among people and varies according to cultural background: we pick it up from the stories told to us through interactions with members of our culture

Metacognitive awareness is a controversial area of inquiry, not least because we cannot readily distinguish between all conscious metacognitive processes and all unconscious or habitual processes. This is an important debate for teachers because we can *educate* with a view to improving people's control over their conscious processes, but in relation to their unconscious processes we can only *train* in ways that fall short of true education. The simplest conclusion to that debate may be located somewhere in the following view (Jakobson, 1980; Piper, 1988): communication involves constant and mutually independent oscillation between conscious processes of control and unconscious processes, rather than control of the one by the other.

Where the effects of metacognitive language skills are clearly seen at work is in the move from spoken language to writing, especially in mastering the formal requirements of spelling. A simple example of a metacognitive skill used in English spelling is one or other of the many rhyming rules that children can learn as an aid to remembering spelling 'irregularities' (e.g. "'i' before "e" except after "c"'). Very often the exceptions to rules of this kind make the rule itself less than helpful; it is much more than these simple mnemonics that language awareness refers to in this knowledge area. As mentioned R. Young (1983) writes about a 'school communication deficit hypothesis of educational disadvantage'. His point is that, on the evidence of many teachers' own public language behaviour in classrooms, they provide a less than adequate model of metacognitive skills in action for children to base their own use of skills of this kind upon. Many children do not receive frequent exposure to these skills in use outside schooling and as a result when they enter schools they are placed at a disadvantage when compared with the performances of other children who receive a relatively greater sensitisation to communication-related cognitive skills.

Here are some examples of these skills at work: talk about the relationships between statements and evidence; explicit reflection on the logic of argumentation and the appropriate procedures for engaging in it; category distinctions between statements of different classes; analysis to create a clearer distinction between two ideas; and, more generally, explicit allusions to the methodology of classroom learning. Clearly from Young's evidence teachers themselves are certainly engaged in these higher order metacognitive activities. In fact they are engaged in them far more than their pupils are! Young concludes that teachers are 'not only doing most of the higher order cognitive work in classrooms' but they are doing it 'without verbal reference of a metacognitive kind' (p. 10). He concludes that teachers need to make these metacognitive processes more public so that their pupils can learn from them.

We can extend this point into discussion under point (9) below in this way: the intricate interaction between conscious and unconscious processes is well captured in studies of semiotics which attend to how well one communicator's control over language impacts upon another communicator's subconscious experience.

(9) Knowledge that any sign system, including a language, depends for its communicative ability upon a set of conventions between the users of the system about the system itself

The central point of 'semiotics' (= the study of signs) is that any system of signs involves the constant matching of content (meaning) with expression (the sign itself). This matching of content with expression depends on conventions for use which users of signs establish with each other about how things are to be understood: how content will be matched with expression. This is a fundamental point underlying any language or system of signs, including such basic things as the clues in detective stories, yet it is one which escapes many young and also older users of language. Expanding the point: there are no rigid rules relating a sign with its meaning; it all depends on conventions of use; the actual form of the sign does not matter, as long as all the users of the sign agree that it be understood in a conventional and regular way. Awareness of this single fundamental point may be enough in this area of knowledge as a starting point for schools to work from in designing their language policies, since it throws up an array of curriculum issues and possibilities that relate to every aspect of language learning and use.

If the point can be communicated to children, in a variety of ways, that a language, like any system of signs, is a form of *contract* between its users, then they will see that the possibilities for language growth, development, reform, improvement, modification, control, translation and evaluation are all affected by that simple point. Linguistic chauvinism is impossible to sustain if we acknowledge that languages are mere contracts between people as users, which we make in order to interpret our worlds; that as our worlds and our horizons change we make new contracts about language to allow new interpretations to be made. We enter into new 'interpretative repertoires' and these new repertoires may transcend the language boundaries which we once thought of as setting the limits of our world.

Note to Chapter 5

1. I draw attention to Hawkins' book even though its first (1984) and second (1988) editions do make a very inaccurate reference to my studies of adolescent vocabularies. On page 79 of both editions Hawkins wrongly states that Corson 'observed a qualitative difference (a "lexical barrier") between pupils who had studied Latin and those who had not'. The salient point in those research studies, however, was that *none* of the children had a background in Latin, even those who favoured a Latinate orientation in their oral and written English. The reasons for these differences, then, are not due in any way to experience of Latin and the differences are not yet satisfactorily explained. Professor Hawkins has undertaken to remedy this error in future editions, since it does provide a gravely misleading reference for educational practice.

6 National language po~~lic~~ies, language projects and LPACs

A language policy at national level tries to do many things. It identifies the nation's language needs across the range of communities and cultural groups that it contains; it surveys and examines the resources available; it identifies the role of language in general and of individual languages in particular in the life of the nation; it establishes strategies necessary for managing and developing language resources; and it relates all of these to the best interests of the nation through the operation of some suitable planning agency. A language policy at national level is as comprehensive and coherent as possible. It marries up with other national goals and must be acceptable to the nation's people in general. By setting out guidelines within which action is possible and desirable, a national policy on languages enables decision makers to make choices about language issues in a rational and balanced way. Australia's 'National Policy on Languages' (Lo Bianco, 1987) is an example of a national policy. This is discussed in some detail below.

Language projects are lesser arrangements and they have smaller targets. These are introduced at national level but they are designed to deal with language questions as they relate to only one problem or only one confined set of problems. The 'National Writing Project' in Britain was an example of the latter. Another example from Britain is the 'National Language Project' foreshadowed in the Kingman Report (DES, 1988) whose rationale is to encourage working groups of teachers to address the issues raised in the Kingman Report itself as a stimulus to classroom-based work across the country.

A policy for languages developed at national level provides evidence to the people of a pluralist country and to the world at large that the country is taking a mature look at its language problems; that it is trying ᵤse solutions to them and to extract as much advantage and equity as ᵢssible for its people from the language diversity that pluralist countries contain. A language policy can be forced on decision makers by circumstances. It becomes a very necessary response at the political level if demographic arrangements in the country create difficulties of administration or education that cannot be resolved in a piecemeal fashion. For example, in a multilingual city state like Singapore, which has four official languages that are all widely used for communication, a policy guaranteeing and implementing a measure of equal treatment for the languages in education was a natural step to take.

On the other hand introducing a language policy can also be motivated by altruistic principles: it can be a reforming task of great magnitude, especially where the language situation is complex as it was in the Soviet Union after the Russian Revolution and where large scale policies of language reform were attempted (see below). Large scale policies like those introduced in the early days of the Soviet Union, however, bring with them all the problems that accompany holistic attempts at social change (Corson, 1986a), problems that the Indian government also encountered in its language planning shortly after independence was won in 1947. In the first flush of achieved nationhood the government decreed that English should be replaced by Hindi as the official language of the new federation, while the many regional languages of India were to be used as the official languages of the states of India which were more or less reorganised along linguistic lines. But this dual language policy failed, partly because of the residual prestige of English in the country as a whole, and partly because of the opposition to Hindi that existed in many areas on political, religious and practical grounds which the original policy makers had overlooked. English was re-adopted as the second official language and the result is that many children in Indian schools now need to learn three languages. According to Pattanayak (1988) India has accepted this 'three languages formula' as a basis for its language education: schooling proceeds through the state language, through Hindi and through English. In those states where Hindi is the state language, another Indian language is taught instead of Hindi.

Holistic planning, in which a decision is taken at the moment of planning that a complete reconstruction of some kind is possible and desirable, is fraught with risks. Holistic planning may be very appropriate for simple organisations where policies can speak unambiguously to participants: in these circumstances policy makers can reasonably advocate a trial of their policies and expect some measure of success if the policies themselves seem reasonable. However in the case of social systems of structural and ideological complexity such as a nation's language community, the diversity of views, values, ends and sensitivities that relate to any broad policy make the design of coherent holistic policies very difficult to attain. Today we have ample evidence that grand schemes of policy change, such as those attempted in the language policy area in India and in the Soviet Union, and many other policy changes in every country have not only fallen well short of their objectives but have produced social costs and private agonies out of all proportion to their limited achievements. From the outset holistic change at national level is usually impossible to control: the greater the changes attempted, the greater will be their unintended, uncontrollable and severe repercussions upon the values, aims and sensitivities of the majority of the participants in the planned reconstruction.

In the modern world a preferable approach to language problems at the national level is a language policy that moves more slowly because its designers are less certain in advance of the outcomes that they can expect from its activities. Later in this Chapter I discuss several approaches to national language policy development, including a very tentative but formal language policy that has been introduced in a pluralist modern society. In contrast to language policies at a national level, a 'language project' has intentions that are less grand; it serves the more limited needs of those countries that are not especially pluralist or whose governments and decision makers prefer to understate the cultural pluralism that they contain.

Language Minorities

Great attention is now being given to language policies because of the great population shifts that occurred over the last two or three generations. These shifts have given prominence to language issues that formerly lay submerged in societies, even in those countries where there were always significant language minorities. Reporting from his studies of OECD countries, Churchill (1986) sees major changes occurring everywhere in national attitudes to minorities. He sees the most potent factor in this move to be the recent development of an international climate of opinion favouring the more open and tolerant treatment of minorities. As an example he uses his own country as a case study which links improvements in the treatment of the Francophone minority in Canada with changes in the structures of social life brought about by increased prosperity and by urbanisation.

Broadly speaking in modern societies there are three main types of minorities: indigenous peoples; 'established' minorities; and 'new' minorities. The first of these, the indigenous peoples, includes those groups long-established in their native countries such as the Sami (Lapps), the Maori, the Inuit (Eskimos), American Indians and Aborigines. Increasingly in places where indigenous peoples are to be found, racist attitudes are becoming socially unacceptable and people of mixed ancestry are identifying more readily with the indigenous minority than once might have been the case. In a place like Tasmania, for example, where the indigenous minority all but disappeared a century ago, a vigorous minority action group has surfaced which takes its lead from larger minority groups elsewhere, like the New Zealand Maori, whose presence as a cultural force has never been in doubt.

Examples of 'established' minorities are the Catalans in Spain, the Acadian French in the United States, the Bretons in France, or Canadian Francophones. 'New' minorities are recent arrivals, including those who are immigrants in the legal sense, refugees including the 'boat people' fleeing from Indo-Chinese countries, foreign workers living semi-permanently in their new home and 'expatriates' serving in countries that are tied in a loose community with one another, such as the British Commonwealth, the Nordic States or the European Economic Community.

There are many possible ways of comparing and evaluating the treatment that minorities receive across countries. One way is to categorise official responses to the issues of minority language rights that are made at national and regional level. Churchill (1986) locates OECD countries at various points on an ascending ladder of Stages depending on their response to recognising minority group language problems and their actions in devising educational policies to meet those problems. The lowest level of development is simply to ignore the existence of special educational problems for minority groups. Most countries were located at this level in their very recent past, but all OECD countries now have some policies reflecting at least Stage 1 or Stage 2 below:

> *Stage 1 (Learning Deficit)*: sees minority groups as lacking the majority language. The typical policy response is to provide supplementary teaching in the majority tongue with a rapid transition expected to use of the majority language.
> *Stage 2 (Socially-Linked Learning Deficit)*: sees a minority group's deficit as being also linked to family status. An additional policy response is to provide special measures to help minority peoples to

adjust to the majority society,such as aids, tutors, psychologists, social workers, career advisers etc.

Stage 3 (Learning Deficit from Social/Cultural Differences): sees a minority group's deficit as linked to disparities in esteem between the group's culture and the majority culture. Additional policy responses are to include 'multicultural' teaching programmes for all children, to sensitise teachers to minority needs and to revise textbooks etc. to eliminate racial stereotyping.

Stage 4 (Learning Deficit from Mother Tongue Deprivation): sees the premature loss of the minority tongue as inhibiting transition to learning the majority tongue and that this occurs for cognitive and affective reasons. An additional policy response is to provide some study of minority languages in schools, perhaps as a very early or occasional medium of instruction.

Stage 5 (Private Use Language Maintenance): sees the minority group's language threatened with extinction if not supported. The policy response is to provide the minority language as a medium of instruction, usually exclusively in the early years of schooling.

Stage 6 (Language Equality): sees the minority and majority languages as having equal rights in society, with special support available for the less viable languages. Policy responses include recognition of a minority language as an offical language, separate educational institutions for language groups, opportunities for all children voluntarily to learn both languages and support beyond educational systems.

According to Churchill's case studies, only the very old bilingual or multilingual OECD states (Belgium, Finland and Switzerland) have reached *Stage 6*. There is some ambiguity in other countries, notably in Canada where policies differ across provincial boundaries and where responses to the Francophone minority can vary from *Stage 6* to *Stage 2* level. Sweden provides the only *Stage 5* enrichment programme in the world for its labour immigrant Finnish minority (Skutnabb Kangas, 1988), although in Sweden educational practice in some places may be lagging behind educational policy. In other aspects it may still be at a *Stage 4* level. In New Zealand the Maori Language Act of 1987 declared Maori to be an official language of the country and anyone now has the right to speak in Maori in legal proceedings. So New Zealand has begun to move towards the enrichment *Stage 5* and *Stage 6*, at least in relation to its Maori minority, but in relation to its very large Pacific Island minorities it is still located variously at *Stage 1*, *Stage 2* or *Stage 3*.

The United States' 'Bilingual Education Act' legislation locates that country firmly at a *Stage 4* level, although the responses of many schools themselves seem to be at a much lower stage. That Act deals with 'limited English proficient' (LEP) students of three types: persons born outside the United States or persons whose native language is not English; persons in whose environment a non-English language is dominant; and American Indians and Alaskan Natives in whose environment a non-English language has significantly affected their proficiency in English. These three categories are broadly similar to the three types of linguistic minorities mentioned above. In dealing with these three types of LEP students, the major goal of all school districts surveyed by Chamot (1988) has been to develop students' English proficiency so that they can participate successfully in all-English instruction. Nearly all districts report that their goal is the development of the academic skills needed for school achievement, while only a small minority of schools indicate that the development or maintenance of the students' first language is a goal. One major reason for these policies has been the belief that they would provide bilingual children with equal access to the educational system and give them achievement scores equal to monolingual children. Achievement score disparities have not been removed however (Philips, 1983).

In practice then the United States is located at *Stage 1* or *Stage 2*. There may be major obstacles to producing much advance on this, given the fact that English has been repeatedly fostered in that country to create an 'American ethnicity' (Fishman, 1987) even though there have always been high concentrations of people using languages other than English to conduct their affairs: Spanish in the South West, in Puerto Rico and in New York; French in some parts of Louisiana and Maine; German in Pennsylvania and Ohio. US Census figures reveal more than 65 languages spoken, in addition to the many indigenous tongues, yet even though a presidential commission has created a National Council on Foreign Language Teaching and International Studies, the image of a rigorous monolingualism is still promoted in the United States. However much the same was said of Australia before the 1970s (Corson, 1985a) and the changes that have occurred there in the last generation offer some hope of development in rigorously monocultural societies elsewhere.

Its major Celtic areas apart, Britain has much in common in its development with the United States. Britain is at *Stage 3* in the attitudes to multiculturalism that curriculum specialists advocate but it is only at *Stage 1* in its treatment of new settler minority language users. Tosi (1988) finds it paradoxical that bilingualism is discussed in schools and colleges as a subject of multicultural interest yet it is still regarded as educationally undesirable. The Swann Report (DES, 1985) rejects bilingual education or mother tongue maintenance at an official school level. Instead schools are urged to teach community languages where possible as subjects in the wider curriculum, equal in status to foreign languages, and to allow communities to use schools as a resource for the transmission of community languages. At least 28 different languages are being taught in over 500 community language schools. Local Education Authorities differ in their policies, with some stressing transition and others allowing for some pluralism. Reid (1988) reports that local authorities have begun the practice of 'mainstreaming' students, using ESL teachers in support roles focussing on the standard curriculum.

New settler community languages in Britain receive some recognition but only in the very early stages of schooling to ease transition to English. True bilingual education has no status; nor is there official recognition of the cultural resource represented by the presence of large numbers of speakers of non-indigenous languages. Indigenous minorities are much better provided for in Britain than non-indigenous groups, but these provisions have been won after a long struggle by the speakers themselves. In the 1981 UK Census 19% of people in Wales regarded themselves as Welsh-speaking and this resource has led to major bilingual programmes. These are discussed in Chapter 7. In Scotland less than 2% of the population speak Gaelic and bilingual education is underdeveloped in comparison to Wales. Outside the United Kingdom in Ireland, as in Wales, the language rights of the Celtic community are guaranteed and extensive research has been carried out to remove inequalities at the school level (Baker, 1988). Ireland is at *Stage 5* or *Stage 6*.

Australia, as its 'National Policy on Languages' recognises, is located at several Stages of development at once. For example, on the evidence of the treatment of many users of Aboriginal languages and some community language users Australia is at *Stage 4* or *Stage 5*; its policies of 'multiculturalism' as a response to the needs of other minority groups locate it at *Stage 3*. Since Australia is second in complexity only to Israel in the diversity of cultural groups that have made it their home, an examination of its language problems and its formal policy responses to those problems is made here.

Language Problems and Policy in a Pluralist Society: The Case of Australia

Australia's language situation is very complex: it is a country where more than 100 community languages are in regular use, where 50 Aboriginal languages still survive and where English is not the mother tongue of a very large minority of the population. In the face of this social and cultural complexity, Australia in the 1970s and 1980s changed its course away from the short-sighted and blinkered monocultural values about language issues that had previously directed policies at national level. Having experimented extensively with national policies based on the vague ideology of 'multiculturalism' (Foster & Stockley, 1988) and following the advice and pressure of its growing multicultural communities, Australia is increasingly recognising its language pluralism as a valuable national resource which enhances and enriches cultural and intellectual life and which is also invaluable in its potential for use in international trade (Lo Bianco, 1987). As part of this change and perhaps a causal factor in it or one of its results, there are strong signs that an ethnic revival has occurred in the country. There is good evidence that people are more ready to take pride in their language proficiency and their ethnic background (Clyne, 1988). There are also indications of a more diverse and healthily volatile language situation developing with a number of new and expanding speech communities.

In the face of its language complexity Australia has taken a lead among developed countries in trying to address its problems systematically. In 1982 the Australian Senate resolved that its Standing Committee on Education and the Arts inquire into and report upon: The development and implementation of a co-ordinated language policy for Australia. The Committee advertised for submissions throughout the country and brought down its report in October 1984. The Report's substantial chapters include a consideration of the following matters:

Australia's National Language;
Teaching English as a First Language;
Teaching English as a Second Language;
Adult Illiteracy;
Teaching English as a Foreign Language;
Australian Aboriginal Languages;
The Language Needs of Persons with Communication Handicaps;
Languages and Australia's International Relationships;
Teaching Languages Other than English;

Translating and Interpreting Services;
Libraries;
Languages in the Media.

In July 1986 a special consultant to the Minister for Education was appointed to coordinate the development of a national policy on languages. In May 1987 the consultant's report, *National Policy on Languages* (The Lo Bianco Report), was tabled in the Senate. Also in May 1987, in the run-up to the Federal Elections, the governing Australian Labor Party announced, as part of its policies, its intention to fund the implementation of the National Policy on Languages. After Labor's election victory the new Government allocated more than $70 million over a three year period for the implementation of the policy. These funds were to introduce five new programmes in key language areas, to supplement the existing 'English as a Second Language' programme and to establish the Australian Advisory Council on Languages and Multicultural Education (AACLAME). The new programmes deal with second language learning, adult literacy work, multicultural and cross-cultural professional training courses, Aboriginal language maintenance, and Asian studies.

In establishing any policy at a national level planners inform themselves about needs and try to match the needs with available resources by putting into place the necessary organisational structures for the collation, allocation and dispersal of those resources. Australia's Advisory Council (AACLAME) is one of the outcomes of the country's policy on languages. That Council's tasks are to identify the role of language and languages in the Australian polity and to devise ways of developing the nation's language resources in the hope of benefiting that polity and maximising life chances and equity within it. As constituted, it is an expert body with members appointed for their knowledge and understanding of language policies and multicultural education issues rather than for their positions of influence in key lobbying groups. Its role includes advising responsible government officials and administering and reviewing the programmes that are established. The country's problem areas have been summarised as follows:

—residual levels of illiteracy among native English speakers;
—poor command of English among some recent and long-standing immigrants and some Aborigines;
—relative lack of skills in second languages among English-speaking Australians;
—the need to identify a category of 'languages of wider learning' to provide a focus for development (i.e. Arabic, Chinese (Mandarin),

French, German, Greek, Indonesian/Malay, Italian, Japanese and
Spanish);
—the erosion of Australia's linguistic resources through the neglect
of potential for bilingualism among the children of families who
speak a language other than English at home;
—imminent extinction of various Aboriginal languages and the
accompanying loss of a significant element of Australia's cultural
heritage;
—lack of sufficient emphasis on practical communication skills in
university courses in some languages;
—unmet needs for interpreting and translating services for non-
English speakers including migrants, Aborigines, the deaf, and
overseas tourists.

The national policy on languages aims to ensure that Australia derives
maximum benefit from its rich linguistic resources. It aims to provide
guidance rather than to be prescriptive. In achieving this it has four key
strategies:

—conservation of Australia's linguistic resources;
—development and expansion of these resources;
—integration of Australian language teaching and language use
efforts with national economic, social and cultural policies;
—provision of information and services in languages understood by
clients.

There is much work to be done in Australia if its language problems
are to be addressed in a way that will resolve other problems of cultural
pluralism and race relations. In the approaches that have been adopted
so far there seem to be some grounds for optimism.

A Policy for Multiculturalism and Language: The Case of Canada

The development of policies to accommodate French and English
language needs in Canada has been a constant challenge which dates back
to the eighteenth century (Cartwright, 1988). While the protection of
French has been relatively easy in Quebec, where it is the majority
language, Francophones have not been as fortunate in the cultural
transition zones of Ontario and Manitoba where there have been social

pressures to restrict the use of French largely to the domain of the household. The Official Languages Act of 1969 declared French and English as official languages of the country at federal level, establishing the idea but not the reality of bilingual districts for both English and French users in those places where they are in the minority. The implementation of this concept depends on legislative support for it at provincial levels. As in the case of the Australian state of Queeensland, which promises not to support language policies introduced at federal level in Australia, there is little political support for recognition of French as an official language in Ontario, in spite of the fact that almost half a million of the province's population consistently claim French as their mother tongue. Of the ten provinces only New Brunswick recognises French and English as its official languages, while Quebec is officially Francophone and the rest are officially Anglophone. Nevertheless the provision of bilingual schooling in Ontario, New Brunswick and Manitoba, which have major minority Francophone enclaves, has increased and this response in education seems to be motivated by the kinds of values that the central government has advocated in its policies.

Like Australia, Canada is a multicultural society of great complexity. The Francophone group represents only one of at least five major clusters of cultural sub-groups (D'Oyley, 1984): the Aboriginal; the Anglophone; the Francophone; the later European; and the later Afro-Asians. Increasingly the federal government's response to this cultural complexity, manifested in a diverse array of languages, has been to place less emphasis on language itself as the distinguishing cultural trait of importance in Canada, and more on the enhancement of multiculturalism as a social value for all Canadians. The new Canadian Constitution of 1982 includes a 'Charter of Rights and Freedoms' which tries to preserve and enhance the country's multicultural heritage and to protect people's rights to use languages other than English and French.

There is a strong contrast, then, in this Canadian approach to language policy when it is set alongside the more recent Australian model. It seems that at official levels Australia as a nation is less prepared to see a basis for social planning in 'multiculturalism' and in the rather vague ideas for reform that arise from this highly abstract notion. In basing its reforms more on 'language', which is an objective entity, rather than on 'culture' which is more ephemeral, Australia may have more chance of reaching its goals since the goals themselves are rooted in something observably a part of the nation's reality. In contrast Canada's policies of multiculturalism may be little more than a vain attempt to paper over a gaping crack in the social fabric. As Cummins (1988) warns: unless it becomes 'anti-racist education' Canada's 'multicultural education' may provide only a veneer of change that perpetuates discriminatory educational structures. It does little to examine the causes of minority students' academic difficulties nor to mitigate variations in achievement that different groups have.

Canada's course is firmly set along the multicultural road but it by no means excludes language considerations and there is every hope that it will resolve language problems. The Canadian Multiculturalism Act (1988) received unanimous passage through that country's Senate. It includes significant aims that are directly related to language issues: the federal government aims to preserve and enhance the use of languages other than English and French, while strengthening the status and use of the official languages of Canada; it aims to advance multiculturalism throughout Canada in harmony with the national commitment to the official languages of Canada. The Act directs all federal institutions to make use, as appropriate, of the language skills and cultural understandings of individuals of all origins. It also describes multiculturalism as a fundamental characteristic of the evolving Canadian heritage and identity, allocating $200 million to the policy over a five year period to be spent on race relations, cross cultural understanding, preserving heritage cultures and languages, and strengthening community support.

As an enduring part of its language mosaic Canada's indigenous minority groups have long been engaged in a struggle for language and educational rights. By 1980 there were 450 Indian bands who were administering all or part of their educational programmes, with large numbers of band-operated on-reserve schools. Three Inuit (Eskimo) school boards were also operating. Like Australia, though, Canada's indigenous minorities are relatively small in number and weak in influence. The diversity of the tongues spoken makes it impossible for them to be seen as official languages outside very localised domains.

A Successful Indigenous Language Struggle: The Case of New Zealand Maori

In New Zealand one matter sets the country's language problems firmly apart from Australia's and Canada's: the key place of the Maori language (*Te Reo Maori*). The sheer diversity of Australia's and Canada's aboriginal languages makes it impossible for any one of them to become a national language in their respective countries. However compared with other aboriginal languages the Maori language has only minor dialectal differences across the country. As a result it already has the *de facto* status of a national 'language in use'. Because of this, and because of its obvious historical and cultural place, *Te Reo Maori* is unquestionably one of New Zealand's two mother tongues. There are those who would disagree with this view or who would perhaps see English threatened by this recognition. But there is no reason to see this recognition of Maori as a threat to the status of English: it is a tenet of this book that the place of 'language' in a community will prosper when several languages thrive alongside one another.

There are many who misunderstand or simply overlook the place of *Te Reo Maori* in the New Zealand polity. These misunderstandings are common among non-Maori people and come from many sources: ignorance of the language's culture, which even today is little understood or valued by non-Maori people; ideological opposition, largely based on the habits of the past, to the culture and its people; ideological opposition to the revival of a long-term subject people who have been excluded from a voice in New Zealand's affairs and who are now 'blamed' for having been excluded; and vague fears that have their roots in racial prejudices which are particularly strong in an isolated country like New Zealand as in many countries that were once the colonies of Northern European countries. The suppression of the Maori began with the unlawful exercise of sovereign rule over these indigenous people by the British settlers (Kelsey, 1984). The denial of Maori language rights in the nineteenth and early twentieth centuries is well evidenced in attempts to stamp out their language through education in ways which contravened and continue to contravene the Treaty of Waitangi, signed in 1840 between representatives of the two parties.

The non-Maori majority's acceptance of the status quo in New Zealand allows the inequity of the linguistic repression that is still visited on the Maori to be seen as normal and natural. For example, even some people associated with the New Zealand Association of Language Teachers, who are concerned with second and foreign language teaching and who could see the Maori language issue more clearly than many, are surprised that many Maori people are less than willing to become closely associated with the 'second languages' movement. But it is no surprise that Maori people should keep themselves and their language separate, since their language is the first language of New Zealand. It would be politically unwise and probably culturally destructive if the speakers of *Te Reo Maori* allowed it to be seen as just another of the 'second languages' to be taught in New Zealand schools. If they were to allow this to happen it would locate New Zealand's treatment of its own aboriginal people at the same level as contemporary Britain's treatment of its new immigrant peoples. French, German, Japanese, Chinese and many other foreign languages all have a place in the school curriculum in New Zealand and in a national language policy. But their place is a lesser one than *Te Reo Maori*'s.

After a long struggle the Maori language seems likely to regain its rightful place as a recognised mother tongue in New Zealand. The Maori Language Act of 1987 declared Maori to be an official language of the country and anyone now has the right to speak in Maori in legal proceedings. This enlarges Maori's domain of usage considerably and means that more accessible interpreting and transcription services of quality must become more available. Since 1983 all New Zealand teachers' college students have spent time studying the language. Although the Maori people are the most economically disadvantaged sector of New Zealand society (Benton, 1986) changes of this kind have developed largely because of the intiatives taken by the Maori people themselves to establish educational arrangements conducive to the maintenance of the language. The *Kohanga Reo* (language nests) movement, for example, began in 1982 and now operates in more than 300 centres. It tries to compensate for the fact that so few young Maori parents now speak the language fluently. It offers a pre-school all-Maori language and culture environment for children from birth to school age, aimed at fostering complete development and growth within a context where only the Maori language is spoken and heard. Because English is freely spoken elsewhere in the community, the movement allows the young to become naturally bilingual in Maori and English. Arguing from these beginnings, the Maori people are now well-placed to demand a greater range of bilingual schooling provisions for their children. There are problems that need to be sorted out very quickly: firstly to provide for the transition of bilingual children from *Kohanga Reo* to primary schools; secondly to provide for the transition from new bilingual primary schools to 'ordinary' secondary schools. To meet aspects of the first of these problems, junior school teachers now receive special training to allow them to cope with the influx of bilingual children and official bilingual primary schools are increasing in number.

With these victories behind them the Maori minority in New Zealand has every prospect of reviving Maori in the community and elevating the culture that it embeds. Although recognition of the equality of English and Maori as national languages in New Zealand is the starting point for any national language policy, the languages of other large new settler groups in New Zealand also need to be included in a language policy for the country. These too are different from the 'foreign languages' which we traditionally associate with schools: they are 'community languages', similar in importance to languages in Australia like Italian (spoken regularly by 440,000 Australians) and Greek (spoken regularly by 260,000 Australians). The provision needed for the young speakers of Samoan, Tongan, Niuean and other Pacific tongues may be very like the provision that is made for French-speaking Canadian children in Quebec: for the social and intellectual well-being of Francophone children, the French must be maintained and developed; but for everyday convenience and for wider participation in their country's affairs, they also need to have complete fluency in English. Similar needs occur for Welsh-speaking children in Wales and for Finnish speakers in Sweden. Samoan New Zealanders and others have similar needs.

In comparison to its recent treatment of the Maori minority, largely in response to Maori pressure, New Zealand is not very advanced in addressing the language problems of Pacific Island, of Indo-Chinese or of other new settlers. A national language policy for the country would identify local problems and offer guidelines for action that could be applied wherever necessary across it. In microcosm New Zealand's language situation over time may become more like multilingual states elsewhere. Certainly its former days of rigorous monolingualism are rapidly disappearing.

Language Policy in a Multinational/Multilingual State: The Case of the USSR

After the Russian Revolution the new Soviet Union provided a uniquely complex setting for language planning. Lenin's policies in the language area produced extensive and ambitious programmes to develop the languages and literatures of minority peoples, to create alphabets for languages that had only an oral tradition, to extend the spheres of usage of local languages, and to adopt written minority languages into the teaching and the textbooks of higher education (Marcellesi & Elimam, 1987). Inevitably large-scale change of this kind, orchestrated from a central authority, met difficulties of implementation and major mistakes were made. In the early decades policy tended to swing from one extreme to another, with universal literacy in some or other language as the only constant aim. Yet universal literacy has only been achieved in the USSR through educating people in their own languages. While there was an emphasis under Stalin on developing linguistic homogeneity in Russian, with little respect paid to national languages, this policy is now considerably modified. Although universal fluency in Russian remains the primary goal, the experiences of the past have taught Soviet leaders to recognise the power of attachment that minority nations and groups have to their languages.

Today the USSR remains a multinational country whose cultural groups speak more than 130 languages. Of these, 78 languages are used as a basis for national literatures, 42 are used in dramatic productions, 46 provide the languages of journals, 56 the languages of textbooks and 67 languages are used in radio broadcasting (Guboglo, 1986). Russian is the first language of almost half the population, while Ukrainian and Byelorussian are used by a further quarter of the population. The USSR's language policy follows the basic course of promoting bilingualism on a large scale: this means the development of the native languages of the nationalities at the same time as the diffusion among them of the Russian language. This policy recognises the language right of minorities to develop their native languages, through allowing children to be educated in their home language during at least the early years of schooling, while simultaneously making it possible for these people to have access to the world culture through the international language of Russian. About 35% of all children in the USSR are taught in a language other than Russian with this figure rising to 80% in the central Asian republics where children regularly receive most of their schooling in non-Russian languages (McLaughlin, 1986).

Because of its long history of second language teaching and its vast experience in bilingual education, Soviet education offers an important lesson for much of the subject matter of Chapters 7 and 8. Educators in the USSR traditionally lay stress on the role of the first language in learning a second, suggesting that there is a single language competence underlying the learning of both languages. Once this competence is well established in the first language, it is then available to provide the basis for second language learning. The concurrence of these views with contemporary theory and practice in this matter in Western countries will be readily apparent from discussion in Chapter 7.

The Majority Language in a National Policy

If my treatment of majority languages in this Chapter seems a little out of balance, this short discussion here may redress things. As can be seen from my review of Australia's national policy on languages, the centrepiece of a national language policy remains the attention it gives to the country's mother tongue. Other issues related to other languages may be more important for those who have a personal interest in those languages, but in mainly monolingual societies the problems that people have with the majority language will inevitably be the dominant ones for a policy to consider. In all countries a large minority of majority language users may need help in the skills of using that language in certain contexts, functions, styles or modes of language in use. Adult literacy programmes are an enduring need in even the most educationally well-served of countries. Mother tongue teaching in schools, in all the areas covered in Chapter 5, is the major part of the ambit of influence that a national language policy covers. A second language may be a desirable acquisition for everybody, but a firm grasp of the first language, in all its functions and styles, is essential. Mastery of the mother tongue has priority if people are to have a voice in society and control over their own affairs.

Yet with a soundly designed national policy there is no need for a conflict of interest between the needs of mother tongue speakers and second language needs. We can readily enhance the teaching of second languages while still strengthening the mother tongue across the country. The reasons for this are only now beginning to emerge in studies of bilingualism and second language learning that are covered in Chapter 6: the learner who is reasonably proficient in a first language has that proficiency increased, not diminished, by studying a second language.

The Role of the Schools

A national policy on languages is a set of nationally agreed principles which enables decision makers to make choices about language issues in a rational, comprehensive and balanced way. It should form the basis for the allocation of resources for language programmes to suit the interests and needs of all members of the community. A national language project, like the National Writing Project in Britain, quite clearly has the school as its focus of operation. It may be less obvious, but the main site for implementation of any national language policy is also in the schools. This state of affairs has come about almost as a direct entailment of the symbiotic relationship that exists between modern schooling on the one hand and the advance and maintenance of human civilisation on the other. As Haugen remarks:

in our modern world universal education has become a professed ideal
. . . linguistic traditions and their potential innovations are channelled
through educational establishments (1987: 631).

When establishing a policy at a national level planners inform
themselves about needs and try to match the needs with available
resources by putting into place the necessary organisational structure for
the dispersal of resources to the maximum benefit of the country's
population. There is a problem here however: From the evidence that
comes from attempts that I have already mentioned to implement
large-scale programmes for social improvement, if democratic strategies
are not established at the local level, any hope of benefit will prove to be
a vain one. What is needed are grassroots arrangements equipped to
translate the visions of a national policy into strategies capable of
enhancing individual lives. The social institutions for developing these
strategies at the local level are already established throughout pluralist
societies in the form of their schools. It seems a very reasonable thing to
ask schools to be responsible for much of the 'working end' of a national
language policy, since language policy goals are clearly in line with so
many of the aims that schools and their teachers already hold dear.

In consort with national policies and projects about language and
languages, I suggest that a movement to create a climate for the
development of language policies across the curriculum of individual
schools is a reasonable and proper course for education in pluralist
societies to be setting. As this book is at pains to show, the development
of a school language policy depends on a number of factors. Once a
national policy is in place and once it provides the discretionary guidelines
needed for action, all of these factors are within the school's ambit of
control: the commitment of the teaching staff to the needs of language;
a willingness to undertake some research into the language needs of a
particular school community; familiarity with the theory (i.e. knowledge)
that relates to language problems; the openness to consult with parents and
the wider society; and the leadership of the school executive and the
enthusiasm of the whole school community in making the policy development process work.

7 Bilingualism and second language teaching (SLT) across the curriculum

Bilingualism and Bilingual Education

In many countries bilingualism is so common as to be an unremarkable phenomenon: in the countries of East Africa, in India, in various provinces of China many people learn more than one language from their earliest days and accept it as a normal part of affairs. Elsewhere multilingualism is the norm: on the Congo River in West Africa more than 130 languages can be encountered, many overlapping with one another in various contexts; in Papua New Guinea tribespeople who have received formal education to higher levels may have had to learn five or six languages along the way, with the language of their higher education, English, coming last in that list of languages. In other settings for many people bilingualism within a multilingual nation state is the norm. In the republics of the USSR, as we have seen in Chapter 6, there are many examples of this. This form of national multilingualism is the norm within and between Yugoslavia's component republics: in Slovenia, Italian-speaking children attend elementary schools where Italian is their language of instruction; in Croatia, the Italian, Hungarian and Czech minorities receive their early education in their mother tongues; in Montenegro, Albanians receive bilingual schooling; in Macedonia, Albanians and Turks do the same; and in Serbia, Albanians and Bulgarians both receive mother tongue schooling. There are other minority languages in Yugoslavia, each provided for in the system of schooling. All of this occurs in a country whose national languages are Slovene, Serbo-Croat, Croat-Serbian and Macedonian.

Relatively few children arrive in the world's schools with only a background in the majority language that is used in their society. But it

159

would be wrong to conclude from this that 'balanced' bilingualism is common around the world. Most bilingual speakers are able to use the weaker of their languages to serve only limited functions, often to do with the specialised activities of commerce, education or work. True bilinguals, who are able to operate with ease in both languages in all everyday settings, are the rare exception rather than the rule. As a complement to this situation, quality bilingual schooling is a recently developed phenomenon which even now is in the early stages of its evolution.

Bilingual education programmes are developing rapidly in pluralist nation states. These programmes can serve very different national needs: as a step in moving towards a single national language; as an instrument in developing ideological solidarity; as a way of gaining access to national contact with a world language; and as a way of extending language rights to minorities. It is also becoming more common in pluralist affluent societies for parents to offer bilingualism deliberately to their children as a means of keeping them in touch with the culture of some or other language which is not a dominant one in their society (Saunders, 1982). As the prejudices of the past, based on race and culture, begin to fade in multicultural societies like Australia, Canada and New Zealand, more people are seeing the benefit of raising their children bilingually.

It would serve little purpose here to attempt a definition of bilingualism since there are so many definitions (Rivera, 1984b; Mackey, 1987; Skutnabb-Kangas, 1981) and each one may be suitable depending on the context in which discussion is occurring. 'Bilingual education' is another matter. When we apply this phrase to schooling we are not talking about an aim of the curriculum; we are talking about one of the means by which schools achieve their educational goals. Nemetz Robinson offers a helpful definition of bilingual education which contrasts with second language learning:

> Bilingual education is distinguished from foreign or second language education, including the study of community languages, in that bilingual education is the use of a non-dominant language as the medium of instruction during some part of the school day (1978: 8).

Acquiring a language is much more than mere 'language learning'. To a large extent 'bilingualism' always implies some degree of 'biculturalism' for the individual since learning a language involves acquiring many aspects of the knowledge, beliefs, skills and experiences that identify the culture that has produced the language. Chapter 8 looks briefly at 'cultural studies' in the context of foreign language learning but its application is as relevant to bilingual and second language education. The issue is complicated by differences in the value that can be placed on minority languages in the schooling process. According to Lambert (1975) the aims of schooling in relation to bilingualism fall into two distinct categories: 'additive bilingualism', when a second language is acquired with the expectation that the mother tongue will continue to be used; and 'subtractive bilingualism', when a second language is learned with the expectation that it will replace the mother tongue (i.e. the minority language). The former is a 'maintenance' form of bilingual schooling which sets out to use both languages as media of instruction for much of the child's school career. The latter is a 'transitional' form of bilingual schooling which only lasts for the early years of schooling, with the majority tongue taking over as the means of instruction after that.

There is an important social justice issue in these two positions, a contrast made plain by Horvath (1980) when she points out that the United States Office of Civil Rights supports the maintenance approach (which is consistent with seeing cultural groups forming a broad mosaic across the nation) while the United States Office of Education supports the transitional approach (which is consistent with seeing cultural groups eventually shedding their identity in the melting pot of the nation). No doubt there are major financial considerations that inform the Office of Education's view. But for pedagogical reasons, set out below, 'subtractive (transitional) bilingualism' is not an alternative that should be routinely favoured in modern schools. Added to this is the fact that bilingualism implies a degree of biculturalism which can make subtractive bilingualism an improper denial of cultural rights, since loss of language in this way often involves loss of culture. In Chapter 9 I return to many of the social justice issues in this debate.

When bilingual education is introduced it is a public recognition of the school's responsibility for the language minorities within its community. In areas where there are large numbers of children with similar bilingual needs, planning at the school level may be more straightforward than in areas where there are fewer children. The rich opportunities that having many bilingual children offers for using a non-dominant language as the medium of teaching, and also as subject matter for teaching, will compensate somewhat for a school programme that is not individualised. In American, Canadian and Finnish studies this approach has produced more than just bilingual fluency in children (see below): their academic performance and intellectual prowess generally have also developed (Cummins, 1983; Skutnabb-Kangas, 1986).

When there are isolated children with unusual needs, severe educational disadvantages can go unnoticed. For example, severe and often intractable problems exist in planning bilingual education for those children whose mother tongue is a regional variety of a national language, as may be the case for Italian-born Australian or British children (Tosi, 1984; Bettoni, 1985). How can bilingual studies proceed in Italian and English for these children if neither English nor Italian is the children's true mother tongue? Elsewhere social dialects of a language pose problems of a related kind. In the United States many Hispanic students come from very low-income family backgrounds, live in fairly segregated neighbourhoods, and consequently speak a form of vernacular Spanish which is far removed from the literary Spanish which bilingual teachers usually possess (Valdes *et al.*, 1981). Only research at the single school level, coupled with access to outside consultants and the incorporation of decisions into a language policy across the curriculum, can offer solutions to problems that have this degree of specificity.

There has been a radical change in attitude and approach in education to bilingualism as our information about the links between language, culture, self-identity, thinking prowess and educational success has grown. Maintaining the mother tongue is said by many to develop a desirable form of cultural diversity in societies, to promote ethnic identity, to lead to social adaptability, to add to the psychological security of the child, and to develop linguistic awareness (Crystal, 1987). In Holland, for example, a bilingual maintenance approach to the education of minority children is favoured, not just for reasons of social justice and self-esteem, but because it is found to be as effective in promoting majority language learning as other assimilation and transition approaches and actually requires less time to be devoted to the teaching and learning of the majority tongue (Vallen & Stijnen, 1987). Moorfield (1987) reviews programmes over the last twenty years in Mexico, the United States, Sweden and Canada where children began school speaking a minority language or dialect and where that language was used as the main or only medium of instruction. Later for all these children there was a gradual transition to instruction in both the minority and the majority language. Academic progress achieved in each case was much better than in those programmes where minority language children were taught entirely in the majority language. Student self-esteem, pride in their cultural background and group solidarity were also enhanced in each case. In other settings, where the needs for bilingualism and biliteracy are so obvious that the question of their desirability is never even raised, initial and advanced literacy in two languages becomes possible and 'real' bilingualism becomes a natural and necessary acquisition for all children (Garcia and Otheguy, 1987).

One of the countries best known for its advances in bilingual education is Canada where the special needs of the French Canadian population have provided a spur to research and changes in practice; where there are more than 100,000 children in French immersion classes; where cities like Toronto are among the most multicultural on earth; and where the various aboriginal peoples of North America provide an additional set of minority language problems (see Chapter 6). Indeed the Ontario Schools Board is guided by a firm government policy that every school must have a language policy (see Chapter 5). Cummins and Swain (1986) provide a guide to the research in bilingual education currently taking place in Canada. The authors contradict many of the prejudiced views that have been widely held about bilingualism and education:

—they show that the research base for bilingual education is sophisticated and growing;
—they offer strong evidence that quality bilingual programmes have been influential in developing language skills and in contributing to broader academic achievement;
—they deny the conventional view that immersion programmes can only be effective with the very young;
—they suggest that in some respects older learners have advantages over younger ones;
—they report evidence that lower ability children also benefit from immersion programmes;
—they conclude that a quality bilingual programme will support and aid development in the first language.

In later sections I extend this discussion of the Canadian experience and supplement it with evidence from elsewhere. While it is possible to draw a favourable conclusion from the bilingual research as a whole to link quality bilingual schooling with cognitive advantages for the learner, Baker (1988) advises us not to overestimate these advantages, especially in relation to everyday mental functioning. On the other hand there is important evidence to suggest that bilinguals are superior to monolinguals on divergent thinking tests; bilinguals have some advantage in their analytical orientation to language; bilinguals also show some increased social sensitivity in situations requiring verbal communication; and bilinguals may have advantages in cognitive clarity and in analytical functioning.

Approaches to Bilingual Schooling: Majority First Language Speakers

In this section and the next I look at successful examples of bilingual education programmes at work. I begin with those programmes where majority language speakers have been taught using a minority language as the medium of instruction.

The Schools Council Bilingual Education Project in Wales was a carefully planned, monitored and assessed bilingual programme. Beginning in their first year of schooling at four years, children from English-speaking homes were exposed to schooling in Welsh for one half of each day throughout their primary education years. The aim of the project was to equip the children with a level of English/Welsh proficiency sufficient to operate within their culture in either language. Provision was made to ensure that the Welsh language learning was based on activities that had immediate relevance to the children's life interests and experience. After matching the bilingual children at the end of the project with groups of children who had received a monolingual primary education in English, no significant differences were found between the two sets of children, except in one social group category where the bilingual children performed even better in their English than the others (Price & Dodson, 1978). Moreover the majority of the children developed considerable skill in Welsh usage by seven years (Price, 1985). Another study in Wales (Dodson, 1985) found that junior primary age children from five types of school, who were either already bilingual or becoming bilingual, were not handicapped in their conceptual development through undertaking bilingual education.

The St Lambert Project in Canada (Lambert & Tucker, 1972) which provided monolingual Anglo-Canadian children with instruction from a monolingual French-speaking teacher for their first five years of education confirms that second language learning for the young can proceed without harm to the child's first language proficiency and academic development. As important, after seven years of bilingual education the children were able to communicate effectively in French with their Francophone schoolmates. Other studies in North America, since the St Lambert Project, allow us to compare three types of programme: children totally immersed in the second language early in their schooling; children partially immersed early in their schooling; and children totally immersed late in their schooling. Results of the comparison show a trend in all programmes towards better performances in their English language skills on certain academic tasks than do matched control groups (Swain & Lapkin, 1982). There is no evidence that early second language learning by majority language speakers leads to any long term loss in the development of first language skills (Harley, 1986). Two further points emerge from the same North American studies: early immersion seems the most effective method for acquiring the second language; and academic progress or general intellectual ability is not impeded by immersion in a second language. Rather the opposite may be the case.

Cohen (1976) lists basic characteristics that successful immersion programmes seem to have for majority language users:

(1) All instruction initially is in the second language;
(2) In grades 2, 3 and 4 first language skills are taught in the first language;
(3) By grade 5, social science subjects are taught in the first language;
(4) New entrants into the programme have no experience in the second language;
(5) Teachers are usually bilingual;
(6) The first language is rarely used by teachers in the pupils' hearing;
(7) In the first year pupils are allowed to use their mother tongue until proficiency in the second language develops;
(8) After the first year the children are encouraged to use the second language for as much classroom interaction as possible;
(9) The regular school curriculum is followed;
(10) The second language is not taught by structured lessons in the early years;
(11) Voluntary enrolment depending on parental consent is the rule.

Approaches to Bilingual Schooling: Minority First Language Speakers

The children in the immersion programs in the previous section come largely from majority language backgrounds and live in communities where the idea of their language immersion programme was supported or at least tolerated. Parental approval of the programmes and their keen support of the children's development in both languages was an accepted part of the arrangements. We can say then that development in the first language of the children (English) and in the immersion languages (e.g.

Welsh or French) was welcomed and promoted inside and outside the school.

In many countries the needs of linguistic minorities for sensitive bilingual programmes are not always favoured by sympathetic schooling systems. Often these minority peoples are among the relatively powerless in their societies and their children's educational futures are not guaranteed by parents who are affluent and influential. On the one hand these children may be from new settler families who bring with them the knowledge of a culture that may never be well represented in their new country. On the other hand they may come from an ancestral aboriginal culture that has been submerged beneath a dominant colonial culture.

Maori children in New Zealand belong to the latter minority group. Their language is not widely used for everyday communication, having as yet little apparent value in the wider society and little support within those social institutions which determine educational policies (Moorfield, 1987). Many Maori children attend *kohanga reo* (Maori: 'language nests') preschools which offer Maori childcare in an environment which is Maori in action and in language. There is a need for primary schools receiving the graduates of the *kohanga reo* to build on this experience of Maori language and culture and these are developing (see Chapter 6). Similar problems exist for Pacific Island children in New Zealand, as they do for many Aboriginal children in Australia and for aboriginal peoples in other countries where indigenous languages survive precariously and by surviving provide an important link between minority peoples and their culture.

There is a major difficulty to be overcome in designing programmes for children of ancestral minority cultures and for children from new settler backgrounds, all of whom may come to school with varieties of a minority language as their first language: In majority culture schools there are few if any teachers who understand the children's language or much of their culture. The real needs of the children and their different learning styles and values can be overlooked. Worse than this, because monolingual teachers are understandably anxious to induct these children into the majority language, attempts at immersion programmes in the majority language that are not consistent with the linguistic needs of the children can permanently hinder their intellectual development and rob them of their educational chances. What do we know about providing bilingual programmes for minority language children and what are their results?

The study 'Learning English through Bilingual Instruction' carried out by Wong Fillmore in the United States examined effective instructional practices in developing the English academic language skills of Hispanic and Chinese minority language students (Chamot, 1988). Four major instructional factors were significant:

- —high quality teaching, including clear lesson organisation, directions and explanations, appropriate aids, attention to higher level skills, and opportunities for oral activities;
- —high quality instructional language, including clarity, coherence, use of contexts, paraphrasing, responding to student feedback, and discussion of grammar and vocabulary;
- —effective classroom management with stress on academic rather than on non-academic activities;
- —provision of equal opportunites for the practice of English.

Effective classrooms in these studies displayed a balance of teacher-directed and individualised activities. In bilingual classrooms students profited most when the languages were presented separately without translations. But there were differences in the learning styles for the Chinese and the Hispanic students, with the latter gaining most from interaction with their peers and the former learning most in structured and fairly quiet classrooms. Saville-Troike (1987) also reports differences between cultural groups in their approaches to social and learning interaction in the classroom: Vietnamese compared with American children may use differing strategies for dispute resolution; Chinese children in American nursery classrooms rely on a greater use of mediation and compromise when solving problems. These differences often carry over into the content and the teaching methods that are appropriate for children from different cultural backgrounds. In some Polynesian cultures, for example, in the early stages of a task children tend to learn by observation, rather than by participation; they prefer to decide their own rate of involvement which increases slowly until they have reached a level of mastery which they judge to be adequate. Not surprisingly when children and their family groups move to new societies they bring their styles of learning and interacting with them.

Also in the United States a long-term comparison of three approaches to bilingual schooling for Hispanic children has been undertaken. The three approaches are:

(1) immersion strategy, in which content subjects are taught through simplified English;
(2) early-exit or short term transitional bilingual programmes of two to three years;
(3) late-exit or long-term transitional bilingual programmes of five to six years.

Comparisons found long term bilingual programmes to be most effective in promoting progress in both Spanish and English and that immersion programmes promoted a greater use of English by students in school itself (Chamot, 1988). Elsewhere in the United States, Spanish dominant children attending schools in California (Campos & Keatinge, 1988) benefited both academically and in their English language acquisition by having their mother tongue used as the language of instruction in the early junior school years.

In Sweden a policy of 'active bilingualism' has been the goal for immigrant pupils' language learning since 1975 and it has been a legal right since 1977. The official Swedish promise of 'freedom of choice' to its immigrants in their decisions about maintaining their own cultures and languages means in practice that every immigrant child, from a minority group which is large enough, must be given the opportunity to attend a mother tongue medium class. Classes for the large Finnish minority in suburban Stockholm, segregated into classes using Finnish as the medium of instruction with Swedish taught as a second language, are among the longest established (Hagman & Lahdenperä, 1988). After nine years of operation researchers have based their conclusions on extensive comparisons with other Finnish children and with other immigrant groups, who have not had a rich history of instruction in their mother tongues. Briefly the segregated Finnish maintenance children, by the end of their compulsory schooling, have still managed to integrate themselves into their Swedish comprehensive school while building up their academic self-confidence, identity, and their proficiency in Swedish. Moreoever the students from the Finnish maintenance classes show considerably higher figures for entry to further education.

In Britain the MOTET project in Bradford (Fitzpatrick, 1987) assessed the effects of bilingual education in a one year experimental programme with infant children whose home language was Panjabi. The class programme aimed to preserve a 'parity of esteem' between English and Panjabi by allotting equal time and space to each language across the curriculum. The study concluded that there were no negative effects from bilingual education. Instead there were the positive effects of mother tongue maintenance as well as a level of progress in English that was equivalent to a matched control group who had not received a bilingual programme. In Holland programmes in Leyden and Enschede (Appel, 1988) for the primary age children of Turkish and Moroccan immigrant workers suggest that minority language teaching for children from these backgrounds has no negative educational or social effects. In short these programmes achieve only good results.

Variable Factors in Bilingual Programmes for Minority Children

Level of language development

Following ideas first expressed by the Finnish researchers, Toukomaa and Skutnabb-Kangas, Canadian researchers Cummins & Swain (1986) put forward their 'threshold hypothesis': there may be threshold levels of language competence which bilingual children must attain in their first and second languages in order to avoid cognitive disadvantages and to allow the potentially beneficial aspects of becoming bilingual to influence cognitive functioning. Theoretical information of this kind is essential for language planning in bilingualism at the school level. On the other hand while these hypotheses explain many different phenomena they still need strong empirical support, especially at the level of language itself. Cummins, for example, assumes that language proficiency is an important mediating variable between bilingualism and education. But he is criticised by some for not telling us much about the specific linguistic advantages that being bilingual brings: the preconditions for literacy in speech, as distinct from the more obvious educational advantages that are spelled out by him rather vaguely as 'literacy related skills'.

Elsewhere Cummins and Swain provide evidence to show that there are aspects of language proficiency that are common to both first and second languages, aspects that are interdependent. This evidence allows us to understand why *less* instruction in the second language often results in higher second language proficiency scores for minority students, while for majority language students *more* instruction in the second language results in higher second language proficiency scores. They also present research evidence suggesting that in some aspects of second language learning older learners are more efficient learners. They go on to offer ideas in programme planning for bilingual proficiency. From Cummins and Swain's discussion three key points can be made about bilingualism and schooling:

(1) a high level of proficiency in both languages is likely to be an intellectual advantage to children in all subjects across the curriculum, when compared with their monolingual classmates;

(2) in social situations where there is likely to be serious erosion of the first (minority) language, there is a need for the development and maintenance of that language if intellectual performance is not to suffer;

(3) high level second language proficiency depends on well-developed first language proficiency.

Putting these three points together we can conclude that children from disadvantaged or oppressed minority groups generally profit from bilingual programmes in which their first language plays the major role, because this lays a language foundation which cannot otherwise be guaranteed. This conclusion contrasts with the findings for children from dominant majority language groups who benefit from bilingual programmes in which the second language is used most frequently (Appel & Muysken, 1987). In the latter case a firm foundation in the first language is guaranteed by the fact that it is the language of wider communication in the society.

The third point, that learning a second language well depends on developing prior proficiency in the first, is broadly consistent with the findings of educators in the USSR, mentioned in Chapter 6, whose experience in these matters greatly outstrips experiences elsewhere (McLaughlin, 1986). Research in Germany too (Rehbein, 1984) suggests strong links between high level development in conceptual information and discourse strategies in the first language on the one hand and second language development on the other.

Because their language is not the language of wider communication, many Maori, Aboriginal, American Indian, Inuit minority children and other children from new settler backgrounds in many countries, may arrive in schools with their first language relatively under-developed in certain contexts, styles and functions of use. As well their grasp of the majority language may be limited to a small range of functions, often passively related to television viewing and the like. For these children intensive early exposure to the majority language may result in low achievement in that language as well as a decline in mother tongue proficiency. Bilingual programmes in the minority language are essential if widespread and discriminatory school failure and its attendant social costs are to be avoided.

Age of acquisition

Very young children (under five) given the necessary environment, such as that offered by the Maori *kohanga reo* centres, acquire a second language quickly and seem to pick up two languages simultaneously without much difficulty. Although most theorists agree that there is some advantage in a very early start in second language learning, the causes and the nature of that advantage are far from clear. The situation becomes more complex for older children.

Skutnabb Kangas and Toukomaa in Sweden (Skutnabb Kangas, 1981) found that Finnish children moving to Sweden and learning Swedish early in their school careers lost much of their proficiency in Finnish; others who moved later (at ten years) maintained a level of Finnish very close to their age mates in Finland while also acquiring proficiency in Swedish. Even allowing, as Harley (1986) suggests, that different social influences might have influenced the younger children's academic performance, arriving as they did so young in a new culture where they were negatively stereotyped, it is the case that similarly adverse social factors often affect young language learners in a new culture: the age related results of the Swedish study are significant whether we explain them in purely linguistic or in sociocultural terms as well. Support for this view of mine comes from Canadian studies of immigrant Japanese children, and there is evidence from Holland and Indo-China too that older children manage to maintain and develop cognitive and academic skills in their first language to a greater extent than younger immigrant children (Cummins *et al.*, 1984) and children between nine and twelve years also make more rapid progress in academic aspects of their second language than do children between five and eight years (Appel & Muysken, 1987).

It seems very important that the child's first language (i.e. minority language) be given maximum attention up to the stage of middle schooling so that skill in using it to manipulate abstractions develops and also so that it can be used to perform the cognitive operations necessary for acquiring the second language. This is not happening in many places, notably as Chapter 6 suggests, in most public school systems in the United States, in Australasia and in Britain. Nor is it happening in radically different places like Hong Kong, where English-medium schools, in an overwhelmingly Cantonese-speaking city, seem to adversely affect many Cantonese mother tongue students' educational attainment (Yu & Atkinson, 1988). At the same time, in learning the majority language as a second language, it would seem that older SL learners up to the age of early adolescence at least have a cognitive advantage over younger ones when educated in school settings on academic SL tasks that are context reduced (e.g. abstract and difficult) (Harley, 1986). Combining these two conclusions, there seems to be a strong argument for deferring formal bilingual programmes until quite late in schooling and concentrating on mother tongue development. Certainly the value of beginning formal second language education should not be considered as a separate issue from the learner's first language development.

Social background, ability levels and learning difficulties

Other influences on children's performances in bilingual programmes are the respective roles of high ability and level of family affluence on results. Baker (1988) summarises the scanty evidence that is available: children from low-income backgrounds and of average or below average ability may all be successful in bilingual schooling. This tentative conclusion also extends to schools that are sited in exclusively low-income communities and to children of below average reasoning ability. The evidence in favour of bilingual programmes for children with learning difficulties is less conclusive but there are promising indications at least that second language immersion does no harm for special education pupils (Bruck, 1985).

For children in some bilingual communities there is an important interaction between the motivation to use the majority language that they receive from the social setting and their age level. Social pressures can pull adolescent students in particular towards a use of the dominant language (to the extent that they can use it) and these pressures may frustrate attempts in school to use the minority language for instruction. Wald (1984) reports language preferences among early adolescent Hispanic children in the United States. In some cases the preference for English existed even when the children had far greater conversational ability in Spanish. This is a complex issue for the sociology of language use and our knowledge in the area of age and language solidarity is only beginning to develop.

In summary

Three principles that Cummins and Swain propose for bilingual education bear repeating here:

(1) putting the child's first language first in school on the grounds that this provides an essential social and intellectual basis for language and academic learning in both languages;
(2) using the two languages separately rather than concurrently in instruction so that each can be exploited to its limits;
(3) seeing bilingualism as a bonus in education through teachers'

understanding and explaining to others the political, economic, cultural, psychological, linguistic and cognitive advantages associated with bilingual proficiency.

Bilingualism and Minority First Language Maintenance: Policy Issues

The broad policy goals that schools might adopt in relation to bilingualism are many. Below is a taxonomy that shows the range of approaches that schools can adopt. It should be clear from discussion so far in this chapter and in Chapter 6 that this list begins with undesirable responses and moves to the more desirable ones. The situation described in (i) has all but disappeared from modern affluent societies. As discussion in Chapter 6 suggests the situations in (ii) to (v) are still very common in a range of OECD countries. Responses (vi) and (vii) are more rare but seem to represent the future direction that school policies will take in pluralist societies:

(i)   no encouragement of minority language in or outside the school;
(ii) official encouragement but no resource commitment;
(iii) using the minority language as a short-term transitional medium of instruction (i.e. less than two years);
(iv) teaching the home language as a subject in school hours;
(v)   using the minority language as a transitional medium of instruction for long periods;
(vi) recognising the minority language as an official or quasi-official medium of instruction for much of schooling;
(vii) creating a separate system of education in the minority language.

This last option does not necessarily mean separate schools and schooling systems. In the USSR, for example, as in Sweden, there have been trials of parallel medium instruction with children from different language backgrounds attending the same school, mixing socially, but receiving all their instruction in their own language while following identical curricula (McLaughlin, 1986). Russian is used as the language of play and of extra-curricular activities. In these trial programmes minority children are thought to learn more Russian, even while doing all their learning in their own tongues. In this way the undesirable features of completely separate schooling or of dual medium instruction are avoided. The use of two languages at different times for instruction (the dual medium practice common in transitional bilingual programmes in many

English-speaking countries) has been forbidden in the USSR since the 1930s (Lewis, 1972).

In a pluralist society, institutions like schools may be the only places where minority first languages can be maintained and developed. There are many reasons why schools need to do what they can in this area. Clearly the maintenance of a heritage language is vital for the self-identity and esteem of its speakers. We have seen too that the cognitive and academic achievement of children whose home language is not the dominant one is likely to be enhanced in school situations where the home language is used as the medium of instruction. For monolingual majority children there are also academic advantages when they are encouraged to do some learning using another language as the vehicle for that learning. In designing an LPAC that deals with these matters, there are many issues to consider. A specimen policy from a pluralist primary school appears at the end of this chapter:

(1) How and when does a school discover the languages represented in the school and in specific classes?
(2) What steps need to be taken to provide staffing arrangements that promote first language maintenance and development?
   —staff/pupil ratios?
   —community involvement?
   —itinerant specialists?
(3) How can bilingual speakers be involved in the school's programme?
(4) How are minority languages used in school and class?
(5) What materials and resources representing the minority first language can be used?
   —is there technical written material in the minority language?
   —is there a literature in the minority language?
   —should literacy in the minority language be a priority?
   —can a working group write and collate original written materials for literacy development in the minority language?
(6) What in-service provisions are being made to develop staff proficiency in language maintenance?
   —helping transitional students ?
   —differences in classroom methods between majority and minority language learning?
   —pupils who are linguistic minorities in their own homelands
(7) How can each community language be used in relations between the school and the wider community?
(8) What information can the school offer to parents to encourage

them to maintain and develop their home languages?
(9) What procedures need to be introduced to implement bilingual programmes for those children who need them?
—for community consultation?
—for bilingual teacher appointments?
—for providing aids and resources?
—for attracting adequate funding?

Community language maintenance and the multicultural school

A school may be frustrated in its efforts to promote bilingualism among its minority students by a reluctance among minority members in the community to use their language outside the home. For the children themselves motivation is inevitably reduced if the language has no apparent prestige in the wider community. The school may have an important role to play here. Fishman (1980) speaks of the need to create 'reward systems' in the language community that require the use of the minority language and in this way motivate and repay those who do use it. This simple idea finds its expression in those countries where bilingualism is at the root of social organisation; where schools, governments, the law, libraries and other instrumentalities demonstrate by their actions and policies that status and dignity attach equally to minority and majority languages. In schools, similar approaches are possible on a small scale: using the language resources of the community in the official school programme of events; using adult speakers of the minority language with respect in the school's curriculum; deploying signs in school, written in the several languages of the school; having older bilingual children work with their younger peers in vertically grouped classes; encouraging children to compile explorations of the emigration patterns of each others' families; and developing narrative stories of family histories. Twitchin & Demuth (1985) offer further suggestions for multicultural teaching in the primary grades. Houlton (1986) looks at the UK experience as it relates to the primary school. He suggests ways in which infant, junior and middle schools can give a truly multicultural dimension to their work.

The role of the parents in all of this will have to be carefully considered, especially in the light of issues raised in Chapter 4. As part of its LPAC a bilingual school will need to address the following questions:

(1) do parents have a role in the school to supplement what teachers can offer? where? when?
(2) will the ideas of language across the curriculum be promoted

through parental involvement?

(3) would some formal introduction to the school's bilingual aims and approaches be valuable for parents who regularly mix with students in lesson time?

(4) how far will the school extend into the home in respect to language matters?

Second Language Teaching and Learning

For many children in pluralist societies bilingualism is not a matter of parental choice, of cultural preference, or a natural acquisition that comes from living in a bilingual language community: it is a matter of necessity. Many 'language in education' theorists make a distinction between this kind of second language learning, born out of necessity, and true bilingualism. The reason for this is not so easy to see: while different kinds of educational experiences may be needed to promote development in the bilingual child from those needed for deliberately teaching a second language, there is obviously much overlap as well.

Various SL instructional methods are possible. It is not easy to think of a possibility that has not been tried by school systems somewhere or other. Some schools have used programmes of complete immersion in the second language in which the children must sink or swim. Some have linked special tutoring in the second language with a use of that language in the classroom. Some provide additional education in the child's first language as a bridge to learning the second (without bilingualism as an explicit aim). Some work with younger children and provide all their schooling in the first language, including initial literacy, followed by a gradual phasing in of the second language. This last approach might not have bilingualism as its aim, although it might well be the result.

Age and time as factors in SL education

The children of new settlers, in those English-speaking societies where community languages are still in wide use across whole residential areas, may not encounter much English before they begin formal schooling. For these children a deliberate second language programme in the school will be necessary to give them a basis on which to build their natural learning of the language. The immigrant Australian children from low-income family backgrounds who provided data in studies reported elsewhere

(Corson, 1985b) arrived in their primary schools with little or no knowledge of English; these children needed three to four years of ESL teaching, on a withdrawal basis, before they were fully ready to participate in classrooms on an equal footing with their peers. But by the end of their primary schooling they were independent users of English and still retained a command of their Macedonian, Italian or Portuguese mother tongues. Of note is that all of these children proceeded to secondary school and most enjoyed better than average success.

Studies elsewhere (Wong Fillmore, 1983; Cummins, 1981) indicate that for most children it can take four to six years to acquire a second language to a level of proficiency adequate for dealing with ordinary classroom activities. The ability that most children have to pick up everyday usages of a language quickly and easily can be misleading when making judgments about their language proficiency. Research in the Netherlands (Verhallen *et al.*, 1988) compared the language of minority children and Dutch children in nursery schools with regard to the children's use of different language functions. Bilingual minority children, who seem to have a good command of Dutch, may still have serious language problems when they have to carry out the more academic classroom tasks. These researchers found that monolingual Dutch children used more functions of language in the classroom to perform more complex tasks than did bilingual children, especially those bilingual children who were judged to have a lower proficiency in Dutch as a second language.

On the other hand, even when there is no pressing need for children to learn a second language, they can achieve remarkable proficiency provided that conditions, resources and motivation are right. The study above by Lambert & Tucker (1972) of monolingual Anglo-Canadian children exposed mainly to French in their first five years of schooling confirms that second language learning for the young can proceed without any harm to the child's first language proficiency and academic development. However a rider must be placed on applying this finding outside the context that produced it, since the Anglo-Canadian children in this special programme lived in environments which placed a very high value on their first language. There are no doubt complex psychological factors at work that need to be considered. For example in the Dutch studies mentioned above (Verhallen *et al.*, 1988) even very young low and high proficiency bilingual children were able to express complex language functions in the second language, although they did so less often than their monolingual classmates. What is often absent in the SL setting is appropriate motivation and facilitation for the use of more complex language functions: the Dutch researchers conclude that pupil-centred conversations in the classroom and instructional exchanges potentially are the best means for stimulating the use of more complex language functions.

Usually schools are called on to provide SL education for children whose first language is not the majority tongue of the culture. As we have seen already in this chapter there is strong evidence to suggest that mother tongue maintenance of some kind in the early years of schooling is necessary for children when their mother tongue is not maintained anywhere else but in the home. Exposure to the second language may impair academic progress and general linguistic development. Skutnabb Kangas and Toukomaa in Sweden (Skutnabb Kangas, 1981) make the point that the child's first language (i.e. minority language) be given maximum attention up to the stage of middle schooling so that skill in using it to manipulate abstractions develops and also so that it can be used to perform the cognitive operations necessary for acquiring the second language. In the United States, in Britain and in Australasia this is not happening on a broad scale and students who have entered ESL programmes at ages five to seven without prior schooling in their first language are found to be significantly behind those who have started their initial education in their native countries (Collier, 1987). Many other things being equal (and recognising always that the ideal time for learning a second language is probably during the pre-school years) a later introduction of the SL will improve results for school age children. The best savings (in time spent on teaching) occur when the formal teaching of an SL is introduced to children aged around ten to twelve years, but more intensive exposure to the language over several years is needed for this to work.

Skutnabb-Kangas summarises the position well: a second language which children hear spoken all around them anyway 'may well be formally introduced later, especially if this gives a low status mother tongue the chance to develop' (1981: 174). She is assuming here of course that the school curriculum is being routinely presented in that low status mother tongue so that the children are not disadvantaged in other ways. Unfortunately this is not an assumption that is possible in many contemporary educational settings and we need to plan to make the best of the present situation even while advocating changes for the future.

Organising for second language support

Most students who need second language support fall somewhere on a continuum between these two very broad categories:

(1) They are students with little or no knowledge of the second language who are newly arrived in the country. They need to acquire the language of the new country rapidly for basic social communication so that they can begin to relate to what is going on in the classroom, school and community.

(2) They are students who are fluent in social communication in the second language but who have difficulty in academic communication. Often they have been in the country for some time and might even have been born there. They may be members of an indigenous minority group. Occasionally children in this category are wrongly identified in school systems as being below average in reasoning ability.

It is easy to overlook the fact that students placed between these two points in SL needs differ in more than just their experience in the second language. For example there will be as wide a spread of academic and learning potential in these SL groups as in other groups of children. There are some findings concerning children with specific learning problems who are also SL learners (Bruck, 1984): given appropriate pedagogical treatment and the same special conditions that they receive in their first language education, these children can learn a second language with no hindrance to their first language and to their general cognitive development. This is but one of the many priorities that schools often have to determine for themselves in providing SL assistance. The list below is a summary of responses by principals and ESL specialists in Australian schools (CSC, 1984) who were asked to rank those groups of students for whom they aimed to provide priority help in English language:

(1) Recent arrivals with virtually no English skills, and 'first phase' learners ('first phase' refers to those students functionally unable to cope with the language demands of a normal classroom).

(2) Second or third phase learners ('second phase' usually refers to post-first phase learners who can meet the language demands of most class activities; 'third phase' usually refers to students who function at levels similar to comparable native speakers, but experience difficulties in some situations).

(3) Students unable to participate in mainstream classes due to lack of English language proficiency.

(4) Students whose parents speak no English.

(5) Students unable to participate in mainstream classes due to lack of content knowledge and/or skills.

(6) Students in transition from junior to secondary school and from

junior to upper secondary school.
(7) Students who are socially isolated.
(8) Students in the early years of primary and secondary school.
(9) 'Gifted' SL students.

In dealing with the needs of students who fall within these nine categories, schools may need to make policy decisions that cover at least the following contingencies:

(1) how are these students to be identified?
     —consultation between administrators, SL and class teachers?
     —interviews with parents and students?
     —diagnostic tests for determining SL proficiency?
     —liaison with intensive language centres?
     —liaison with feeder schools?
     —a combination of methods?
(2) how are their needs to be assessed and how is progress to be evaluated (see 'Approaches to Assessing SL Proficiency' below)?
     —what are the SL learning needs of the children?
     —in using what functions of language do they need most assistance?
     —what language modes are priority areas (i.e. speaking, reading?)
     —are children present in sufficient numbers for the school to set up groups at different stages of SL development?
     —what linguistic distance is there between the children's first language and the second language (see Chapter 8)?
     —are students literate in their first language?
     —how much schooling have they had in their home country?
     —have they studied the SL as a foreign language?
     —how long should a programme continue before proficiency is likely?
(3) what external support will be needed to provide for them adequately?
(4) how can the students' first languages be used in learning the second?
(5) what non-threatening environment can be provided for language learning (i.e. one where the students feel able to take risks in communicating)?
(6) what form of motivation to learn the SL would suit the needs of students?
     —what SL teaching styles are preferred (see 'Approaches to

Teaching a Second Language' below)?

—how will SL learning be linked with school reward systems?

(7) how will the school display a positive attitude towards the students' first languages and towards the users themselves?

(8) what provisions for using language for listening, speaking, reading and writing would ensure a balanced approach to learning?

—how many hours per week of SL instruction is a fair allocation for students in various levels and phases?

(9) how will students get feedback on their performance in the new language?

(10) what additional staffing levels are desirable and possible?

(11) is a second language coordinator necessary for the school?

(12) is there need for an across the curriculum language support team?

(13) how will in-service training be provided for classroom teachers?

(14) how will in-service training be provided for SL teachers?

(15) what organisational arrangements best suit the needs of the students and the school (see 'School Organisation for SLT' below)?

(16) how will children with specific learning difficulties and other mainstreamed pupils be integrated into the programme (see Willig & Greenberg, 1986)?

(17) at what point and how are the SL provisions to be evaluated?

Obviously the SL teacher cannot be fully responsible for the learning of all the students who have SL needs in a school. Indeed in some countries SL teachers are dwindling in number as more generalist teachers are equipped with SL training as part of their teacher training (Reid, 1988). The responsibility for SL work has to be shared across the curriculum with the work done in many specialist SL settings supported and extended by other teachers who come into contact with the SL students. Second language teachers are certainly the SL experts in the school; they are the ones who will have special insights into matters of language development generally and into individual students' strengths and weaknesses that can be shared with other staff. But the need for cooperative planning in SLT is a facet of an LPAC that deserves highlighting as a public commitment by all staff members. While the presence of SL teachers will make things easier, by building on this presence there are many ways in which a cooperative and committed approach can be integrated into the school's organisational patterns.

School Organisation for SLT

The second language problems that schools encounter will determine the organisational responses that they will make. A range of problems will mean a range of responses. Difficulties arise when schools try to stretch a single solution to cover a plurality of SL problems. As part of a coherent policy and depending on their SL needs and school capacities, schools located in pluralist communities often provide more than one of the following options

(1) *reception units*: placed inside or outside the school and providing intensive work for the whole school day mainly for new arrivals and other first phase students. Their aim is to prepare students as quickly as possible for integration and gentle transition into the school's regular programme. They usually incorporate a variety of methods (see later in this chapter), including structural elements (such as pronunciation), functional/notional activities (like role play and drama), language experience activities aimed at cognitive growth, and 'special purpose' study of the SL in the contexts of school subject areas.

(2) *integrated and cooperative teaching*: provided across the curriculum with the SL teachers either working in one curriculum area at a time or working alongside class teachers but mainly with SL students. Both SL and class teachers are concerned with the full development of the children in their charge across the curriculum. Shared responsibility of this kind can produce maximum rewards for SL students, especially when the SL teacher is seen as a full and equal colleague and not as a mere aid to the classroom teacher.

(3) *paired teaching*: with SL teachers teamed with class teachers to plan, implement and evaluate programmes. Both types of teacher have equal status in the arrangement.

(4) *parallel teaching and programming*: with the SL teacher and the class teacher planning together but teaching independently. The SL teacher takes a class of mainly SL students and teaches one or more subjects or topics in a block, at the same time as other students are being taught the same subjects or topics. This is more common in secondary schools, especially in language arts and social science subjects. It can allow an economical use of time, stability in management, flexibility in curriculum content, and provide the SL teacher with autonomy and status.

(5) *withdrawal teaching*: where SL students are removed from normal classes, either partially or totally, into special small-group units for intensive SL immersion work or on blocks of specially prepared material based on their regular curriculum. These may involve vertical grouping of children by age or horizontal grouping of children by their achieved proficiency in the SL. A group of three to four students can provide a rich opportunity for individualised instruction. Where withdrawal is partial, care in selecting the subject area for withdrawal is a priority. Care is needed since some SL students are disadvantaged unreasonably by leaving the regular class, either because they lose touch with regular curricular content or because they miss an opportunity to excel in some special area where they are proficient. Withdrawal teaching with non-SL teachers or teacher-aids can concentrate on survival skills, based around brief excursions to shops, banks, places of recreation etc. On the whole, though, withdrawal teaching is not favoured unless made absolutely necessary by circumstances. It serves little real purpose 'across the curriculum' since it reduces the variety of language situations available to SL learners. It can also stigmatise children too readily, perhaps promoting low self-esteem and negative attitudes towards learning the SL.

(6) *SL extension*: as an option in secondary school, SL students receive SL extension work, perhaps for some special purpose or in some technical curricular area, while other students take other regular optional units. An alternative is to provide SL extension as an optional subject in place of the same language as a school subject (i.e. in place of the subject 'English') and for this option to be a school-based or publicly accredited course.

(7) *correspondence school enrolment*: where students are proficient SL users in most contexts but need special purpose development which the school is not equipped to provide.

(8) *peer support systems*: where the school employs a 'buddy' system that teams the SL student with a willing SL competent peer (see Glynn & Tavener, 1989).

(9) *enrolment in SL evening classes*: where mature students are proficient SL users in most contexts but need special purpose development which the school is not equipped to provide.

(10) *first language support*: where schools recognise the child's first language as an important learning tool for gaining proficiency in the SL and make use of content materials prepared in the student's first

language by SL teachers familiar with that language. First language maintenance has other values that are already discussed in this chapter and seems very desirable for children in their early to middle years of schooling.

(11) *development of study skills*: for the more proficient SL students there may be a need to concentrate simply on study skills as they are applied across the curriculum. Several of the organisational approaches already mentioned can be linked with this activity.

(12) *familiarisation programmes*: where the students need an orientation to schooling as it is conducted in their new culture and schools support their SL induction programmes with a familiarisation programme in the children's first language that is aimed at giving them the conceptual foundations about schooling itself that their SL can be based upon.

(13) *language support across the curriculum*: where students need special support materials to match up their own language proficiency with the intellectual demands of specialist subjects. These materials are prepared by SL teachers after closely observing the SL students at work in the subject area. Although new arrivals seem to pick up a reasonably high level of SL proficiency within two years of arrival, there is much evidence to suggest that their ability to cope in face to face communicative situations usually disguises severe weaknesses in coping with the academic demands of English-in-use across the curriculum. Support for five to seven years may be necessary if academic difficulties are to be avoided.

(14) *incidental teaching*: for the more mature students, occasional personal tuition is provided at the student's request. An SL teacher is known to be available in the school for consultancy work of this kind and an adequately private room is provided where individual students can bring their difficulties, usually related to difficulties in assignments set by their classroom teachers. If the SL teacher is also proficient in the subject area of the student's problem then this valuable kind of personalised teaching service will be widely used.

(15) *rotation teaching*: where the SL and regular teachers share the total pool of students and rotate them so that every teacher at some time in a school week works with every child, concentrating on the teaching strengths and interests that each teacher offers.

(16) *special purpose teaching*: where the language teaching is deliberately matched to the specific needs and purposes of the

learners, usually in relation to the technical demands of some curriculum area. In 'studies in work across the curriculum' too there may be a need for SL students to engage with the register of the language that is used for communicative purposes in some special work setting.

Integrating the SL teachers into the school and the supervision of minority language teachers

Successful integration of SL teachers and their pupils into the work of the school cannot be left to chance. There may be special difficulties if the SL teachers are itinerants serving the needs of several schools, because they will be relative strangers to regular staff members. There are teachers who resent the presence of another teacher in the room, especially one who is not on the permanent staff of the school, or who find collaboration with an SLT colleague to be a difficult exercise. SL teachers themselves may need to be diplomatic to gain access to some classrooms: for example, by offering their initial services only in the reading programme. As teachers come to see that the SL specialist has something of value to contribute then the way may be smoothed a little for greater collaboration. SL students in secondary schools, who are moving to and from specialist classes, are helped when flexibility of movement in and out of parallel classes is a regular and accepted feature of the school pattern of organisation. They feel less stigmatised and can also progress at their own rate, moving into and out of classes as they judge their needs to be met.

SL teachers of the majority language are usually trained in SL methods, but often SL teachers of a minority language are untrained. Although it is very desirable that minority language teachers be both bilingual and well trained, if a choice has to be made between a trained monolingual teacher and an untrained bilingual teacher, the latter will usually be preferable: the priority is that the teacher can understand everything that the minority children say in their first language and be able to accommodate to their needs. For this reason Skutnabb Kangas & Cummins (1988) suggest that a bilingual teacher without any training is usually a better choice than a monolingual well trained teacher, especially where the second language is widely available outside the classroom. Where there are numerous SL needs to be met then a number of teachers, drawn from the minority communities without professional training, will often be needed. This adds another dimension to the special policy demands that are placed on schools which have SL teachers on their staff:

(1) how will the school ensure that its SL teachers are not accorded a second-class status?

(2) how are SL teachers to overcome the isolation from their colleagues that comes from teaching outside the school's main programme?

(3) how are they to be helped in motivating the very young in minority language activities where minority language teaching competes with activities that young children may find more enjoyable?

(4) how is the inspection of minority language teaching to be carried out and how is quality control to be maintained?

(5) how will the untrained SL teachers be helped to carry out their teaching roles through on-the-job and in-service training and supervision?

Withdrawal and grouping of minority language students

If the school's aim is to equip minority language children with the majority language, while still maintaining their mother tongue, then a withdrawal programme is probably needed if classes are largely majority language speakers. This programme might provide special immersion arrangements, similar to those already recommended in earlier sections. If the school programme cannot extend to this ideal of first language maintenance, then I have already mentioned reasons why withdrawal may not be necessary or even desirable. The first question for a policy to address in this area is the following: is withdrawal really necessary for groups of minority pupils?

Assuming that bilingual immersion provisions are available or that withdrawal for other reasons is absolutely necessary, other questions will follow:

(1) how will the school ensure the provision of skilled teaching?

(2) how will the school ensure the provision of adequate well-ventilated accommodation?

(3) how will the school ensure the provision of a good supply of suitable books, bilingual dictionaries and culturally sensitive audio-visual aids?

(4) how will the school ensure that wholehearted cooperation between teachers releasing pupils and those receiving them is
demonstrated to confirm for pupils that their success in the
withdrawal programme is important?

Sometimes other patterns of organisation are possible or necessary.
Sometimes people from indigenous cultures or from other cultures that
are very different from the majority culture prefer arrangements that
differ from those provided for the children of immigrants coming from
cultures rather similar to the dominant one. Following the wishes of
groups in the parent community itself, the school may need to make
different types of arrangement reflecting cultural preferences. For
example: a dispersal of the minority group into classes mixed with
majority language students (analogous to the 'mainstreaming' of special
education pupils in some countries) is preferred by some groups of
Pacific Island immigrants in New Zealand and by some Panjabi speaking
groups in Britain. These people prefer to take the responsibility
themselves, outside the school, for passing on their own culture and they
want nothing more from the school than that it give their children full
access to the dominant culture and the majority language. Others ask
that their children be concentrated in separate groups, at least for some
of the time, so that the culture can be preserved. Among the Inuit
native people of Canada the episodic teaching of highly dispersed small
groups by itinerant teachers is common and quite practical. Elsewhere
there is a recognition of pupil preferences in grouping, especially the
wishes of older children. Some balance, then, needs to be maintained
between pupil and parent preferences in these matters.

The school will need to know the cultural and social role of the first
and second languages in the minority pupils' lives: what is the place of
the minority language in the children's lives in relation to the majority
tongue? A school's response to this question will shape the planning of
a language learning sequence for the minority children. The needs of
children from different cultures may be very different. Is there need for:

(i)   immediate immersion;
(ii) short term teaching of some subjects in the minority tongue
      along with intensive majority language instruction;
(iii) long term teaching of most subjects in the minority tongue
      followed by entirely majority language instruction?

Alternatively a favoured approach may be some form of parallel or
concurrent second language instruction providing:

(i)   additional or remedial language tuition after transfer to majority language tuition; ·
(ii) gradual transfer programmes with two languages used in the same class;
(iii) long-term study of the majority language as a formal school subject.

The effective organisation of SL programmes does not end with simple language provisions. There are at least three other issues that need to be addressed in a school policy where cultural pluralism is part of the social context: how is the school to approach the cultural features of minority groups; what is the 'official' attitude of the school to the minority cultures; and what place can members of the minority culture have in school governance?

The Cultural Characteristics of SL Minority Groups

In formalising school approaches to the cultural characteristics of minority groups, several options are possible. Whether schools feel ready to adopt these options may depend on policies established at a national or system level, especially a national language policy of the kind discussed in Chapter 6. National policies of this kind reflect commonly agreed social values and try to offer a guide to what is possible in any community that is part of the wider society. As important again will be the wishes of adult members of the culture itself which need respecting: some will prefer full integration for their children; some partial integration; and some separation for much of the time. An early option, then, will be the matter of grouping pupils of same or similar cultures together. Other matters are less problematic: multicultural schools obviously need to work at eliminating negative stereotypes from the curriculum and at making teaching and administrative staff sensitive to minority cultural characteristics and needs. Culturally relevant information may need disseminating to groups, other than the minorities, so that community understanding of the school's LPAC in this area can be promoted and maintained.

There are further steps that schools in progressive pluralist countries are taking: appointing staff of the same culture; introducing subjects into teaching programmes that are related to the minority culture; recognising minority languages as vehicles of instruction for minority children; and recognising that minority languages have a place in the education of all children.

Official school attitudes to the minority culture: Participation in governance

In identifying the range of attitudes to the minority culture that are present in the school, policy makers might ask themselves and their colleagues which of the following four perceptions of the minority culture are commonly held by staff members:

(i)   seeing the minority culture as a deprived environment to be compensated for;
(ii) seeing the home culture as a topic of interest in the school;
(iii) seeing contact with the minority culture in school as an enduring need of the minority group;
(iv) seeing an understanding of the minority culture through the curriculum as an enduring need of the majority group.

As a professional development activity, staff might be asked to debate which of these four possibilities is the ideal that should prevail in their school. Other ideas may come from this debate, such as the possibility of involving minority members in school management.

Encouraging the participation of minority group members in school governance is a step of great significance. Taking that step will provide a signal to the community that the school is interested in becoming organic to its community and putting an end to its status as an island of cultural isolation within it. Again there are several ways in which participation might occur. The ideal may be a combination of strategies involving minority group members:

—in a direct decision-making capacity;
—in a consultative role;
—through participation and visibility in school operations as aids to its programmes;
—through participation and visibility in school operations in salaried posts;
—through pupil grouping and separation from majority pupils for joint activities celebrating aspects of their culture.

Small but growing moves in all of these directions are well within the reach of every school.

Approaches to Teaching a Second Language

This section provides no more than a brief outline of this complex subject area. Extensive training in SL or foreign language (FL) pedagogy is a prerequisite in the modern world for those planning to be second language teachers. There are many texts that offer the general reader a more detailed coverage of this section's subject matter (e.g. Finocchiaro and Brumfit, 1983; Bell, 1981; Alatis et al., 1981; Littlewood, 1981; Brown, 1980; Savignon, 1983). What follows is an overview of some of the major theoretical positions and issues which may be of use to school administrators trying to organise for SL education across the curriculum.

From research on teaching and learning in SL classrooms (Skutnabb-Kangas, 1981; Krashen, 1982; Chaudron, 1988; Fitzpatrick, 1987) there is good evidence to support all the points in the following list. This list supplements other language learning factors discussed in Chapter 8. There is still much research to be done and although the research that has been done is extensive, very little in this list will surprise experienced teachers:

—learning efficiency is improved as the strength of instrumental motivation (examination success; job etc.) increases;

—motivation increases when pupils are allowed to decide for themselves when they are ready to produce second language utterances;

—high motivation is linked with pupil understanding of the educational objectives and with pupil sharing in the task of setting objectives;

—learners need input in the target language at a level that can be understood; learning efficiency is improved as the strength of affiliative motivation (joining a respected group) increases;

—a low level of anxiety is needed in the learning setting;

—anxiety is reduced by a supportive learning environment and by non-authoritarian teaching;

—learners need a high level of self-confidence and a low level of self-consciousness in relation to the learning task;

—input needs to be just ahead of the learners' stage of rule development for it to support or disconfirm interlanguage rules that they already possess;

—group work may be superior to teacher-led activities in increasing coverage of content, amount of interaction or production, and accuracy of production;

—teacher-led activities may be superior in providing input that is extensive and needs a high level of accuracy;

—communicative games and information gap tasks can extend interactive behaviours in the second language significantly and this facilitates learning;

—learner proficiency correlates positively with the amount of production in classrooms;

—brief repetition and rephrasing of a message by teachers in the second language assists immediate learning;

—many learners will benefit when teachers draw attention to the learners' progress by interpreting the learners' SL production and relating it explicitly to knowledge of the rules of the language;

—peers used as models of language-in-use improve learning;

—learning at more advanced levels is improved by rich interaction with adults and by a range of social contacts.

A starting point in planning an SL programme is to be aware of the physical and administrative conditions in which the programme will have to operate. This is limiting enough for any teacher. It makes little sense to limit the programme further by adopting some narrow approach to SLT that excludes areas of competence simply because they are not part of a theoretical framework that justified the narrow approach. All of the approaches to SLT fit along a continuum stretching between two broad categories: 'part-to-whole' or 'whole-to-part'. These categories are not dichotomies since even the most extreme approach will inevitably include elements further along the continuum. In this section I look very briefly at six approaches to SLT. The first three approaches ('grammar translation', 'audio-lingual' and 'structural/situational') are more 'part-to-whole' approaches; the second three ('functional/notional', 'language across the curriculum', and 'communicative competence') are more 'whole-to-part'.

The *grammar translation* approach has been widely used in foreign language teaching (FLT). Here the stress is on reading ability, on the meticulous study and learning of grammar as an aid to reading comprehension, and on written and to a lesser extent on oral translation. In this approach spontaneous oral work has been little emphasised with greater attention paid to wide and repetitive reading of graded materials and with the language broken down into component parts for ordering into a sequence for learning. There is relatively little attention paid to language used in a natural and non-literary context

The *audio-lingual* approach has also been widely used in FLT. It was the favoured approach for the intensive training in spoken languages that was given to servicemen in World War II: its aim was to promote quick proficiency in everyday language situations involving speaking and listening. This approach emphasises language drills based on specific grammatical patterns and the need to 'over-learn' these patterns so that they become automatic. The student is expected to transfer knowledge of these drills to the natural language situation and to be able to communicate effectively in such situations without knowing much about grammatical rules or about how to move into a wider range of linguistic experiences.

In the *structural/situational* approach the language fragments to be learned are also divided into small grammatical segments and each segment is taught one at a time, with emphasis placed on repetition, on drills and on acquiring 'good language habits'. This approach can even be found in first language education (Dannequin, 1987). One underlying dogma here is that language is first and foremost seen as a sequence of sounds. In order to acquire mental representations of those series of sounds, it is believed that pupils need to repeat accurately what they are taught. Another underlying dogma is the belief that language is essentially a skill subject, comprising four basic skills: understanding, speaking, reading and writing. It follows from this dogma that much of language teaching becomes a process of skill development, based on the repetitive practice of isolated features. To this rather simplistic learning theory, however, the 'structural/situational' approach adds a more sophisticated rider: the idea that these isolated features of language should be taught and used as parts of whole utterances or sentences that are to be applied in meaningful contexts, which means that language should be taught in simulated real-life situations. While the 'structural/situational' approach recognises the importance of meaningful communication in meaningful situations in language teaching, language is still seen by many strict exponents of this approach as a set of grammatical and lexical units. So a major weakness of this approach, which it shares with the other 'part to whole' approaches, is its tendency to highlight a grammatical feature to the exclusion of practical application of language in real situations: in contexts of functional, pragmatic communication between human beings.

Of the three 'whole to part' approaches, the *functional/notional* approach starts from the view that a learner needs to be an active participant in the learning process (Chamot, 1983). This approach emphasises communicative acts and conversational analysis, with grammatical structures and techniques of over-learning relegated to a subordinate role. The content of a course is organised around the perceived meanings or 'notions' that learners need to possess to communicate in particular functional contexts: notions such as the expression of time, dimensions, sequence, quantity, location and motion. Language is seen in more functional terms and extensive lists of these functions are used as bases for syllabus design (see Widdowson & Brumfit, 1981). Each function is potentially applicable in an endless variety of situations: functions such as evaluating, persuading, expressing emotion, and drawing social distinctions. Similarly catalogues of situational types and topics have been compiled along with lists of grammatical categories and classes (*ibid.*). The aim of this approach to SL teaching is to help students 'crack the code' of the new language: to move from the stage of imitation to a spontaneous use of language that will enable new language users to communicate in whatever situation they find themselves. To achieve this the learner must meet a much greater variety of linguistic forms from the outset. Some of the characteristics of a 'functional/notional' approach to SLT are as follows:

—a well-designed curriculum begins by specifying the language needs of the learners;
—the context for learning is located in an activity or in an experience that is rich in natural language potential (usually a theme or topic related to a school subject area);
—the language functions (e.g. describing, explaining, asking, questioning, telling etc.) are taught and practised using communicative activities suited to the lesson or task and these activities may be very like the first language oral language activities that were discussed in Chapter 5 (Corson, 1988a);
—the approach involves both receptive and productive language since language heard in context is later to be produced in a similar context;
—there is usually as much individualising of instruction as is possible, with natural oral language interaction given priority.

While the 'functional/notional' approach provides a means of developing structural categories while still considering the functions of language, one criticism of it is that it still presents language as an inventory of units, units that are notional/functional rather than structural, but still isolated from 'the natural whole'. On the other hand the functional approach may in fact be more realistic on this question. Soviet educators, for example, make much of the fact that language learning in the classroom is inevitably a different process from learning it in a natural context.

The *language across the curriculum* approach has the same theoretical basis as the 'functional/notional' approach but also gives attention to the very doctrine that underlies this book: the view that language plays a central role in all learning right across the curriculum. No matter what the subject area students assimilate new concepts and a range of new insights into topics largely through language, so students need to be exposed to the language of maths, science, music etc, if they are to have mastery of the subject matter of those fields of study and through that mastery a command of the language that permeates the subject matter: language develops primarily through its purposeful use in all curriculum areas. It is not easy to see this approach standing on its own without integration with one or more of the others. The idea that language contributes to learning in special fields, however, is an insight that can be added to all of the other approaches discussed here.

The *communicative* approach highlights the SL learner's ability to function in a truly communicative setting. In any process of communication all speakers adjust the way they speak to suit the situation, the purpose that motivates them, and the relationship between themselves and the people they are addressing. Certain ways of talking are appropriate for communicating with intimates, others for communicating with non-intimates; certain ways of putting things will convey politeness, rudeness or anger. Learning to use a language, on this account, involves a great deal more than acquiring some grammar and vocabulary along with a reasonable pronunciation. It involves the competence to suit the language to the situation, to the participant and to the basic purpose. Conversely and equally important, it involves a competence in interpreting other speakers to the full.

The choice facing the SL (or FL) teacher is not the simple one of opting for one or other of the approaches outlined above. A skilled professional might see merit in all of the approaches and apply them in some way at different times and with different pupils, since the nature of the language problems themselves determines the approaches that suit. The need may be to develop techniques that combine the teaching of the traditionally necessary aspects of language — grammar, vocabulary and sounds — with an emphasis on the meaningful use of language both across the curriculum and in natural communicative settings. Providing the student with an all-round communicative competence is the aim.

In the discussion in Chapter 8 of foreign language teaching, communicative competence is presented as a complex idea that includes at least six sub-competencies (van Ek, 1986): linguistic, sociolinguistic, discourse, strategic, sociocultural, and social competence. Each of these components of communicative competence is an important goal in the SL and first language classroom too. For example, we would judge first language users who had graduated from some lengthy process of education but who did not have proficiency in one or other of these components in their first language to have been failed by that process of education. They would be viewed as 'uneducated'. Similarly SL students who fail to develop a reasonable level of proficiency in any one of these components cannot be considered expert users of the target language; they will be disadvantaged in their interactions with their peers, in relating to their new culture and in society.

The final goal in SLT is always to reduce the social distance between the SL students, their peers and the culture of the second language. The best way of doing this, of course, is by equipping SL students with a communicative competence that is very similar to that possessed by their first language peers. While doing this there is a constant need for liaison and cross-reference between the activities of the SL children and the regular curriculum activities of their peers. Teachers need to decide on the level of language competence that is needed for the children to enter a normal stream classroom, they need to strive in that direction and try to recognise efficiently when that level has been reached. Along the way, teachers can explore ways in which the SL children can integrate into normal class activities (movement, singing, assembly, art and craft, sport and games, excursions) and maximise the opportunities for this integration. It follows in doing all of this that teachers need to have formal methods for judging the achievements of their students in learning their new language and their readiness to interact with others.

Approaches to Assessing SL Proficiency

While changes have been occurring in approaches to teaching second languages, changes have also been occurring in the way that the results of that teaching are evaluated. Again these changes reflect other changes in values about language that are held more generally. While there has been a movement in emphasis from a 'part to whole' approach to a 'whole to part' approach to SL learning and teaching, theorists have also changed their views about which aspects of language are important for assessment purposes. Instead of measuring the more visible and highly recurring features of language, like pronunciation patterns, vocabulary use, and grammatical usages, other aspects of language learning now attract more attention and this move has occurred as the 'whole to part' methods of SLT have gradually become more prevalent. Performing a simple observation of 'language in use' has become a basis for the more favoured methods of language assessment, although this is not to say that other methods are discredited.

In this section I discuss a range of approaches and then focus on only one specific method: communicative proficiency assessment is a holistic approach to language assessment especially if supplemented, as I recommend, by naturalistic observation using ethnographic methods. Ingram (1985) provides a more substantial overview of assessment approaches to SL schooling.

A point always to consider in assessing pupils using a language which is not their mother tongue is that for them the assessment procedures themselves will be viewed rather differently from the way a first language user might view them. While the assessment procedures for children entering SL programmes need to be cognitively demanding, as Cummins (1984) warns, they also need to be clearly embedded in the context (i.e. not too abstract: based on interpersonal involvement in some kind of shared reality) since SL speakers will have experienced mainly this kind of SL face-to-face use. Later when pupils are graduating from an SL programme the measures used to assess their proficiency should be both cognitively demanding and context reduced (i.e. where a shared reality cannot be assumed and messages need to be elaborated) since this type of explicit language use is closer to the communicative demands of an English-only classroom.

Tests of SL student performance can perform a variety of functions: to determine proficiency, to determine achievement, to diagnose weaknesses, and to forecast aptitude. Shuy (in LaFontaine *et al.*, 1978) offers five broad approaches to language assessment:

(1) *Discrete-point tests*: the widely used 'Test of English as a Foreign Language' (TOEFL) is a good example of this kind of test. It is based on multiple choice items to probe knowledge about isolated facts of language. The popularity of discrete point tests may stem from their ease of use. The chief weakness in tests of this kind is that they are usually applied away from any naturalistic context of language use, thus isolating the language component from a real-world context. As Ingram (1985) observes: when language is used in real life, all the components are together, supporting each other in meaning and dependent on each other structurally; skill in using language includes being able to put all the components together and to understand them when they are received together.

(2) *Integrative tests*: these contrast with the discrete-point approach in assuming that proficiency is best assessed over a number of sub-skills of language in use. Comprehension tests are examples that will be familiar to many teachers who use them in first language teaching and learning: a paragraph of text is presented to students and they are asked to answer questions based upon it. Other examples are cloze analysis (see Savignon, 1983), where a percentage of words are

omitted from a text and need to be filled in, written dictation tests where verbatim repetition is the goal, written composition, oral interviews, reading aloud and multiple choice tests of reading comprehension (Rivera, 1984a). The results of integrative assessment procedures are more dependent on the interpretation of the person giving the tests than are discrete-point tests, so they have a lower scorer reliability. On the other hand if carefully chosen their construct validity can be very high since the range of competencies that they can be used to assess offers the kind of breadth that is recommended by recent developments in language learning theory.

(3) *Direct rating methods*: when properly carried out these tests are close to ideal in accuracy, but they are expensive and time-consuming. The speaker's language is assessed by trained observers including a native speaker, across a range of contexts, functions and skills. The Ilyin Oral Interview is one example of direct rating methods (Savignon, 1983). These methods are widely regarded as offering the highest degree of content validity of all known testing procedures.

(4) *Self-report ratings*: these may appear to have little use because of unavoidable problems of subjectivity, however the insights that they can offer should not be overlooked. Older second language users spend a good deal of their time monitoring their own performances; very often they possess levels of critical awareness about their language in use that may be denied to the independent observer. The difficult task is to design a rating system that will make it easy for students to reveal their knowledge of their own strengths and weaknesses.

(5) *Direct observation*: this involves an assessor observing the use of language by children in a range of natural contexts and perhaps recording it in some way. The results of that recording can then be analysed by other assessors who isolate aspects relevant to their assessment agenda. This approach to assessment is not unlike the methods of assessing first language learning that are favoured by contemporary teachers of English (see Chapter 5). My discussion of naturalistic observation methods, at the end of this section, tries to take direct observation methods as far towards the ideal as is possible in conventional schooling.

Communicative proficiency assessment

One approach to direct observation testing, which attends more directly to the students' skill in using language for various natural purposes in realistic situations, uses 'communicative proficiency assessment' instruments'. There are similarities here with 'integrative tests', although communicative proficiency assessment goes much further: it focusses on what learners can do with the language, on the tasks they can carry out and how they carry them out: on their total language behaviour and its productive capacity (Ingram, 1985). Canale (1984) suggests five components that instruments of this kind could contain. These five components offer one set of benchmarks that schools could use to measure their own procedures for assessing global SL competence:

(1) Tests of Listening Comprehension
(2) Tests of Reading Comprehension
(3) Tests of Oral Interaction
(4) Tests of Written Expression
(5) A Self-Evaluation Questionnaire

Canale's suggestions for scoring the results of tests of these kinds are also relevant. Scorers need to attend to:

—the *information* communicated by students (i.e. its relevance, clarity, factual correctness and amount);

—the *grammaticality* of utterances used (i.e. vocabulary usage, word formation, sentence formation with attention to separating minor errors from major ones);

—the *pronunciation or spelling* of responses;

—the *appropriateness*, depending on such contextual factors as topic, role of participants, setting and purpose;

—the *discourse*, which involves the extent to which utterances function together to produce unity in the text and suggest coherence of thought.

A school SL assessment programme which included improvised, worthwhile tests of language covering each of the five components above would be close to providing an adequate baseline profile of student ability for placement and policy purposes. Once this information has been gathered *naturalistic observation* should be included as a check on the assessment of all students, especially those graduating from an SL programme into the English-only mainstream of the school's curriculum or those who have already been judged as proficient but about whom there is some doubt. Simich-Dudgeon & Rivera (1983) offer 'an ethnographic approach to bilingual language proficiency assessment' which they have subjected to a field test. They call their approach a 'teacher observation system' (TOS). It is not necessary to include the whole system here; it is very detailed and comes with a manual. Most teachers concerned to implement some similar scheme in their SL assessment could devise their own version of the TOS by thinking carefully about how they could make judgments, based on their own observations, that would respond to the questions below that the TOS approach addresses (Rivera, 1983: 117):

(1) What kind of functional language skills does the language minority student bring to school?
(2) In which language(s), social contexts, and for what purposes does the student communicate best?
(3) In which language(s) does the student have the widest contextual range of communicative abilities?
(4) What kinds of communicative skills does the student need to master in order to participate appropriately as a member of the school speech community?

Assessing the language of learning disabled minority language pupils

This topic is too specialised for it to be covered in detail here. Yet because of its importance and the fact that most special education candidates are now being placed in mainstream classes in many countries, it needs to be treated in a discussion about school level language policy. Cummins (1984b) provides a major reference in this area. The ethnographic approach outlined above, based on naturalistic observation, seems very relevant to Cummins' recommendations. I summarise some of his points below:

(1) for minority children already diagnosed as having language disorders, assessment and instruction should be primarily oriented not towards the production of language forms but towards helping children to interact with others or with a written text; the task in assessment is for teachers to separate the effects of the children's language barrier from the effects of their language disorders and this can only come from attending to their practical competence in both the first and second languages;
(2) for minority children already diagnosed as hearing-impaired, descriptive assessment in both languages (including perhaps a sign language) is of more value than normative assessment; the focus will be on what children have developed rather than on what they lack;
(3) for minority children who may be candidates for gifted and talented programs, teacher observation must play a major role in

identifying them; one piece of evidence may be rapid progress in learning the majority tongue (assuming that 5 to 7 years is the average time needed for minority children to catch up in their use of the language for academic work); a major factor in allowing these children to display their talent will be curricular and extra-curricular activities that encourage that display; an important point is that these children will be no less represented among the minority children than among the majority.

Resources and Materials for Second Language Teaching

Unsuccessful SL programmes often lack bilingual materials and there can be no organisational substitute for this deficiency. High quality materials that are culturally sensitive, not imported from another culture and do not impose alien cultural values are really necessary. Good quality bilingual dictionaries are essential for children who have developed levels of literacy in their first and second languages. The following are some policy items that schools will need to consider when considering resource materials and resource people:

(1) Is there a staff member with recognised responsibility for coordinating language learning among children with SL needs?
(2) Can this person be better used than at present in providing staff development in SL learning pedagogy and acting as a consultant on the best use of available resource materials?
(3) How might resource people in the wider education system be used more fully?
(4) How might the children themselves and community members be involved as resources for learning?
(5) Are their culturally appropriate assessment procedures available for new students with SL needs?
(6) Is there a role for an education support committee, involving ethnic groups, to liaise and work with the school?
(7) What large resource items for SLT should the school include as part of its long-term planning estimates?
(8) Is the school's budget fairly allocated to meet the language learning needs of all children?
(9) Does the local community itself offer any sources of funding that might be directed towards the school's needs?

*   *   *

The task of putting the ideas contained in this chapter to work, as part of a language policy, is not an easy one. As only a guide to this task, included below is an appendix to the chapter which provides two specimen policies: the one is oriented more towards addressing a school's need for SL provisions and the other is oriented more towards the first phases of mother tongue maintenance provisions.

Appendix: Specimen Policies

(1) A language policy across the curriculum for a pluralist primary school

The draft policy below has been developed for use in a highly pluralist primary school which is only beginning to address its significant language problems (Otahuhu School — see Chapter 1). In its present form the tentative policy has not yet been subjected to error elimination in the school context. It represents a conjecture about what is possible, based on informed theorising by the school's executive. It was prefaced by a set of principles that stressed the twin roles of language as something learned and as a tool for learning, the three basic tenets of LAC (see Chapter 5), and the key role that language has in cultural maintenance and in shaping ethnic group solidarity. The policy blends position statements with plans for specific action based on information contained in Chapters 5 & 6 of this book. One feature is its commitment to the needs of the range of minority children who form the vast majority in the school's population. The policy provides only a starting point in a serious and committed campaign to address the school's language problems (McDonald, 1988). I present the policy uncritically:

Introduction
  (1) The further development, refinement and implementation of the policies defined in this document will be the school's priority task in the coming year.
  (2) The process of policy development, refinement and implementation will be guided by an acceptance of LAC principles and a corporate commitment to cultural pluralism.

Organisation and management of the school
(1) *School and class organisation*
  (1.1) Class organisation will be based on composite vertical groupings.

(1.2) Other organisational structures will be researched and evaluated with a view to introducing further innovations in the coming year (such as cultural units, peer support systems, rotation teaching, mother tongue maintenance etc.).

(2) *Staffing and deployment*

(2.1) Advertisements for all teaching vacancies will require applicants to have an interest and ability in assisting with the development and implementation of multicultural programmes, ESL programmes and/or minority language programmes and indicate the desirability of fluency in Maori, Indo-Chinese, Samoan or other Pacific Island languages.

(2.2) Discretionary part-time staffing granted by the employing authority for 'special needs' will be utilised as follows:

(i)   provision of support for second language learners within their home classrooms;

(ii) individual and small group instruction in reading on a withdrawal basis.

(2.3) Where necessary and appropriate, provision will be made for the release of teachers with expertise in Maori and/or Pacific Island cultures to enable them to develop programmes in these areas.

(2.4) Responsibility for the supervision and monitoring of special needs programmes will be delegated to Syndicate Leaders (i.e. deputy principals and associate principal).

(3) *Professional leadership and guidance*

(3.1) A curriculum team responsible for 'language and multicultural education' (LAME) consisting of a senior teacher and two others representing the junior and senior school will be established. The principal will be an *ex officio* member.

(3.2) Responsibilities of the LAME team will include:

(i)   general oversight of language and multicultural education programmes;

(ii) promoting language and education issues within the school;

(iii) initiating and coordinating the implementation of the policies outlined in this document and recommending additions, deletions and amendments where necessary.

(4) *Teacher development*

(4.1) The teacher development programme during the coming year will give priority to LAC issues and to the promotion of cultural pluralism within the school.

(4.2) The LAME team will be responsible for planning and implementing the teacher development programme.

(5) *Resources*

(5.1) From the coming year's school budget and special purpose grants (i.e. library, free textbook scheme) 15% will be tagged for the acquisition of appropriate minority language resource materials.

(5.2) A suitable area will be developed specifically for the storage of multicultural resource materials.

(5.3) The LAME team will be responsible for:
  (i)   the evaluation, acquisition and organisation of resources;
  (ii) identifying, evaluating and enlisting the aid of the various consultancies and support services available in the community.

(6) *Buildings and facilities*

(6.1) Representations will be made to the appropriate authorities seeking the conversion of the 'open-space' classrooms in the junior school to 'variable space'.

(7) *Community consultation and involvement*

(7.1) The Board of Trustees and the school community will be consulted and kept fully informed of all proposed developments and policy decisions.

(7.2) The staff will support in principle the notion that the various ethnic groups in the school community be represented on the Board of Trustees, by co-option if necessary.

(7.3) The staff will support in principle the concept of community involvement in curriculum development (e.g. curriculum planning groups) and actively seek a practical means of involving parents in the development and implementation of the language policy.

(7.4) Every effort will be made to tap the pool of linguistic expertise available within the community and to involve volunteers in multicultural programmes.

(7.5) The LAME team will be responsible for promoting and organising community participation and involvement.

The Curriculum

(1) *Multicultural education*

(1.1) Multicultural education will be recognised as a legitimate curriculum area in its own right and included as a separate section of the School Scheme.

(1.2) Scheme development in multicultural education will be guided by a commitment to supporting the revival of the Maori language and to the importance of assisting pupils from other ethnic minority groups to maintain their mother tongues.

  (1.3) The LAME team will be responsible for developing a School Scheme in Multicultural Education.

(2) *Oral language*

  (2.1) The School Scheme in Oral Language will be revised during the coming year.

  (2.2) Scheme revision will be guided by the following principles:

    (i)   an acceptance of the principle that oral language occurs across the curriculum and that it is both something learned and a fundamental tool for learning;

    (ii) a recognition of the primacy of oral language and its role in providing a base for both reading and writing;

    (iii) a recognition of the importance of oral language in the development of self-esteem and its role in cultural transmission;

    (iv) a recognition of the need to develop and promote pedagogical strategies supportive of minority language speakers in the classroom.

  (2.3) The LAME team will be responsible for revising the School Scheme in Oral Language.

(3) *Written language and reading*

  (3.1) Revision of Schemes in these subject areas will be delayed until after this policy has been evaluated.

  (3.2) In the meantime existing policies in those subject areas will remain in place but should be interpreted in the spirit of the principles and policies enunciated in this statement.

Conclusion

This policy is intended to be current for one year only. At the end of that time progress will be evaluated and a further document prepared as a guide for action during the following year.

(2) **An introductory policy for a pluralist primary school with bilingual needs**

The policy below has been developed only as an introductory language policy for a very culturally pluralist primary school with bilingual needs (St John's Otara — see Chapter 1). The policy was prefaced by broad guidelines that lay stress on the school showing respect for the children's home languages, on the need in future to develop the home languages of the children along with their access

to English, and on the uniquely pluralist place that the school has in
its community. The policy in its present form is little more than a
tentative effort by the school to adapt itself to coping with major and
longstanding language problems that are now seen in the new light
of many of the findings already discussed in this chapter (Ford, 1988).
I present it uncritically:

Current practices supporting an across the curriculum policy

(1) Upon enrolment attention is paid to the language spoken in the
    children's home. In many cases this is a mixture of Samoan and
    English.
(2) In June each year an ethnic survey of the school roll is undertaken
    to assess any changes the school may need to make.
(3) Encouragement is given to appointment of staff members who are
    of the same culture as the children. Reference is made in
    advertisements to the multicultural nature of the school.
(4) More opportunity has been given for the children to have access
    to the school's very large and recently improved library.

New practices

(1) Specific data will be gathered on language practices within the
    school across a range of contexts, functions, styles and varieties
    of language-in-use.
(2) A policy process for the development of new policies will be
    discussed and adopted by the staff as a group.
(3) There will be more consultation with the parent community
    about the purposes and curriculum of the school. Staff will
    become more informed about the languages and cultures of the
    children and their families.
(4) A teacher-induction process will be developed reflecting the
    cultural aspirations and language needs of the children and
    helping teachers to avoid stereotyping.
(5) The physical environment of the school will be developed so that
    it reflects more of the nature of the school population.
(6) Every encouragement will be offered to the children and
    teachers to use their home languages in school situations both
    informally and formally.
(7) Administration will provide more opportunities for staff to visit
    schools where strong bilingual programmes are operating to
    discuss their advantages and problems.
(8) A teacher reference file on bilingualism and teaching English as
    a Second Language will be developed so that teachers can have

easy access to high quality information concerning these.

(9) The school will develop a policy on evaluation which will try to reflect the positive aspects of pupils' learning and treat them as individuals.

(10) The current policy for the ESL class will be critically evaluated to consider whether or not it is meeting the objectives for which it was originally developed (should there be more mother tongue maintenance for younger children?)

(11) The selection of material used in school programmes will be monitored to ensure it is drawn from the users' cultural environments wherever possible, avoids gender and racist stereotyping, and that language components are recognised and effectively catered for.

(12) A wide variety of quality material will be made available in the pupils' first languages.

(13) Local resources and staffing will be used where possible and necessary to assist in first language maintenance.

(14) A monitoring and evaluation programme will see that the objectives of this policy are being met and will provide for regular up-dating and revision.

8 Foreign language teaching and cultural studies across the curriculum

Foreign Language Teaching (FLT)

This chapter follows quite directly on from discussion in Chapter 7. Although foreign language teaching in this chapter is implicitly linked with cultural studies teaching, I am not trying to set FLT artifically apart from SLT since they are clearly located on the same continuum. All language learning has much in common to the extent that it provides and requires a window on some or other culture. But because SL learning takes place *within* the culture to which the language relates, formal cultural studies has a lesser place in SLT than it has for FLT where the school needs to provide vicarious contacts in its curriculum with what is lacking in the wider context: namely a natural engagement with the culture of the foreign language. A programme of cultural studies can compensate for the very real disadvantages that foreign language teaching has when compared to second language teaching. Consider the several clear advantages that the SL situation has over the FL: a second language has more significance for the learner since it can be used immediately outside the classroom; it can be learned more quickly because as the native language of the country there is constant and abundant exposure to its physical manifestations; and the extrinsic motivations to learn the language are ever-present and urgent ones. In contrast the FL context is almost exclusively fabricated by the FL teacher; reinforcement and revision will not be incidental, nor will they take place at all unless the teacher plans for them; tests will focus necessarily on aspects of 'correctness' rather than on wider communicative competence; and, assuming that the students are willing candidates, responsibility for motivating their performance or failing to do so lies almost exclusively with the teacher. This can be a recipe for the failure in FLT of those pupils who receive no extrinsic motivation towards learning a foreign language from their families or from their lives and experiences outside schools. This first section provides only an introduction to the formal areas of study of FLT. Like SLT it is an area of complex skill and understanding that requires expertise far beyond the resources of this book. Many books are available to assist the school administrator or policy maker who wants to know more about pedagogical approaches to FLT. Some of these cover both SLT and FLT (e.g. Brown, 1980; Alatis *et al.*, 1981; Littlewood, 1981; Savignon, 1983; Hyltenstam and Pienemann, 1985) and others deal exclusively with FLT. My purpose here is only to introduce some of the issues and problems that a 'non-FLT-specialist' school administrator or policy group might need to address in organising an LPAC that includes FLT matters.

A full understanding of relevant factors in successful foreign language teaching and learning is still a long way off. Crystal (1987 p. 371) provides an overview of many of the relevant factors. I elaborate on his list below to show the complexity of the task:

—*the importance of having an 'aptitude' for FL learning*: almost anyone can learn a language given time and effort but certain personality traits do seem to help. Empathy, adaptability, assertiveness, independence, drive and application are all useful, as is a good memory, good articulation, and skill in seeing patterns in data and patterns in sound sequences. I should add that in education now we are a long way past the view that 'aptitudes' are stable possessions that people are born with and carry around throughout their lives. The things that go to make up 'aptitudes' are certainly influenced by the environment, especially by experiences in early childhood. Children who are bilingual from their earliest years, for example, will probably have their aptitude for FL learning enhanced relative to monolingual children.

—*the importance of knowing how to learn a language*: useful strategies including silent rehearsal, techniques of memorisation and paraphrasing can all be treated as syllabus items deserving deliberate learning activities for their development (see the discussion of 'strategic competence' below).

—*the importance of regular exposure to the foreign language in both spoken and written forms*: the most valuable exposure aims to teach 'little and often', avoiding fatigue and superficial levels of learning. Regular exposure to native language users and to texts drawn from the real world is a major benefit, especially if the exposure relates to other work in the educational programme and if children can move within the FL environment. Immersion programmes introduced in some places (see Chapter 6) provide the student with greater competence in the foreign tongue than is usually achieved by students in traditional programmes (Genesee, 1984).

—the importance of graded teaching objectives: realistic progress especially for slower students may depend on a careful selection of objectives. The objectives should vary according to the modes of language to be covered (see Chapter 5), the order of their presentation, the number of languages to be learned, the varieties of the language, and the kinds of skills and techniques to be mastered.

—the importance of flexible teaching methods: some attempt at an individualisation of instruction is recommended and this should be woven into the resources and time available. Desirable methods in oral work can be much the same as those recommended for oral language classwork in mother tongue teaching (see Chapter 5). A range of method 'schools' exist for FL teaching and these are broadly similar to the range of SL approaches already covered in Chapter 7. At different pupil ages there will certainly be a need for variation in the approaches used.

—the importance of motivation: it is necessary to take the language out of the classroom as much as possible so that students can see its use by real people and realise that the language is respected by people whom the students can respect. Teachers also need to be motivated by the knowledge that their students are willing members of FL classes who intend to take their learning further. This means that pupils and teachers must know that opportunities for studying the foreign language will be available in later years. Students may also be motivated if they are able to decide for themselves their point of entry (i.e. grade level) for studying a foreign language.

—the importance of age: In recent research a slightly better performance in listening comprehension for students beginning a language at age 8, rather than at age 11, has been reported (Harley, 1986). It is true that under ideal conditions, with limited teaching objectives, with specialist teachers and with methods suited to the interests and intellectual levels of junior school children, an early start in learning a foreign language can work as well as an early start in SL learning by majority language speakers (see Chapter 7). Without these conditions the results may not be worth the expenditure of time and effort involved. There was an era of optimism, when people were enthusiastic about teaching a foreign language to junior school

children, but this era has passed. Stern (1976) laid to rest many of the more extravagant claims: clearly early age school instruction does not itself guarantee success and it is likely that the ability to learn foreign languages overall, like many abilities, improves with age. Skutnabb-Kangas (1981) concludes that older learners are better, quicker and more efficient in most aspects of FL learning and that any advantages younger children possess can be compensated for by using different teaching approaches with the older students. For the cultural studies side of FLT the early years of secondary schooling may be the best time for broadening student understanding and lessening their cultural insularity (Nemetz Robinson, 1985). In general, traditional forms of FL teaching may be better postponed to the post-primary years[1], although there are several knowledge areas for language awareness development that are very suitable for introduction in the junior grades (see Chapter 5).

Foreign Language Teaching Policy Items

Most of the following points are for the guidance of a policy group planning an FL programme in a school where no foreign languages are presently taught or where major changes are intended. Schools that already teach some foreign languages will have special constraints and these are mainly addressed under point 2 below. Some of the questions that I have asked require straightforward answers which depend on the human, physical and financial resources available. I have not added any discussion to these more straightforward points. Some of the questions deal with pedagogical matters that are covered elsewhere. Others raise issues that are more complex and these may require extensive debate and some small scale research into attitudes and needs (see Chapter 3).

FL Questions

(1) **how many languages should be taught?**

(2) **which language(s) should be taught?**

The question of which languages should be taught in a school can be very controversial in a pluralist society. There is much at stake when individual people have their language roots or their major foreign language experiences in a language which is a candidate for inclusion on a school's curriculum. National and school traditions, student and community needs, and staff inclinations will all come into the debate. When the participants in the debate are also employed as teachers of some foreign language who are worried by the prospect of its possible removal from the curriculum, then a bitter dispute is quite possible. What criteria can the school use to resolve this problem?

In an existing school the availability of teachers is clearly a constraint on any decision that is taken. But perhaps all or some of the available teachers are linked to languages that are of declining value in the school and in the society, relative to other languages. In dealing with these cases a policy might provide a transition period during which gradual efforts will be made to introduce the more desirable languages and reduce teaching of the less desirable ones. Other things being equal, as in the case of a completely new school, the following points might provide a rationale for choosing foreign languages for a school's curriculum:

(i)   can the language easily be made relevant to the lives, interests and experiences of the children to whom it is to be taught?

(ii)   is the language widely used as one of the country's second languages?

(iii) is the language widely used as a local community language?

(iv) is the language spoken in nearby countries?

(v)   does the language provide a *lingua franca* with neighbouring countries?

(vi) is the language generally regarded as an international language?

(vii) is the language linguistically close to the mother tongue or is its distance likely to be a handicap to early learners? [Italian, closely followed by Spanish and French, is nearest in linguistic distance to English; German is further away; and Russian is further still (Crystal, 1987). The nearness of the learner's first language to the foreign language exerts a strong influence in the early stages of learning, facilitating learning especially in the areas of lexis and syntax. Although linguistic distance may not produce inevitable learning problems, it is the case that if the beginning learner is able to perceive similarities in the two languages some important learning problems will be avoided (Ringbom, 1987).]

(viii) is the language a language of commerce with any of the country's major trading partners?

(ix) is learning the language likely to be especially useful to the child in extending language awareness in the mother tongue?

(x)   is the language identified as an official 'language of wider learning' at government or national language policy level (see Chapter 6)?

If affirmative answers can be made to many of these questions, then there is a strong case for including a given language on the school's curriculum, subject to resources and staffing being available. But using this questionnaire will not resolve all of a school's problems. In some countries many of these questions may be relevant to most schools and it may be the idiosyncracies of the local context that will provide the final arbiter. For example, in the pluralist context of Australian schools any of more than 100 languages might be supported by answers given to questions (i) and (iii); any of a dozen languages by answers given to questions (i), (ii) and (iii); several languages by answers given to questions (iii), (iv), (v) and (x); Chinese (Mandarin) would be supported by answers to (i), (ii), (iii), (iv), (v), (vi), (viii) and (x); Japanese by answers to (i), (iv), (viii) and (x); Indonesian/Malay by (i), (iv), (v), (viii) and (x); French by (i), (ii), (iv), (vi), (vii), (ix) and (x); Italian or Spanish by (i), (ii), (iii), (vii), (ix) and (x). In Canada, the United States or Britain the range of possible languages might be as large, but they would be different groups of languages.

Very often FL learners come to have more knowledge of the foreign language they study than SL learners have of their second language. The difference is that the former have less control over their knowledge (Ringbom, 1987). A cultural studies approach, across the curriculum, can inject the extrinsic motivation needed to develop control, provided that the languages chosen for inclusion in a school's curriculum are appropriate ones. Where the relevance of a language to the child's world is marginal, a cultural studies programme, targeted on that culture, will probably remain as marginal as the language it relates to. Again schools need to take care in choosing the languages that they offer and also the cultural studies programmes that they relate them to. For example, in a country like the United States with a high and visible Hispanic population, Spanish seems a sensible inclusion as a foreign language in a school, even if there are few Hispanics in the immediate community of the school. It may be less important to teach French as a foreign language in the south west of the United States, in spite of French's international standing. On the other hand, in Australia and New Zealand French is a language of several close Pacific neighbours and this may prompt its inclusion on the curriculum of schools in those countries. However cultural studies programmes, linked to these languages across the curriculum, might pay less attention to the 'cultures' of metropolitan Spain or France and more attention in the

United States to the cultures of Hispanic and Latin Americans and in Australasia to the cultures of the Melanesian francophone nations in the Pacific.

(3)   to whom should they be taught?

On balance, students who are already extensively bilingual have an advantage over monolingual students in learning another foreign language (Ringbom, 1987). Another related factor is the role played by met-alinguistic awareness in foreign language learning: conscious awareness of language as a system may provide special support for language learning (Thomas, 1988) and some of the recommendations made in the final section of Chapter 5 will be relevant here too. The section discussing 'variable factors in SL learning' under 'bilingualism' in Chapter 7 is also related to this point.

(4)   how much of the languages should be taught to each group?

(5)   how should they be taught?

(6)   how can cultural studies related to the foreign language be included across the curriculum?

These last three points comprise the subject matter for the rest of this chapter.

Communicative Competence and FLT

Communicative competence relates to two questions (Hymes, 1987): how do cultures themselves shape language acquisition and how does this acquisition continue throughout life? The complex of skills, attitudes and knowledge that the term 'communicative competence' covers can be broken down into at least six sub-competencies (van Ek, 1986). A point to extract from this list is that the development of communicative competence generally depends on acquiring 'a whole' which is much more than the sum of its parts. Development also depends on a ready integration in teaching and in learning of aspects of these competencies. I list these below and later say a little more about each one:

(1) *linguistic competence*: the competence to use and interpret structural elements of a language;

(2) *sociolinguistic competence*: the competence to use and interpret language with situational appropriateness;

(3) *discourse competence*: the ability to perceive and to achieve coherence of separate utterances in meaningful communication patterns;

(4) *social competence*: empathy and the ability to handle social situations;

(5) *sociocultural competence*: familiarity with the sociocultural context;

(6) *strategic competence*: the ability to use verbal and non-verbal strategies to compensate for gaps in the language user's knowledge of the code.

Many of the audio-lingual language learning methods that are now less favoured gave a prominent place to the development of *linguistic competence* by stressing that language learners perform a range of structural operations. Earlier generations of FL teachers were able to promote a good deal of high level linguistic competence in pupils by dividing language into the broad skill areas of speaking, listening, reading and writing and by then instructing for carefully measured development, within each area, in the sub-skills of phonology, lexicon, semantics and syntax. Indeed this level of linguistic competence was sometimes beyond the level of knowledge that the students had about their own mother tongue. This strong concentration on skills and sub-skills very often failed to capture language as it is actually used in communication. Too often there was minimal concentration on meaning in these tasks and excessive attention was paid to the structural changes that had to be made in manipulating fragments of language. This does not mean that structural practice needs to be excluded from the FL teacher's repertoire of pedagogies. Linguistic competence of this kind may be a very necessary acquisition, provided the other competencies are not ignored. As Littlewood (1981) remarks, we are still too ignorant about language learning for us to be able to say dogmatically what can and cannot contribute to its processes.

Relating language to the social meanings that it carries and using it for social interaction means that a language learner must acquire the rules of use and of discourse that make up *sociolinguistic competence*. This begins to develop when the students come to use their language in a meaningful social context, interacting naturally with others rather than in response to the artificial prompting of the teacher. The stress here is on appropriateness of meanings (such as the expression of attitudes, the use of speech acts and the presentation of propositions) and on appropriateness of forms (such as register, non-verbal expression and intonation). Discussion in Chapter 7 on the functional/notional approach to SL teaching is relevant to developing this kind of competence. A syllabus for work of this kind might be based on an integration of functions, notions and activities, moving from simple patterns of interaction involving restricted cooperation, through less restricted cooperative activities, to higher level patterns such as sharing information and processing it in discussion and evaluation.

Mastery in combining forms and meanings to establish integrated spoken or written texts in different genres indicates the possession of *discourse competence*. There are two major aspects to this kind of competence: the ability to use cohesion devices to link fragments of text together (such as pronouns, transition words and parallel structures); and the ability to use coherence rules to organise meanings (such as repetition, progression, consistency and relevance of ideas). The ability to teach in this area requires a high level understanding of what constitutes cohesion in discourse in a language and what techniques can be used to promote that cohesion in any text where it is lacking. This may seem a rather advanced level of FL teaching. However its introduction and use in a spiral of curriculum development can begin with the earliest and simplest texts that students produce and it can develop in range and effect as the complexity of the student texts develops.

Interaction in a classroom is very different from true social interaction. The latter requires a degree of *social competence* in putting the language to work. This involves being able to conform not just to the functional requirements of a situation but also to the social conventions that govern behaviour between people in real-life settings. This is a highly sophisticated acquisition since many people, even in their mother tongue, feel inadequate in certain social situations. Children at certain ages or from certain backgrounds, for example, feel inadequate in most social situations where adults are present and here there is a real gain to be derived from work in studying a foreign language. The role play activities that are useful for developing social competence in a foreign language can give the child some appreciation of what it means to have social competence more generally. Again most of the approaches to mother tongue oral language work discussed in Chapter 5 are useful FL activities for social competence development: whole class and group discussions; improvisations; role plays; simulations; public speaking and debates can all have a place at different levels.

Major difficulties are encountered in learning languages well that demand dimensions of social competence that are very different from those that learners are used to. In the Japanese culture, for example, much information is transmitted through non-verbal communication and it is in a code with which non-Japanese people have little acquaintance. Context is all-important in using Japanese to good effect in Japan itself. When used in its cultural setting, Japanese is very high in level of 'information implicitly contained' if it is placed on a scale with other languages used in their cultural contexts, ranging from those like German and the Scandinavian languages, which require a low level of context information, through those like French, English and Italian which are intermediate in their levels of context information (Hall, 1976). The meaning of vocabulary items in Japanese (as in Polynesian languages) is also highly dependent on context and this interaction operates in ways that are largely beyond the understanding of people who are novices in the culture.

Background knowledge of a language's culture and of the societies where it is used is essential for high level competence in a language. This *sociocultural competence* provides the backdrop of meanings, the 'interpretative repertoires', against which the language can be set. The rest of this chapter addresses aspects of this kind of competence. The vast range of knowledge types that it touches upon includes all of those fields of knowledge that users of the language place value upon in its natural setting. A sophisticated grasp of sociocultural competence in a language also includes knowledge of what differences there might be between people in 'social competence' within the foreign culture, even between different cultural groups who are users of that same language. For example, Erickson & Schultz (1982) found that White and Black American speakers have different conventions for eye gaze in speaking and listening settings: White speakers let their gaze wander; Black speakers look at the listener. Having knowledge of a simple fact like this may allow a new language user to interpret situations better by employing this item of sociocultural competence so as not to misinterpret these non-verbal cues that accompany language in use.

Since the early 1970s *strategic competence* has attracted special interest because it is this competence that allows students to grow beyond the rather limited range of language proficiency that has been offered to them in traditional classrooms. It has been found that the control students have over their learning strategies can be improved by classroom instruction. This finding means that students can continue FL learning outside the classroom using self-directed and individualised learning methods. 'Strategic competence' refers to two broad sets of processes: the operations that learners use to solve problems in receptive and productive second language use (see below); and the learning strategies themselves that cover operations used to increase second language knowledge and its accessibility. This second ingredient in strategic competence is an easier thing to understand than it is to pass on to others. It is the kind of proficiency that good SL or FL teachers offer their students through the example of their own teaching practices. It requires a consistent, deliberate and regular display of the metacognitive skills 'in use' that are needed for independent language learning, along the lines that were discussed for first language teaching in the final section of Chapter 5.

The first ingredient in strategic competence involves understanding and applying the operations needed to interact appropriately in the language. 'Conversation analysis' is one developing area of study which tries to identify those regular aspects of social order that allow the operations of conversational interaction to occur and grow (Button & Lee, 1987). Perhaps the word 'versatility' captures much of the point of this kind of competence: students show that they are versatile across a range of contexts in negotiating or constructing interactions. For example, they are able to:

initiate new topics of conversation;
shift the topic of conversation;
make back references within the conversation;
change registers or styles or the level of formality of an interaction;
relate what is said to the knowledge, beliefs or experiences that
interlocutors are assumed to share;
detect and correct misunderstandings;
show appreciation;
provide reasons for conversational actions;
clarify instructions that are received;
make arrangements for the future;
include asides in dialogue;
repair or edit their own or others' utterances.

There are ways of achieving all of these things in respect to any single language, but it would be wrong to conclude that these strategies have the status of 'cognitive universals'. Some of them are reasonably regular across human discourse; others are culturally relative and context bound, so they cannot be taught as 'syllabus items' in the same way to all language learners. In these, as in other respects, FLT has moved far beyond the earlier conception of the learner's task which saw it as a passive one. Now the active role of the learner is recognised, with individual differences in learner personality traits and motivation levels directly influencing the results of teaching. Nor is it just individual differences in learners that we are dealing with here: Chapter 7 mentions differences in learning styles between Hispanic and Chinese students of English; Chapter 9 gives a much fuller coverage of differential treatment of abilities, as it affects children from diverse cultures. As Kasper (1988) points out, cultural differences in learning strategies are very apparent across a range of circumstances: for example, showing lack of knowledge in or out of the classroom may be experienced as face-threatening by members of some cultures; or failure to understand a teacher's utterance may be embarrassing for the student, indicating disrespect for the teacher, and may result in few requests for information or clarification from some students. It is necessary, then, in any SL or FL programme for schools to keep the possibility of cultural and individual differences firmly in view.

* * *

This chapter has said less than it might about the design and management of a 'cultural studies programme across the curriculum (see Corson, 1989a). For the interested reader Byram (1988a; 1988b) suggests conventional approaches to skill and knowledge acquisition as a way of linking FLT with cultural studies. Nemetz Robinson (1985) provides some simple principles and ideas that may underlie the complex process that takes place when a person from one culture begins to understand a person from another.

The task of putting to work the ideas contained in this chapter, as part of a language policy, is not an easy one. As only a preliminary guide to this task, below is a specimen SL and FL policy which is oriented towards the needs of a conventional secondary school located in a country that also has an indigenous minority language. It provides a plan for action.

A second and foreign language policy

The preliminary SL and FL policy below is being developed for use in a conventional secondary school (Selwyn College — see Chapter 1) following an extensive survey of staff opinion by members of its modern languages department (see Chapter 3). In its present form the tentative policy still lacks references to communicative competence and cultural studies issues. It was prefaced by a set of principles that stressed the value for pupils of learning another language, the need for a selection of foreign languages to be available in secondary schools for all who wish to study them, the importance of experience in the language itself as a basis for choice, and the need for continuity of offerings in the languages area. The policy blends position statements with plans for specific action (Glenny, 1988). It opens with a commitment to the country's minority language (New Zealand Maori) as one important SL offering:

Te Reo Maori

(1) the school affirms both recommendations of the national curriculum review:
—the school system accepts its role in the promotion, retention and preservation of Maori language and culture
—Maori language is available to every student who wishes to learn it or learn through it
(2) the Maori language programmes introduced into the school in recent years should receive every assistance in becoming established in accordance with nationally declared obligations.
(3) it is vital that these courses be placed on the timetable irrespective of their class sizes.

Foreign languages

(1) French and German will remain the established foreign languages in the school.
(2) Japanese will be offered when a staff member capable of teaching it can be employed.

Course structures

(1) in the new entrants' year introductory courses in Maori, French and German will be taught to all classes. This programme will be language based but will also include a cultural studies component.
(2) in the second and third years the three languages will be offered as option subjects.
(3) in the senior school (fourth and fifth years) courses leading to external examinations in the languages will continue to be offered.
(4) in a future year a beginners course in German will be offered in the fourth year subject to enrolment numbers. This will meet the objective of providing a second entry point for language learning in the school.
(5) the school will undertake to guarantee classes at the next level in all languages where the need exists regardless of class sizes.
(6) class sizes in the junior school will be kept below 30 and not allowed to rise to compensate for smaller classes at senior level.

Approaches

(1) in the junior school a strongly communicative approach is used. The initial emphasis is on listening and speaking, only later on reading, and writing has a lower profile until senior levels.

(2) in the senior school a theme-based approach is used: this allows the listening and speaking skills to be maintained and allows scope for reading and writing skills to be developed further.

Notes to Chapter 8

1. Recent developments in Italian primary schools may soften this claim. Titone (1987) reports large research studies conducted across Italy: the Italian experience indicates that English, French and German can be taught with considerable success as foreign languages to Italian primary school children, provided that the best possible learning environment is offered.

9 Social justice issues and language policy

This chapter opens with a discussion about the links between language, power and schooling in modern societies, arguing for the development of 'critical language awareness' as a goal of schooling. It continues by addressing several key social justice issues that provide a backdrop to designing language policies in pluralist schools: the debate about bilingualism and education; the debate about gender, language and education; the debate about language, culture and knowledge; the debate about the differential treatment of ability; and the debate about how far schools can go in compensating for social inequalities. The purpose of this chapter is to provoke school policy makers to see these issues as challenges that they need to address in their planning. We offer few straightforward solutions.

Language, Education and Power

Matters of social equity and justice are central to designing language policies. It is a disservice to Education if school administrators and teachers proceed on their professional course blind to the issues of power and influence that sit along the borders between schools and society. These are matters that the members of a school executive have to confront, especially as they relate to language since access to language and a wide command of it is empowering for the individual and politically liberating for social groups. There is great relevance for all these matters in the ideas advanced by Pierre Bourdieu. A brief consideration of his cogent arguments about language and education seems a good starting point in linking language policy with social equity and in discussing social justice issues (1977a; 1977b).

'Theories of cultural reproduction', such as Bourdieu's, examine factors in societies and their cultures that are important in maintaining and reproducing (desirable and undesirable) characteristics of those societies and cultures. Obviously language is a key factor in reproducing and maintaining the features of cultures and societies, since a rich access to the dominant language gives individuals and groups power over their own affairs and influence over the affairs of others. As a result they are able to shape societies to serve their own ends and maintain them in the form to which they are accustomed. They do this partly through controlling and changing the conventions for language use and imposing them on others who are without such power. Children, of course, offer the prime example of those who are without power over the conventions of language and who by default are obliged to accept the conventions established by others. There is nothing necessarily sinister about this process (although in totalitarian societies, and elsewhere too, it is used and can be used to serve sinister ends); this is one of the ways that societies work since the purpose of a social organisation is to protect and further the interests of its members: those who control the conventions of discourse and who have the loudest voices most often have their interests promoted. At the same time those denied rich access to the dominant language and the power to make their own language more influential are hindered in expressing themselves, in drawing attention to their needs, and in commanding the support of others in the culture.

Bourdieu uses the phrase 'cultural capital' to describe those culturally esteemed advantages that people acquire as a part of their life experiences, their peer group contacts and their family backgrounds: such things as 'good taste', 'style', certain kinds of knowledge, abilities, presentation of self, norms for language use, and language forms. He argues that the cultural capital that is valued in schools is not equally available to children from different backgrounds, yet schools operate as if all children had equal access to it. By basing their assessments of school success and failure and their award of certificates and qualifications on children's possession of this high status cultural capital, which is unequally available, schools act in such a way as to reproduce the social arrangements that are favourable to some but which disadvantage other social groups. In this way, Bourdieu contends, *de facto* inequalities are translated into *de jure* ones and the value of the cultural capital passed to the next generation is reinforced yet again. This whole social process is described by Bourdieu as the application of 'symbolic power' (the power to constitute the given simply by stating it) by dominant social groups who inflict 'symbolic violence' upon non-dominant groups. This symbolic violence is a form of oppression which imposes arbitrary symbols of knowledge and expression upon those who often do not recognise the symbols as arbitrary but accept them as the way things must be. The members of some social groups, as a result, come to believe that their educational failure, rather than coming from their lowly esteemed social status, results from their natural inability. They come to believe that social and cultural factors are somehow neutralised in the educational selection process and that the process itself is fairly based on objective educational criteria, like possession of knowledge about the culture and the language necessary for expressing it.

Traditionally teachers assume that they share a common language with most of their students and a common set of values related to that language. On Bourdieu's account, however, this is only the case when the students share approximately the same cultural capital as their teachers, which is a rare event in non- selective forms of schooling. Teachers have also traditionally assumed, on this basis, that their judgments about children's abilities to use the language of education, with its complex meanings, allusions and shared conceptual frameworks, are fair to all concerned. The reality we now know is rather different.

Language is the most important aspect of the cultural heritage that each of us receives and there is much evidence that 'language' operates in a discriminatory way in educational settings. Apart from the obvious aspects of language, like its syntax, sounds and vocabulary, each of us acquires in our socialisation certain attitudes towards words and their use which we use to make judgments about which forms of expression seem to us to be superior to others. Captured in these relationships is the significance allotted by formally educated social groups to academic culture, the social institutions set up to transmit it and the language judged to be necessary for that transmission. The theory of 'the lexical bar' (Corson, 1985b) examines only one aspect of these issues: the mediating place in educational success and failure of the high status vocabulary of the English language.

The lexical bar points to the educational significance of having a high-status vocabulary whose possession and use confers sociocultural prestige on those who know the appropriate place and manner in which to use it. In English, coincidences of social and linguistic history have combined to create a lexical situation that is unique among languages: most of the specialist and high status terminology of English is Graeco-Latin in origin and most of its less abstract terminology is Anglo-Saxon in origin. English in this respect, relative to other languages, has a fairly clear boundary drawn between its everyday and its high status vocabularies. Although the etymology of the language does not 'cause' the lexical bar in English, it does offer us a means for recognising this bar which is not as clear-cut in other languages. Because the children of certain social groups in their final stages of schooling have unequal active access to high status words and because teachers and schools make judgments about their students' grasp of the culture using for much of their evidence the students' performances in language, we can say that specialist word usage stands as an important mediating factor between social group background and educational success or failure.

We find strong support in these studies for Bourdieu's theories: because educational selection processes are based upon a long-term display of access to that form of cultural capital which is the high status lexicon of the language (partly on the reasonable grounds that a display of this kind indicates possession of a conceptual framework steeped in the high status aspects of the culture) the bar serves to reproduce different attainment rates in education for children socialised into the language norms of different groups. In this way the influence in the culture of conventionally dominant groups is reinforced. But one's access to and use of vocabulary is only one of the discriminatory factors. As I point out below, there are many other forms of cultural capital whose possession discriminates between groups on grounds that are related to ethnicity, gender, class background and more general aspects of language code.

There are points of criticism that can be brought against Bourdieu's theories (for a fuller critique see Thompson, 1984) and these need to be considered by those taking his ideas further. For an applied field such as language planning in schools there is one outstanding difficulty in Bourdieu's ideas which is very illuminating. This concerns striking a balance between a view of language which sees it as 'socially' valuable on the one hand, and a view of language which sees it as 'intellectually' valuable on the other. In his approach to language Bourdieu over-emphasises the form or the style of language used (i.e. its social value) at the expense of considering the content that language can be used to express (i.e. its intellectual utility); he seems (unwisely) to dismiss the idea that linguistic expressions might have any force other than the power derived from the authority of the social institution in which the language is used.

It is true that specialist words, for example, by definition fill up those areas of thought which are the most difficult, the most abstract and which for these and other reasons attract high regard within the culture. But probably the most important reason these areas of thought and the words used to express them attract high status in the first place is because people from a diverse range of ideological backgrounds over the centuries have recognised their importance: they give access to meanings which allow us to advance the course of civilisation, to criticise and improve it, and to advance considerations of justice and equity and other humanitarian concerns that are so much at the heart of Bourdieu's own theorising. Indeed without these high status areas of thought and their attendant language, Bourdieu's theorising itself might not exist; certainly his theory would not have an adequate form of language for expressing its own existence.

My point here is that while schools need to consider these ideological concerns very carefully, in order to decide the most equitable approach that they can adopt in making judgments about language, schools are not inevitably the willing dupes of power forces that are outside their control. Schools through their language policies can do much to end the injustices by widening children's mastery over their own language. Let me make the points clearly:

—teachers are right to use their students' language as some sort of evidence about their thinking processes but they are wrong to think that oral and written language is the only evidence available to them or that it is never misleading evidence;

—teachers are right when they teach some forms and styles of language in the belief that they give access to meanings and uses that are very important for children to have;

—teachers are also right when they teach some forms of language in the belief that those forms of language are non-arbitrarily (i.e. neutrally) important for the cultures and societies that the children inhabit and for the species that they are a part of.

Teachers and schools can strike a balance in their thinking in this area: between valuing the language of the children's home cultures on the one hand (by not forcibly separating the children from their language origins) and on the other acknowledging that children need to be equipped with the wherewithal to live within, derive benefit from, contribute to and criticise a civilisation which, for all its faults, is infinitely better than no civilisation.

There is a related practical point about the short-term goals for their graduates that schools always have to make and face: an unrestrained access to communicative and analytic competence in the culture's language, in all its forms and functions, is the major part of the knowledge that gives children power over their own affairs and an influence in their society. Obviously schools cannot compensate for injustices in the wider society. I address this point more fully below. But nor can schools postpone acting on children's educational needs until reforms occur outside schools to reduce social inequalities. They must do the best they can within that status quo, but they must do this while equipping their graduates with the critical skills needed to change and improve that status quo. What has been suggested in some areas is the need for children in schools to acquire critical language awareness.

Critical Language Awareness

A starting point in being constructively critical about anything is to admit that as human beings we can never be completely objective about complex matters. When we tell ourselves that we are managing to be neutral about things we often run the risk of reinforcing prejudices and errors in our judgments of what we see. 'Critical Language Awareness' takes this claim as its starting point: it denies the possibility that we can be absolutely objective in making judgments about complex language matters. It is very different from the rather descriptive approach to 'knowledge about language' that was discussed in Chapter 5 and which is known as 'Language Awareness': most language awareness activities employ an approach to 'language' that accepts the descriptive account of language as a given; it takes norms of language behaviour that have been established in conventions of use over time and assumes those norms to be unproblematic and uncontested. Critical language awareness goes beyond this approach and these assumptions. This 'critical language study', as it has so far been developed (CLSL, 1987), works from ten theoretical claims summarised below:

(1) Critical language study tries to explain and not just describe the discourse of a society;
(2) Socially dominant forces have the power to shape the conventions that underlie discourse just as much as any other social practices;
(3) Conventions of language and discourse tend to be 'naturalised' (they are accepted as unproblematic givens);
(4) Conventions of language (i.e. rules of use) receive their value according to the positions of their users in systems of power relations;
(5) Different conventions embody different ideologies;

(6) Critical language study needs an historical orientation to link it with the past events that structure language and determine its forms and the future effects that its present structures might have;

(7) Discourse is determined by its conventions but it is also a voluntary and creative activity that allows its users to reflect on its conventions;

(8) Discourse is both socially determined and creative;

(9) Discourse is itself a site and practice of struggle;

(10) Critical language study is a resource for developing the consciousness and self-consciousness of dominated people.

If schools and teachers are to implement 'critical language study' a good starting point would be to implement a more critical approach to the exercise of discourse in their own institutional practices. The methods for doing this are already outlined in Chapter 4: constructing effective school policies depends to a large extent on developing an ideal speech situation out of which the policies can emerge. But in this section I am discussing a critical activity made available to children that is itself twice removed from policy construction. Firstly it may require, as I am suggesting, a policy that itself emerges out of a critical use of professional discourse. Secondly it may also require individual teachers to adopt a more critical approach to their teaching practice, especially as it relates to the use of language and discourse. None of this can happen in a vacuum since emancipatory discourse of this kind presupposes a commitment at every institutional level to uncovering and explaining the conventions of discourse that obtain. Part of an LPAC might be to lift the lid a little on discourse practices that tend to oppress or exclude people and to suggest how they might be modified to reduce the oppression that they cause. Another part of an LPAC might signal how teachers can alert students to oppressive conventions of language. For example, by discussing the frequently pretentious use of high status Graeco-Latin words in school discourse teachers might encourage students to transcend in their own language an affected use of these words and to think less about impressing with their language and more about communicating their true meanings.

The approach to critical language awareness identifies three major categories of issues (CLSL, 1987):

(1) Promoting social awareness of discourse. The kinds of work that children in schools might do include: examining why access to certain types of discourse is restricted; examining how imbalances in access determine the individual's power over affairs and self

(e.g. between teacher and student, doctor and patient, judge and witness etc).

(2) Promoting critical awareness of variety: examining why some languages and varieties are different in status from others and are valued differently in different settings; examining the historical events that have produced different valuations of language varieties; examining the effects that devaluing a language variety has upon its users.

(3) Promoting consciousness of and practice for change: examining how social struggles and changes in power relations can change language; examining the potential for change and the constraints on change in current societies; examining how purposeful improvements can be brought about.

A sophisticated language policy in a school would address these points directly; they are fundamental to the intellectually liberating and critical activities that schools need to provide and which are dear to the hearts of many teachers. For a start these points would certainly provide good discussion openers in staff development work. If teachers in general were persuaded of their place and value, the next step would be discussion about incorporating them in some way in an LPAC. A school policy that offered children access to this kind of language awareness and which was assented to and followed by all teachers would go much of the way towards providing a vehicle for protecting the language rights of individuals: Article 19 of the 'Universal Declaration of Human Rights' asserts this as 'the right to communicate'.

Bilingualism and Social Justice

It is clear that language is a social justice issue yet we need to acknowledge that language is only one of the components that go to make up a person's 'cultural capital': other socially prestigious aspects of capital may be more powerful than purely linguistic factors in creating stereotypes by which people are judged and in influencing school achievement. Indeed purely linguistic factors, such as the possession of the dominant language or some variant of it, may be simply second or third order reflections of the social and cultural contexts of schooling (Troike, 1981; 1984). Discussion in Chapter 3 points to the harmful effect that stereotypes seem to have in providing the content of social categories: they influence the way we process information; they create expectancies about others; and they create self-fulfilling prophecies. Prejudices and stereotypes, then, affect the life chances of all groups when those groups are obviously different in some way from dominant groups. Clearly it is a duty of the school to try to minimise the impact of those prejudices and stereotypes wherever they might distort just arrangements for education. But this act of separating discriminatory judgments about people, from judgments that we may feel we have good reasons for holding, is not always a straightforward matter, since discrimination varies not just between peoples but also across contexts. Troike instances the case of Finnish immigrants to Sweden who as a group are viewed rather negatively there since they are seen as the inhabitants of a former Swedish 'colony', while in Australia Finnish immigrants have a relatively prestigious place among immigrants which comes about because they are perceived as 'Scandinavians' with all the positive attributes that that label connotes. The important point to note from this is that in Swedish schools the Finns do poorly as a group; in Australian schools they do rather well.

The complexity of these matters is increased by the frequent interaction of aspects of social class, ethnicity and language. For example, school achievement in the southwest and west of the United States is clearly stratified, with Blacks as a group at the bottom, Hispanics in the middle, and Anglo-Americans at the top. Yet while the Blacks are native speakers of English and the Hispanics have usually gone through a programme of subtractive bilingualism that might not augur well for their educational achievement relative to native speakers of English, like Black Americans, it is the Hispanics who achieve better as a group in schools. In my research (1985b) in Australia's most cosmopolitan city, immigrant children (Italian, Portuguese and Macedonian) from low-income backgrounds, who had learned their English in school as a second language, out-performed their Anglo-Australian classmates from equally low-income backgrounds on a battery of language instruments and in school achievement examinations, even though the latter spoke English as their mother tongue and were matched in non-verbal reasoning ability with the former. In Canada, across all socio-economic categories, groups of Canadian born children from immigrant language backgrounds (Italian, Chinese, Ukrainian and German) outperform groups of children whose mother tongue was English (Cummins, 1984a). Clearly in all these cases there are other variables in the equation which may or may not have much to do with language: on the one hand both the Hispanic and the immigrant Australian and Canadian children had rich experiences in two languages, a contact denied to their monolingual peers and this might give real advantages; on the other hand Blacks as a group in parts of the United

States are the victims of racial discrimination in almost every social context, not least in schools, and this could outweigh language strengths that they might have relative to Hispanics. Teacher attitudes towards a particular group coupled with other forms of discrimination may raise or depress academic achievement in ways that can modify many of the linguistic advantages or disadvantages that children might possess.

Horvath (1980) argues that it is issues of social justice and the value of cultural diversity that motivate the introduction of bilingual education. It is usually aimed at the needs of the socio- economically disadvantaged. Yet even in bilingual programmes, as we have seen in Chapter 7, there is the real possibility of a disguised form of social injustice occurring: when instead of a 'maintenance' approach to bilingual schooling, which sets out to use both languages as media of instruction for much of the school career (additive bilingual education), a 'transitional' approach to bilingual schooling is substituted (subtractive bilingual education). The important social justice issue in these two approaches is clearer if we remember that the United States Office of Civil Rights supported the maintenance approach (on grounds of social justice) while the United States Office of Education supported the transitional approach (on grounds of educational efficiency and economy). For pedagogical reasons I have already argued in Chapter 7 that 'subtractive (transitional) bilingual education' is not an alternative that should be available in modern schools, even though it is the approach that is most commonly found. Baetens Beardsmore (1986) adds another reason: in additive bilingual programmes teachers are bilingual themselves, even though they may use only one language, and they act positively towards both cultures in the environment; in transitional programmes the teachers are usually monolingual and are often unwittingly hostile to the bilingual element in the child's make-up. The discussion that follows deals with criticisms of 'additive bilingual education'.

Bilingual Education: A Critique

In many places, on pedagogical grounds and for social justice reasons, this book has advocated the cause of 'additive bilingualism' for children from minority first language backgrounds. I begin this section by presenting the other side of the case. There is a range of respected opinion in favour of transitional second language programmes that needs to be investigated and considered. My airing of that opinion here does not necessarily imply agreement with it.

Ethnic group identity and language as group symbol

Resolving a social justice debate about minority language rights depends heavily on the position one adopts on the link between ethnic group identity and language. Although research does suggest that ethnic group members identify more closely with those who share their language than with those who merely share their cultural background (Giles *et al.*, 1973), the matter is less clear-cut than this finding might imply. J. Edwards (1988) tries to see the link between language and ethnic identity more clearly. After wide reflection he concludes that the survival of ethnic identity does not depend on the preservation of an ethnic group's language, at least not on its preservation in any ordinary communicative form. His points are consistent with Lieberson's (1970) study of the language situation of ethnic groups in Canada: Lieberson found many instances of ethnic groups with distinct languages and also many instances of distinct ethnic groups sharing a common language. He concluded with the obvious point that ethnic differences do not always find parallels in linguistic differences.

Although language is a highly visible marker and a central component of ethnic identity which closely unites communication and sentiment, this is not enough to justify supporting minority languages that are on the edge of extinction. If a language is at risk and language shift is under way, this is because of factors that are outside language, such as contact between groups and economic influences: language shift is a symptom of that contact not its cause. There are many factors at work here and generalisations made can be very wide of the mark. Our knowledge is not great enough at this time to be able to integrate all of the evidence into any single explanatory framework. For example, in the pluralist Australian context Smolicz (1979) finds Polish and Greek immigrants maintaining their original language while in contrast Dutch immigrants tend to lose their language by the second generation. He explains this by pointing to language as one of the 'core values' that unite Poles or Greeks, while language for the Dutch is not as central a factor in that cultural group's cohesion and identity. This may provide one answer. On the other hand McNamara (1987) finds that rates of language loss, similar to the Dutch, occur among Israelis living in Australia, but he suggests other reasons for this: by the second generation wider changes in social identity for the Israeli-Australians accompany and account for their major language shift towards English.

Yet another matter is the symbolic value of languages. By ignoring the distinction between the communicative and the symbolic importance of language, social policy makers may make proposals that are quite unsuited to the real problems that they have to face. For example, in Ireland few people who do not speak Erse as their mother tongue bother to learn it proficiently, yet the language still has a widespread symbolic value and group-marker status. A contrasting example is to be found among the Maori of New Zealand, as among the Navajo of the United States and other cultural groups elsewhere. While these groups' languages have a central and unavoidable symbolic value for all those who identify themselves as Maori or Navajo, they also have a level of communicative importance which extends far beyond ceremonial use. Maori and Navajo will inevitably survive as languages as long as there are surviving members of the cultures that embed them.

J. Edwards sees better grounds in general for supporting transitional over maintenance education and his case for this is a strong one if we allow him to argue as he does from an all-society or utilitarian point of view. He argues that because maintenance involves a direct administrative promotion of identity retention, it cannot work because this is something that outside intervention cannot affect. He also claims that there is little evidence that such intervention is actively supported by large segments of populations, either majority or minority. Instead Edwards suggests that schools should provide atmospheres that are tolerant of groupness, reflective of heterogeneity and also multicultural but only to the extent that all good education is multicultural. More active intervention on behalf of minority identity may be undesirable and impractical. In the matter of languages that are at risk, on the evidence intervention is not a practical exercise since it involves a 'wholesale reworking of history' and a 'broad reweaving of the social fabric' (p. 210). There is much to consider in this argument: schools planning a policy response to their community's language problems, without the guidance of some national policy on bilingual education, may need to make judgments on values issues that cannot be resolved without a reliable census of community opinion. Even then there are other factors that will affect what schools can reasonably try to do.

For the sake of argument let us assume that additive bilingualism is a possible alternative for a school or a school system to adopt. How might its strengths and weaknesses as an educational policy be measured? Baker (1988) offers seven points that are sometimes presented as major criticisms of additive bilingual education, at least of the approaches to it that are practised in Canada and considered for export to other countries. Below I summarise these criticisms and comment on their relevance to the debate on bilingual education:

(1) *Immersion bilingual education for majority language pupils is different from immersion bilingual education for minority language pupils:* This is not so much a criticism as a statement of fact. In examining the evidence from bilingual programmes, schools do need to avoid making the category error of applying the findings from the one kind of programme to parallel practices in the other. Creating bilinguals out of majority monolinguals is not of direct relevance to minority students who begin school either as bilinguals or as minority language monolinguals. The discussion in Chapter 7 which presents the two types of programme in rigorously separate sections may help.

(2) *The social, political, cultural, economic and educational differences that exist between countries make it impossible to export a model for bilingual immersion education from one national setting to another:* This is a warning that advocates of new bilingual education programmes need to reflect on and to take note of. It offers a good reason for them to pause and reflect on their own social context. They should then press ahead with bilingual schooling arrangements that are suited to the sociocultural context that they are in.

(3) *Many factors determine the success or failure of bilingual programmes including parental cooperation, positive pupil motivation, the social background of pupils, the status of minorities in society and pupil self-esteem:* This too is not so much a criticism but an observation about the context of bilingual programmes. A fully developed, negotiated and trialled LPAC for a school will go much of the way towards removing this difficulty.

(4) *Cultural pluralism is often seen as an outcome of bilingual education that is positive, but pluralism can increase inequality, divisiveness and fragmentation:* This too is not a criticism of bilingual education itself. Rather 'cultural pluralism' is one of the justifications that some offer in support of bilingual education. I return to this point below.

(5) *Much of the research on bilingual education has been carried out by people who have interests in seeing results produced that are favourable to the cause of a bilingual form of education; people's support or criticism of bilingual education is influenced by their ideological presuppositions:* This too is not a criticism of bilingual education but it does properly question the objectivity of those claims that are made about it, in the same way as the claims of any social or educational innovation can be scrutinised on the 'cui bono'

principle. There are underlying political, social and cultural assumptions which do need prior and urgent consideration since there is much more to the business of bilingual education than just adding a language to the child's repertoire.

(6) *Support for bilingual education is mostly from academics:* If this situation ever existed it is changing. The greatest support for extending bilingual education within formal systems of schooling comes from minority groups themselves, such as the western Indian bands of Canada, the Maori (but not the Samoans) in New Zealand, Australian Aborigines in the Northern Territory, Welsh speakers in Wales, and some Hispanic communities in the United States. This development is occurring often in spite of the lukewarm support that the various causes receive from the majority of academics in the respective countries.

(7) *Assimilation into a mainstream society can be attractive and sought after by groups and individuals; rather than being the result of coercion it may be chosen by many in preference to the separation that is implied by belonging to bilingual communities:* This is a major policy issue for schools to confront since it is clear that there are differences between minority groups and between individuals within them in their willingness to maintain the separate cultural identity that can come with being bilingual. Perhaps those minority groups and individuals, who are not well disposed towards the preservation of their language links, are not as aware as others of the advantages that might come with bilingual education or perhaps they rate this matter more lowly in their scale of values or perhaps they see it as a community rather than a school responsibility. As mentioned already, the maintenance of the minority mother tongue is said by many to develop a desirable form of cultural diversity in societies, to promote ethnic identity, to lead to social adaptability, to add to the psychological security of the child; and to develop linguistic awareness (Crystal, 1987). On the other hand, as point (4) above suggests, full bilingualism in a society can lead to social instability. Permanent social divisions can arise and a narrowness of outlook can replace the cultural awareness that was an orignal aim, especially if social institutions like churches and clubs, which have an inevitable ideological purpose, reinforce this narrowness.

Chapter 2 mentioned that form of socially discriminatory diglossia which exists when there is unequal social esteem between two forms of the same language or two different languages, an inequality that can affect the respective users' access to power and privilege in their societies. It is sometimes found even in a relatively uniform bilingual society like Paraguay, where most people speak both languages, that there are clear disparities of esteem between the two languages. This is a possible consequence wherever two languages co-exist, since in most bilingual societies only one of the groups in contact usually feels the need to learn the language of the other. Any inequities in this diglossic situation are worsened if most of the users of the one language remain in an inferior economic and political position. But is this likely to happen?

What is becoming clearer, on the scanty evidence from those countries where additive bilingual education for minority peoples is gaining respect, is that the community of minority tongue users themselves can begin to rise in esteem and in political influence along with the rebirth or strengthening of their language. This is a complex phenomenon and there is no simple cause-and-effect relationship between, on the one hand, increasing levels of bilingualism and, on the other, an increased social standing for the minority language's users. But where the minority community itself is in charge of the schooling process the entire pro-gramme of schooling is directed towards elevating the status of the community and questioning the role of schooling in that process. Language questions become subsumed under much more important issues, among which language is only an all-pervading and sometimes distracting factor (Garcia & Otheguy, 1987). When minority language maintenance is initiated in a community, the minority members of that community become the experts: they are the advisers and real controllers of the bilingual education programme; their values shape the educational out-comes. Political mobilisation with real purpose can begin to occur. Community attitudes are laid bare and discussed. Local people receive formal training as teachers. Parents participate in the activities of the school to a greater degree and they acquire skills that were previously not their own. All of these things, and many more, contribute to the elevation of the minority group. Political consciousness awakens where perhaps previously there was none. And the language of the minority becomes available as a recognised political voice at the same time as their political will begins to assert itself.

It is likely that schools controlled and run by remote bureaucracies and staffed by teachers whose culture is not the culture of the local community get in the way of all this. When majority culture educators look at minority children they tend to focus on what those children lack and usually what they see is the absence of a high level proficiency in the majority language. This lack becomes the focus of the schooling that they offer those children. It is a commonplace for observers of educational reform to claim that policies of compensatory, multicultural and anti-racist education, imposed from afar, make little difference to educational inequality. These policies ignore the root causes of that inequality which is very often linked to an absence of bilingual provision within the curriculum of specific schools. Sometimes that bilingual provision can be aimed at mother tongue maintenance, sometimes at enhancing the cultural esteem of minority groups, sometimes at some combination of these aims. Only a local community can really decide what is necessary. When communities themselves are in charge of education, when they themselves have the respect and the dignity that goes with deciding the future of their offspring, they themselves come to see education in a much broader way. They begin to ask each other about the best way to educate their children and about what is wrong with the alternative processes of schooling that they are familiar with.

In some societies the cultural diversity that they contain is pointed to as a prized possession, as something to be celebrated. Even a country like Australia, which was on the surface staunchly monocultural and monolingual in the 1960s, has gone a long way within a generation towards reversing its social values on these matters. For many in societies like Australia it is the monocultural and monolingual people who are now seen as deprived. In these societies too the maintenance of minority and community languages is seen by many to reflect a future view of the society in which cultural pluralism and linguistic diversity can be used as statements about the nation's view of itself and the world. Elsewhere, on the other hand, and often in parts of the same countries, transition to the majority language is supported by the majority of people who have a vision of their society as a homogeneous and a united nation state. In between these two polarised views there are many other views, held by individuals and communities, often reflecting ethnocentric or xenophobic attitudes and often in stark opposition to the nation's official policies on these questions. Because these viewpoints reflect attitudes that are supported and stabilised by local groups and communities, only a local agency can really come to terms with addressing the community values that lie behind the relevant point of view. It is here where the school has a vital community education role, not merely in accommodating the values of its community to the school's practices, but also in modifying those values (where it can and where it needs to) in the broader interests of the community itself. Perhaps nowhere is the school better placed to modify community values than through the example it offers in dealing with matters of gender, language and education. Perhaps nowhere else is there a potential for widespread change that could be socially transforming.

Gender, Language and Education (by Jan McPherson)

In the last fifteen years, with the impetus of the Women's Movement, research interest in gender and language has grown considerably. This growth has been accompanied by the realisation that notions of language, gender, and the relationships between them are problematic. It has come to be generally accepted that 'gender' categories are based on ideas about what is to be regarded as appropriate male or female behaviour. These ideas change over time and place. There are no fixed social characteristics which are the sole prerogative of an individual according to their biological sex. Similarly, there are not distinct and different male and female languages which cannot be spoken by members of the opposite sex. However, it would seem that there are styles of language which are differentially accessible to, and valued by men and women. In this section I will try to disentangle some of the ideas about gender and language which I feel have relevance to schools and education. These ideas raise questions which should have implications for any language policy across the curriculum.

Talking about men and women

There is a considerable body of literature dealing with ways in which language has denigrated, excluded or made women invisible (see Thorne et al., 1983: 166–207, for a comprehensive, annotated bibliography). Efforts to change sexist language, both in schools and beyond have often been trivialised and ignored.

There are a number of ways in which teacher language and teaching materials contribute to the maintenance of sexist attitudes in educational institutions. It would be impractical to suggest that teachers could avoid all sexist material, however it is important that they are aware of sexist implications where they exist, and that these matters are not presented to students as neutral. Sexist attitudes may be reflected in:

Overt sexism: The use of sexist jokes, derogatory terms for women, verbal or physical touching, patronising attitudes and so on. Stanley (1977) found 220 terms describing sexually promiscuous women, but only 22 for sexually promiscuous men. This imbalance gives some clue to the extent of sexist attitudes in our culture, and an indication of how these are reflected in language.

Gender stereotypes: School materials often depict girls and women in passive roles, in unpaid work, or only in caring professions; men and boys on the other hand are seen in a wider variety of settings in which they are active participants, working in a variety of jobs. As an example Whyld (1983) cites an analysis of the Caldecott prize-winning books in the USA, which revealed that the only adult women depicted, apart from wives and mothers, were a fairy, a fairy godmother and an underwater maiden. Not one woman in the sample held a job. Such stereotypes often go unchallenged, and are reinforced in teacher–pupil interaction: 'Could I have two strong boys to help me carry this table?'.

He/man language: He/man language refers to the use of masculine words (e.g. 'he', 'his', 'man' etc.) to mean both males in a particular sense (e.g. 'man and wife'), and males and females (e.g. 'man overboard') in a generic sense. Attempts to change this sort of language have met with considerable resistance and derision, if not hostility. Work by Martyna (1978, 1983) indicates that the use of he/man language is not perceived neutrally, but in effect amounts to psychological exclusion: females find it much more difficult than males to imagine themselves members of groups referred to as 'he', or 'man'. A small number of males also resist identifying with human groups referred to in these discriminatory ways.

Ignoring women: Women are often made invisible by ignoring both their contributions to social life and their existence within it. In an analysis of children's schoolbooks, Graham (1973) found that male pronouns outnumbered female pronouns by almost four to one. But this was not primarily due to generic use: 97% of the uses of 'he' referred specifically to male humans or animals. We find that women are consistently absent from school materials as individuals and as groups (either actively or passively). For example, the 'famous names' approach to poetry, painting, medicine and so on frequently ignores the contributions of women in these areas, and also ignores the contributions that women have made in areas of lower prestige (e.g. embroidery, friendship, herbal medicine: See Whyld (1983)). The pervasive belief that it is necessary to 'keep the boys happy' by presenting stories with male protagonists, or covering subject areas which are likely to be of more interest to boys (and therefore represent more men and boys) also functions to exclude women and girls.

Talking in the classroom

Prior to the mid-seventies, most of the work on gender differences in classroom interaction stemmed from a concern with the comparatively poor performance of boys in elementary schools. In an overview of the research on teacher–student interaction, Brophy (1985) notes that critics alleged that schools were 'too feminine', and that female teachers were unable to meet the needs of boys. Since that time, concern has shifted with a recognition that girls' relatively high achievements in early schooling are not sustained in secondary classrooms, particularly in mathematics and science.

Some of the studies of classroom interaction have produced contradictory results. Kelly (1988) notes that while some authors claim that boys almost invariably receive preferential treatment in class, others suggest that such allegations are 'nothing more than the figments of feminist imagination' (p.1). Such inconsistencies may in part be due to changing patterns of gender interaction according to the age, social class and ethnicity of students, the level of schooling, the subject matter, the sex of the teacher, and the style of classroom organisation and interaction encouraged by teachers (e.g. teacher-centred versus pupil-centred). Despite some apparent contradictions in research findings there do appear to be general trends. Although these are not necessarily typical of all classroom settings, they may be of use in helping teachers become more alert to interaction patterns that might exist in their own classrooms.

Maltz & Borker (1982) suggest girls and boys seek to accomplish different aims through language. Girls use language to create and maintain close and equal relationships with others; to criticise others in an acceptable way; and to interpret the speech of other girls accurately. Boys on the other hand use language to assert their position of dominance; to attract and maintain an audience; and to assert themselves when others have the floor. These different styles are reflected in the dynamics of classroom discourse. Kelly (1988) undertook a review of literature concerning differences in teacher–pupil interaction. Her results indicate that:

—teachers consistently pay less attention to girls than boys (although this varies, it still occurs across all age groups, it occurs in various

socio-economic and ethnic groupings, across all subjects, and with both female and male teachers);
—girls get less of all kinds of classroom interaction (this discrepancy is most marked in behavioural criticism, but they also receive fewer instructional contacts, high-level questions, academic criticism and slightly less praise than boys);
—girls volunteer to answer questions as often as boys;
—girls are less likely to call answers out;
—these differences occur despite teachers' assertions that they do not treat, nor wish to treat girls and boys differently;
—teachers are often unaware of their differential treatment of girls and boys.

Brophy (1985) suggests that there is a need for 'thicker' descriptions of classroom events, with more attention to the qualitative nature of interactions. Swann & Graddol (1988) looked more closely at the ways in which turns at speaking were allocated, and the roles played by teachers, by quieter and by more talkative pupils in classroom interaction. They suggest that the distribution of talk in their studies derived from a collaboration between pupils and teacher. Underlying classroom transactions is a 'competitive dynamic' in which 'first in gets the floor' (p.60). Teachers' non-verbal cues, particularly gaze-attention was important in systematically offering boys more opportunities for participation, and cuing them to answer earlier, even when the floor was apparently open to all. Their description of one girl's strategy for remaining silent is revealing:

> Emma, the quietest pupil, often raises her hand and on playing the video for the first time we were puzzled as to why she was selected to speak so little. However, closer analysis of interchange openings suggested she was 'playing safe'. Emma tended to raise her hand just as the teacher's gaze turned towards the pupil she was about to select to speak. And with the teacher's ability to select the first hand (from an apparent flurry) Emma's manoeuvre must have required extreme sensitivity to the behaviour both of the teacher and other pupils. It seems to trade on the fact that the way of minimising the chances of being selected to speak in this class is to volunteer, but with careful timing (p. 59).

Research addressing gender inequalities has tended to ignore the implications of race and class in gender relations. There are a small but growing number of studies which try to redress this imbalance. Wright's (1987) study of relationships between teachers and Afro-Caribbean pupils in a British school indicated that there the experience of girls and boys was very similar. Both groups perceived themselves as being 'picked on' by teachers, and they did in fact receive a disproportionate amount of the teachers' time. Wright also draws attention to the fact that, while friendship patterns have generally found that pupils move in single-sex cliques, this was not true of the Afro-Caribbean students either inside or outside the classroom. Their common experience as Black pupils seemed more salient than differences due to gender. Jones (1988) also points out that a focus on gender inequalities may obscure power relations that exist between pupils of the same gender but of a different race or class. In studying classroom interaction within a single-sex girls' school in New Zealand, she found that working class Pacific Island girls were offered only limited, subordinate opportunities to participate in classroom talk. Middle class, Pakeha (European) girls received the bulk of the teachers' attention.

A number of studies indicate that teachers are unwilling to admit that they might treat girls and boys differently (e.g. Fennema & Peterson, 1985; Morse & Handley, 1985). Teachers claim that they respond to the behaviour of children as individuals, rather than as girls or boys. While this may be true, it is likely to consolidate rather than change interaction patterns in the classroom. There is also evidence that indicates that teachers may not notice gender inequalities in classroom interaction. This may be because male domination in societies is so normal that it is literally invisible. Imbalance in classroom 'air time' may be perceived as balance (Megarry, 1981).

Women and men talking

Overall there seem to be good reasons to suspect that girls and boys experience education differently. To extend our understanding of these differences it is necessary to consider schools within a wider theoretical perspective.

Challenging the stereotypes

Early accounts of ways in which women used language were based on intuitive judgments. Perhaps the most pervasive of these ideas was that women were supposed to be extremely talkative. Their use of vocabulary and sentence structure was reckoned to be relatively simple and limited, though with a tendency to hyperbole, and saturated with words that were sweet and chaste. It was thought that they were more inclined to break off their sentences without finishing them (because of lack of adequate thought before they opened their mouths). And finally their speech was considered to be shallow, lacking in both eloquence and soul (Jesperson, 1922; Coates, 1986).

Much of the early work in sociolinguistics, which attempted to take the study of language use beyond the realm of folk linguistics, looked at social class. It became obvious that other variables such as age, ethnicity, gender and social context were also important (e.g. Labov, 1972). Within the dominant traditions of this type of research a relationship between the speech of women and other disadvantaged groups was proposed. These approaches tended to regard the speech of any group that was not White, male, protestant and middle class, as a deviation from that norm. Women's language became defined as language that was not male (Threadgold, 1988).

The empirical findings of sociolinguistic research have challenged and refuted many stereotyped beliefs about women's language, but in some instances have produced new stereotypes of their own. An example is Lakoff's (1975) work on the use of question tags. She claimed that women use more question tags than men, and that this was a feature of the uncertainty and hesitancy that characterised their speech. Subsequent research has questioned both the generalisability of her findings and her interpretations. Women's and men's use of question tags vary in different contexts, and the question tags themselves may be interpreted as having several different functions (e.g. seeking to include another speaker, sustain interaction, demand agreement).

Overall research indicates that although men and women may speak differently in certain situations, there are very few specific differences which are generally applicable. However there appear to be three recurring differences:

—women talk less than men in cross-gender interactions;
—women and girls tend to choose standard, or 'correct' forms more often than males (e.g. Trudgill, 1974; Macaulay, 1977; Romaine, 1978);
—women use a wider range of pitch and more intonation than men (McConnell-Ginet, 1983).

Despite these findings stereotypes of women as talkative gossips whose chatter tends to lack coherence and consistency persist. This may in part be because our perceptions and interpretations of what is said are influenced by the sex of the speaker. For instance, the same baby's cry was interpreted as 'fear' when the child was believed to be female, and 'anger' when it was believed to be male (Condry & Condry, 1976). Spender (1980) suggests that the myth of women's talkativeness persists because:

> Women have not been judged on the grounds of whether they talk more than men, but whether they talk more than silent women . . . when women are supposed to be quiet, a talkative woman is one who talks at all (Spender: 1980: 42–43).

Feminist approaches

Rather than looking for differences in female/male language which are 'true' in every situation, more recent research has taken language as only one aspect of a wider social context. This means a fundamental shift in the way language is viewed. Language is seen as being 're-created' in transactional relationships between people in different situations, rather than having some sort of objective reality in itself. Meanings derive from the whole situation, rather than residing in specific linguistic forms and words. Thus there has been more focus on the styles or genres which women and men adopt in particular settings and with particular others. Much of this research has developed from feminists' concerns to explore ways in which unequal power relationships between men and women are mirrored and maintained in language. For example, P. Fishman (1983) found that in household conversations between male and female partners, women consistently have to work harder than men in maintaining the conversation. They ask more questions, support and encourage their partners contributions, do more 'maintenance' and 'continuation' work, but at the same time fail in many of their attempts at interaction because their partners do not respond. Fishman suggests that in this way men are able to control the content and rhythm of conversation. They talk only when and about what they want; they are able continually to 'establish and enforce their rights to define what the interaction and reality will be about' (P. Fishman, 1983: 100).

This type of research has been important in showing which genres are made accessible to women in varying contexts. Historically women have been excluded from public rhetoric and denied access to literacy, bureaucratic language and the written word. However this exclusion is not always blatant and research such as Fishman's has been important in showing how women often do not have the power to determine how language is created in interaction. There has been considerable recent work in this area, which has sought to show that women and men talk differently in both mixed and single sex groups. This work questions assumptions made about the relative 'powerlessness' of women's language. For example, while in the context of a mixed group a tendency to avoid interruption may lessen access to verbal participation, in an all-women's group this may be a feature of a less hierarchical, more collaborative approach to transaction. Supportive listening, sharing and sensitivity are only perceived as weak in situations in which they are contrasted with their opposites.

An outcome of this type of research has been an emphasis on 'difference'. It is often implied that in effect women and men speak different languages, with different meanings. Talk in all-women groups is described variously as: cooperative, communal, other-directed, supportive, sharing, personal, emotional, subjective, speculative, accepting of disorder. Men's talk on the other hand is typified as: gladiatorial, competitive, assertive, impersonal, orderly, logical, rational. It is important to note that not all 'male' attributes are necessarily valued as morally good, even while they tend to be valuable in terms of traditional (male) notions of power.

In using this idea of 'difference', some feminist approaches have emphasised the special nature of women, the richness of their own resources, culture, understandings and relationships. This celebration of women's qualities has been crucial in overturning the simple -/+ dichotomy that is often applied to female/male differences. However notions of difference are problematic on several counts:

—Concentrating on difference between women and men tends to obscure differences between women, who as a group are wrongly regarded as much more homogeneous than the dominant male group;
—There is a danger that difference will be seen as an attribute of the individual or group rather than as a part of the complex social situation within which gender differences are construed. Thus it might (wrongly) be felt that equality can be attained by changing the way that women speak (by encouraging them to become more assertive, use deeper voices: become more 'masculine'). This approach would fail to address the whole question of power and control; in essence it suggests that 'women can only aspire to be as good as a man, there is no point in trying to be as good as a woman' (Spender, 1984: 201).
—Within mainstream Western thought difference is understood to imply hierarchical opposition: good–evil; presence–absence; reason–emotion; male–female. In each pair qualities are viewed as

mutually exclusive; they are defined in terms of what the other is not. In addition they are not considered to be of equal value; the first member of each pair is accorded higher status.

The work of Derrida, and the subsequent work of French feminists such as Irigaray, Kristeva and Moi has been important in exposing the hegemonic assumptions implicit in notions of 'difference' which involve opposition and hierarchy (wherein 'female' is defined in terms of what is 'not male', with the lack of the phallus as central to this concept). In their view dominant 'phallocentric' discourse not only represses women's language but denies its existence and silences it (Threadgold, 1988; Hare-Mustin & Marecek, 1988). Difference, as hierarchical opposition, is destructive. However if difference is conceived of in terms of potentially valuable alternatives, which are not seen as mutually exclusive, then it offers opportunities for the creation of new meanings and new understandings of 'male' and 'female'.

In summary

These ideas have direct relevance to the ways in which we can understand schooling and education. In early attempts to change gender bias in schooling, the assumed goal was an 'untheorised equality' (Branson, 1988: 97). It was thought that if girls were given equal access to the whole curriculum, equal opportunity to participate in classroom interaction, equal encouragement and attention by teachers, and if textbooks and teacher language were ridded of their gender biases, then the results of schooling would be equitable in terms of post-school participation in the workforce and in tertiary education. Crudely put, this approach assumes that equality means treating girls 'as if' they were boys. It fails to question the whole structure of schooling. Schools are essentially 'male' institutions, that are shaped by 'male' values. The knowledge that is valued in schools is 'logocentric' (see below) and mechanistic, rather than aware of human, relational aspects of context; assessment is based on individual competition rather than on collaborative sharing; and classroom interaction favours those who are most adept at accessing and using 'male' genres. Branson (1988) holds that in such a setting girls are required to live a cultural lie, forced to compete in a male mode which stands in opposition to socially constructed notions of what it is to be female. Within education 'the sensitivities of women must be rediscovered, acknowledged, used and respected' (Branson, 1988: 105). The absence of the female from education impoverishes boys as well as girls by denying access to genres beyond the restricted and restricting 'male', thereby belittling and inhibiting their development as complete people. What is needed is an awareness of the ways in which educational curricula and practices devalue and ignore what is 'female', a willingness to challenge the current situation and the courage to attempt change.

Language and Knowledge

Describing education as 'logocentric' raises two of the key issues in the 'language and knowledge' debate: to what extent is one's knowledge of language an indication of one's knowledge; and to what extent can all of one's knowledge be put into language? Plainly if as was argued in Chapter 5 schooling is based almost entirely on 'knowledge displayed' in some or other language mode, then education *is* tilted towards the logocentric. Does this mean that other important forms of knowledge, that are ineffable, have little place in conventional education? In the last section Jan McPherson suggests that the bias of schools towards the logocentric is a problem that needs to be addressed if they are to become fairer places for boys and girls (and better places generally). But this bias of schools towards the logocentric has other discriminatory effects, especially for the members of cultures which view the role of language in knowledge and learning rather differently.

For schools in pluralist communities the importance of thinking carefully about the link between language and knowledge cannot be overstated. Modern education is largely founded upon the belief that 'knowledge displayed through language' is a measure of knowledge of the culture. Most of our assessment techniques assume the accuracy of this claim. But this view is directly challenged in some cultures where language knowledge, of the kind that is valued in academic settings, does not approach a full representation of all the knowledge deemed to be important in the culture. Maori and other Polynesian cultures offer examples of this (Bray & Hill, 1973). Traditionally Polynesians see knowledge as sacred, tribal and private to those within the community in which it develops; this contrasts with the secular, universally shared and communicable knowledge that academic institutions place value on transmitting. There are weighty implications in this for education in countries with traditional minorities, especially since Western education is largely concerned with content knowledge rather than process knowledge, while in traditional societies informal pedagogy often has quite the reverse emphasis. The Maori educator below makes suggestions for changes in the education of all children in a pluralist society if that education is to present curricular knowledge about all the cultures that it contains:

> The Maori knowledge which gets into schools in the future must have the authenticity of Maori sources of inspiration to give it the authority it needs and deserves . . . Structures must be created so that Maori people, their perceptions and their understandings of their experience, can contribute fully to the education of all citizens in New Zealand (Penetito, 1988: 26).

The role of language in this Maori knowledge is to provide the means by which things are done; essentially it must always be Maori language for these things to be 'done'. Quite simply for the Maori *te taonga nui a te tangata ko tana reo* ('language is the greatest gift') from which all else follows. More than this, in any traditional culture language almost always preserves levels of perlocutionary force that cannot be separated from the context in which the language is used. Even the meanings of words and phrases cannot be properly understood or translated in isolation from some context or other. In Australia and North America, too, aboriginal people have views on these matters which may suggest modifications to the logocentric emphasis that is followed in conventional schooling. Rigsby confirms this point in relation to Australian Aborigines:

> Aboriginal people generally do not consider knowledge (including language) to be available to any and all. Rather its distribution and sharing are dependent upon social dimensions of kinship, age, sex, and other variables, including power and personal politics (cited in Senate Standing Committee, 1984: 92).

While this degree of contrast with Western views about knowledge may not be common among minorities in most countries, there are still many school pupils in most countries who come from cultural backgrounds that are very different in the kinds of 'realisation of knowledge' that their culture allows them. Language may be used very differently or not at all, on some occasions, to demonstrate proficiency.

The very different forms of socialisation received by children before formal schooling and outside the school itself can produce pronounced differences in the kinds of knowledge that the same children can or want to display, especially children in the early years of schooling or those who are new arrivals in a culture. Discussion in Chapter 2 indicated that minority children can come to school knowing very different kinds of things; they have very different 'interpretative repertoires' that they impose on the world. When they confront the assessment methods that teachers use, it is often the case that they are asked to display knowledge about 'x,y' when what they really know about is 'y,z'. A problem for them can be that in conventional schools they are never asked to display knowledge about 'y,z'. A further problem is that they are often asked to display their knowledge in unfamiliar ways. Again we can use the example of Polynesian children who tend to be more 'oral and aural' oriented in their dealings with the world, while the educational system that they encounter is primarily 'visual' with its heavy emphasis on literacy and its relatively few opportunities for regular peer and group interaction built into the school system from the outset. Seeing the world from the minority culture's point of view is an acquisition that teachers of children from different cultural backgrounds need to possess and allow for. The culture of the child needs to be in the mind of the teacher.

School language policies will take issues such as these into account if they are going to respond sensitively to student and cultural diversity. Differential treatment of minority background children may be required, not to produce educational inequality but to guard against it.

Differential Treatment

In their treatment of children from minority or new settler cultures, teachers are not always sensitive to the impact that being raised in another culture can have on a child being educated within a second culture. As well as the obvious difference of a communicative competence in another language, which cannot be ignored by teachers, there will be other more subtle factors that call for different responses if fair treatment is to be extended to all children. Culturally different children may have:

—memories of another language environment where modes of interaction between people of different ages and status are very unlike our own modes of interaction;
—experiences of a different cultural approach to schooling, where classroom roles and relationships between teacher and student and between student and student are not the same;
—a system of values and personal perceptions of the world that are intricately linked with the other culture, whose possession and use cannot be easily changed in response to the teacher saying that

change is necessary;
—private experiences of family life, schooling, travel, dislocation, war
and violence that may be ineffable but which colour the present;
—different expectations of what constitutes academic success, social
recognition, and claims to leadership;
— a radically different way of looking at life in their new land.

These factors can combine to affect the kind of 'participation' in schooling that is available to culturally different children. Participation in schooling has much to do with the quality of the relationship between students and the degree to which the school curriculum, organisation and climate for learning accords with their experiences, values, interests and aspirations. Schools in English-speaking societies, for example, often place greater emphasis than schools elsewhere on competitive and individualised school performance. This is disabling to those many students who come from class or gender groups and cultural backgrounds where competition between individuals is neither prized nor cultivated, but where there is a positive emphasis on informality, egalitarian behaviour and group activities.

In trying to understand the sense in which I am using 'participation' here, there may be value in two concepts introduced by Ralph Dahrendorf in his book *Life Chances* (1978). He speaks of 'options' and 'ligatures' as the two distinguishing kinds of 'life chances' that societies offer to their members. If we are thinking in this instance about 'education within societies', *options* in education are the range of choices that people receive as a result of their education; the wider the range of options, the greater are the life chances that individuals are deemed to possess. On the other hand, *ligatures* are life chances of a very different kind: these are the bonds between people that are established as a result of their membership in society or their participation in that society's education. The 'Harvard Project on Human Potential' takes up these ideas from Dahrendorf. It offers the example of some groups of Third World women, who seem poor in options and rich in ligatures; but because ligatures provide some of the most important benefits in life, namely, support, structure and motivation and a sense of respect and continuity, it is altogether likely that women in some Third World settings, who have few options, experience their lives as highly satisfying even though Western observers would not agree (Levine & White, 1986).

Among some cultural and social groups ligatures are seen as positive ends in themselves to be cultivated as a goal in life, and not as the instruments to other ends that cynical Westerners sometimes hold them to be. Among the Maori people of New Zealand, for example, even in the midst of the rich options that their country extends to its citizens, it is the ligatures that mean much more, even when that valuing of ligatures leads to a reduction in options. Those few educationists who see the development of ligatures as an important aim for schools often stress the use of community languages, for example, as a means of extending bonds between students; a stress on 'language' of any kind, across the curriculum, increases the ligatures between students while also enhancing their options.

It is a matter of observation that most Western education systems are strong in providing students with options, but weak in providing them with ligatures. In Australasia, Britain and North America many of the clients of contemporary education come from ethnic communities where ligatures are prized. For some, such as the thousands of immigrant 'boat people' from South East Asia, ligatures of one kind or another may be all that remain to them. For others, such as Aboriginal Australians and American Indians, there is a cultural continuity reinforcing the preservation of ligatures that remains largely outside the understanding of their fellow countrymen. It seems a very fitting thing that a language policy should draw explicit attention to this important distinction between options and ligatures and its educational implications.

But current policies in OECD countries favouring differential treatment are new phenomena which go against the grain of traditional nineteenth century monolingual education and the training and philosophies of many teachers. There is a wealth of historical precedent to overcome in many countries: In Britain the 1870 Education Act eliminated minority language schooling in Wales for almost a century; in France, the United States and Germany the use of a single language became linked to nationalistic aspirations and to the development of a modern state; in Australia the myth that the country was culturally homogeneous grew from the commonly held but false belief that national unity somehow depends on having cultural unity. Teachers as individuals are very often progressive in their ideas and practices, but as a group they too can be among the more conservative and even reactionary forces in a society. Churchill (1986) makes the point that schoolroom practices are perhaps the most effectively resistant form of educational language policy: the views and assumptions of classroom teachers form an invisible framework that structures policy discussion and creates a *de facto* language policy.

Returning to Churchill's typology of problem definitions, presented in Chapter 6, we see that the problem definitions in his *Stages 1* to *4* all advance the view that the minority should seek the same social outcomes and educational objectives as the majority. In contrast *Stages* 5 and 6 involve differential objectives and outcomes, of a relatively minor enrichment kind for *Stage 5* (enhanced private use of the minority language and the cultural esteem associated with it) and of a relatively major kind for *Stage 6* (participation in a minority culture which has an equal status in the society with the majority culture). Only in these later Stages is there any necessary abandoning of the values of a monolingual society; only in these later stages too is there a recognition of the value of 'additive bilingual education' rather than the reverse value.

Each of the Stages depends for its successful implementation on the support and expertise of practitioners, notably those in contact with minority group children. More to the point, the greatest degree of adaptation is required in practitioners: if implementation is to be successful teachers need to be more advanced in their thinking and more sophisticated in their values in relation to the context than policy makers at the system level usually can be. There is a need then for social distance to be reduced between policy makers and practitioners if equitable arrangements are to be put into operation. This need can be met in two ways: through widespread and close collaboration between people at system level and people at institutional level; or through the teachers themselves becoming the policy makers. 'In the context of the contemporary nation state' say LeVine and White 'neither official policy nor grassroots voluntarism alone can be relied upon to realize desired potentials; they must work together convergently and synergistically' (1986: 217). Culture becomes a critical term in all this: policy makers and implementers need to share cultural models of life, education and social performance if the possibilities for their collaboration are to be enhanced. Problems can then be explained and understood; small-scale and tentative solutions can be tried out; and some hope of mutual adaptation can be envisaged. Better still is when working policy documents are produced by those who have to implement them, as is the case in a school language policy across the curriculum.

As important too is Cazden's observation (1988) that indigenous teaching staff are a most necessary resource in providing differential treatment. As a small example, there is evidence that teachers from different cultural backgrounds have different techniques for praising and sanctioning students. Erickson (cited in Nemetz Robinson, 1985) contrasts the 'private praise', given by a Latino teacher to a pupil, with the public praise that an Anglo teacher gives. In the former, the teacher's private praise is manifested through a gentle smile, a simultaneous touching of the child's shoulder and a positive head movement; in the latter, the teacher's public praise is loud and enthusiastic so that the whole class can hear. It is likely that children who are culturally different will respond better to different ways of praising and sanctioning their efforts. At the same time the manner in which the Latino teacher in this case showed approval might be a more satisfactory pedagogical model for teachers in general to adopt.

Cazden also presents complementary perspectives on the adaptive action that occurs in schools in the face of cultural differences: the 'cultural difference' perspective asks (as I have been doing so far in this section) that teachers take differences more into account than they do; the 'differential treatment' perspective warns that present differential approaches to pedagogy actually increase inequalities in knowledge and skills that are present when students start school. For instance, in the area of 'beginning reading' much research has been done on the effects of differential approaches to pedagogy: as an example, the way that reading instruction methods are differentiated between high-group and lower group children may actually increase inequalities. In this and a range of areas the problem of 'unintended teacher bias' seems to be at the heart of the issue. Probably Bernstein's advice that 'the culture of the child must first be in the consciousness of the teacher' is one of the places for us to begin in mitigating this bias.

Other factors in schools discriminate against children in ways that may not be linked directly to specific class, culture or gender factors. Some children outside schools experience modes of communication which compensate for what is increasingly regarded as the very poor communicative model offered by conventional approaches to pedagogy. Other children, often but not necessarily from low-income family backgrounds, do not experience these modes of communication outside schools and their disadvantages are reinforced by the school. R. Young (1983) talks about schools suffering from a 'communication deficit'. In Chapter 5 this topic was linked to extending pupils' language awareness through teachers being more conscious about their display of metacognitive skills. But as Young points out there is a limit to what can be achieved by yet another form of compensatory education of this kind. Instead he suggests that something might be done by changing the communicative practices and contexts of schools generally to reduce their emphasis on one-sided verbal and decontextualised learning. He advocates more explicit reflexivity in classroom talk which means changing the dominant pattern. The persistence of this pattern may stem from the belief that it solves certain basic problems of control which teachers and schools struggle with, problems which translate into a poor communication pattern and in turn produce educational disadvantages for some groups of pupils. Elsewhere Young (1989) addresses these problems more forthrightly and in detail. His proposals are not desperate ones: there is much that schools can do which they are not presently doing. At the same time there is a limit to how much schools can 'compensate for society'.

Language Education as Compensation for Society

While language can provide a mirror of a society, language itself is not a cause of social injustice or disadvantage. To change language behaviour other things outside language need to be altered. As J. Edwards (1988: 206) notes in relation to language problems in societies, there can be 'too much emphasis upon what schools alone can do, given that their efforts are often dwarfed by social pressures outside their gates'. Cazden (1988: 198) sees the context of the classroom as the base of a hierarchy of contexts, reaching from a level which is closest to speech acts in schools to the more distant: 'classroom, school, school system, community, and so on; and the classroom context is never wholly of the participant's making'. She warns that 'those who help to shape the contexts that surround the classroom have to realize their responsibility as well'. Bullivant (1981) also addresses this issue when he expresses concern that the transmission of the school's essential common elements could be weakened if it attempts too much on its own: for Bullivant what minority students of all kinds most need, in order to succeed in the wider society, is a core curriculum that is 'general knowledge based'. Branson (1988) and Threadgold (1988) make similar points.

Directly relevant to minority pupils, Paulston (1978) points out that issues relating to bilingual education cannot be understood without reference to the conflict arising from unequal opportunities and from the state of 'structured inequality' in the socioeconomic environment. In Paulston's view the school failure of minority group children is more likely due to their feelings of conflict in the face of unequal status than it is due to factors related to their ethnicity or their language (see also Tosi, 1984). Aspects of 'cultural capital' that are rather separate from language may intervene to frustrate the school's best efforts in promoting equality of opportunity among minorities. Much the same can be said for the children of the poor more generally: education cannot make up for wider socioeconomic disadvantages; it has long been known that at every stage of the educational ladder the likelihood of working class students reaching that stage decreases independently of rated intelligence or level of educational attainment (Nash, 1988). There are massive constraints on schools in their dealings with the culturally different, the socially different and the gender different.

The background to these constraints on schools is more easy to identify than to change. Schools cannot and do not balance differences in cultural capital between children. On the contrary the evidence suggests that contemporary schooling gives an added value to the cultural capital that children bring with them: it increases social inequity. The point for policy makers is a simple one: we inevitably risk the failure of social planning policies if those policies have their target solely or even mainly in the schools; educational planning will always 'fail' if we fail to promote consistent and genuine change and improvement in the social and economic conditions of the poor and of the otherwise disadvantaged at the same time or before we implement those educational policies. Policies of social reform, then, are themselves indirect educational policies.

Restructuring education, curriculum reform and thoughtful pedagogies will make some difference. The point for language policies across the curriculum is that they need to be integrated wherever possible with wider social policies. It may even be necessary for an LPAC to include policy items aimed at promoting small-scale social reforms in the local community on the very good grounds that these reforms are needed before the school can adequately perform its statutory role.

What Else Can Schools Do?

Social reform does not come solely from attempts to remedy economic injustices, since there are groups in all societies that resist economic paternalism and what are often interpreted as attempts at cultural assimilation. Rather than trying to eliminate the strong sense of group identity that exists among sub-cultures in schools in many places, some schools are trying to understand it and allow for it in their programmes. Sub-group identity in the school is a subject receiving more attention by educational researchers (see Walker, 1988) and ways of promoting inter-group harmony are being actively sought. V. Edwards (1986) points to work by social psychologists in the area of inter-group relations which is clearly relevant for those trying to introduce sensitive language policies at the school level.

Our identity as individuals is determined by our knowledge of the different social categories to which we belong and by our estimation of the value that others place upon those categories. If we feel that our own group, while different from others, is still valued by others then our personal identity will be adequate. If a low ranking is placed on our group by others then we may seek a more favourable identity through various means, most of them being expressions of group solidarity in the face of what are seen to be unjust assessments of our group's identity. We may also mount direct confrontation that challenge the assumptions and beliefs of the majority group.

Many schools, especially secondary schools, have students who have found an identity for themselves in groups whose status is not highly valued by the school or by society in general. This low valuation, especially in matters of language, may reinforce differences in language use between the group's members and the higher status language favoured in the school. How is the school to respond to this in its policies? The direct method sometimes favoured is for the school to give a place to the language of the student sub-culture, trying in this way to win the group's allegiance to the school's aims and programme. But the effect of this simple linguistic approach to this major problem may be to increase student alienation rather than narrow it. A better approach may require a wholesale redefinition by staff of the group's attributes so that what were previously seen as undesirable traits are given a recognition closer to the status that the group itself places on those characteristics. These sub-groups are easily identified in most schools, whether they find their identity in ethnic street gangs as is common in New York, in rival football codes as in Sydney, in rival football clubs as in Britain, or in formal organisations of some kind outside the school. For example, in the New Zealand setting Polynesian young people often coalesce in schools in groups that imitate the behaviour of the highly organised motor cycle gangs that are widely dispersed about the country and which provide a rallying point for many young people who may perceive themselves to be otherwise powerless in the highly European-based culture of New Zealand.

Schools might best accommodate to the challenge of socially and culturally different groups of this kind in their midst by seeking out those characteristics of the groups that can be valued positively and by giving a place in school life to rituals and activities that relate to those characteristics. The more secure and positive members of a group feel about their identity, the more tolerant they are likely to be of members of other groups (Gudykunst & Schmidt, 1987). Some groups of Black children in New York, of Jamaican children in London, of Chicano children in Los Angeles, of Francophones in Toronto, of Aboriginal children in Sydney and of socially marginalised children everywhere might resist the work of schools much less if their youth cultures were more publicly valued in this way. In line with our theme here, they may come to view the language of the school, as a result, with less hostility and see it as a more useful instrument in furthering their own interests. For this approach to succeed it needs to be free of tokenism and paternalism; a carefully designed and negotiated policy may provide the necessary starting point. A removal of illiberal 'controls' in other areas of school management may need to be part of the package.

Research studies from Canada and New Zealand (Kehoe & Echols, 1984) found that schools with the lowest levels of truancy, vandalism, anti-social behaviour and the potential for higher levels of achievement were those with a clearly drawn and widely known philosophy for cultural relations in the school. Teachers in these schools modified their textbooks, changed their teaching styles, expected good results from their pupils, avoided giving offence to their students on cultural matters, and adjusted their programmes in the face of pupil failure. Praise and reward for good behaviour rather than punishment for bad was favoured. In contrast schools which practised assimilation had higher levels of truancy, vandalism and anti-social behaviour. They also had problems from ethnic gangs, from teams selected on the basis of race and from widespread negative stereotyping.

In confronting issues of racial discrimination, raised by cultural differences in the communities from which they draw, schools can act positively to promote non-discriminatory policies. Some of the successful methods recommended in OECD countries are as follows:

—recruiting and promoting ethnic minority staff across all the areas of employment within the institution;
—recognising the value of various cultures and social groups to the school and giving space and finance to them within its programme;
—giving a high status to community languages and encouraging bilingualism;
—giving strong support to the learning of the majority language by all students;

—avoiding methods of teaching and assessment that discriminate against minority group children;

—avoiding methods of grouping students which disadvantage ethnic groups and reinforce stereotypes;

—involving minority parents as partners in their children's education for the sense of 'efficacy' that arises and which communicates itself to the children, with positive academic results (Tizard *et al.*, 1982; Ada, 1988).

10 Concluding summary: What a language policy might contain

This final chapter presents its summary of LPAC topics and questions under three broad headings:

A   The Organisation and Management of the School
B   Teacher Approaches to Language Use
C   The Curriculum: Pedagogy, Content and Assessment

Any single LPAC could not hope to address all of the areas summarised in this chapter. In the early stages of policymaking schools will decide those areas that are most relevant to the needs of the children and to the language problems that affect the school and its social context.

A   The Organisation and Management of the School

STAFFING MATTERS

Staff Development and Collaborative Planning (Chapters 3 and 7)
    (1) whose responsibility is staff development in the ideas and practices of LAC?
    (2) what assistance is available for staff who are dealing with transitional language students?
    (3) what training in classroom methods is available for staff coping with students in the same classroom who are at different stages of SL development?
    (4) what in-service provisions are being made to develop staff proficiency in language maintenance?
    (5) what training in classroom methods is available to staff coping

with pupils who are from linguistic minorities (dialect speakers) in their homelands?
(6) how can pupil preferences in language work be taken into close account in planning?
(7) what attitudes towards language varieties and styles used within the school are held to be desirable ones by the staff as a whole?

Language Consultant or LPAC Coordinator (Chapter 5)
(1) is the school to have a consultant or a coordinator?
(2) should the post be full-time or part-time?
(3) what are the limits of the post's responsibilities?
(4) if part-time, what allowances will be made in the staff member's timetable to free him/her to give adequate attention to language matters?
(5) is in-service training in LAC to be part of the role?
(6) can oversight and revision of the LPAC be reasonably left to the consultant/coordinator?
(7) how will this person's duties relate to the control of facilities and resources that are central to language activities?

The Supervision of Minority Language Teachers (Chapter 7)
(1) how will the school ensure that these teachers are not accorded a second-class status?
(2) how are they to overcome the isolation from their colleagues that comes from teaching outside the school's main programme?
(3) how are teachers to be helped in motivating the very young in minority language classrooms where minority language teaching competes with activities that young children may find more enjoyable?
(4) how is the inspection of minority language teaching to be carried out?

POLICY MAKING, RECORDS AND EVALUATION

School-Based Research (Chapter 3)
(1) what small-scale fact gathering needs to be done before a policy can be implemented successfully?
(2) what large-scale research is desirable in the long term?
(3) what advisory or consultancy services might undertake large-scale

research on behalf of the school?
(4) how is any major research to be funded or subsidised?

Official Documents (Chapters 5 and 6)
(1) how do national or system-level policies for education integrate into the schools LAC work?
(2) are there directions in a common core curriculum that need to be translated into the text of an LPAC for application at school level?
(3) do official syllabuses lend support at various points to the policy?
(4) are there recommendations in a national language policy or deriving from a national language project that need to be acknowledged in the school's LPAC?

Record Keeping (Chapter 5)
(1) what form will the school's language record-keeping take?
(2) who will be responsible for updating and securing the records?
(3) what limits will be placed on access to the school's records

Support and Advisory Services (Chapters 6 and 7)
(1) what methods are available for the classification of minority pupils by ability?
(2) what provisions are there for access to adequately normed tests?
(3) is there a central resource for borrowing teaching aids for use with minority language pupils?
(4) how is continuity in language provision guaranteed for minority children moving between schools at the same or at different levels?
(5) what official resource people outside the school can assist planning and implementation of the LPAC (i.e. itinerant teachers, advisers on minority group matters, inspectors and superintendents, resource centres)?
(6) are there financial provisions mentioned in a national language policy or project that might be used to serve the school's needs?

Policy Implementation and Evaluation (Chapters 4 and 9)
(1) does the school have a 'policy about policy making'?
(2) do staff participate routinely in policy making?

(3) whose responsibility is the LPAC's implementation?
(4) how is progress to be monitored?
(5) what are the evaluation methods to be?
(6) at what stage and by whom will the policy be revised, rewritten and upgraded?
(7) is the policy to have a limited life pending the development of a new policy created in line with changing circumstances?
(8) is there a policy on gender in the school that could provide a framework to guide the LPAC's treatment of gender issues?

THE COMMUNITY

The Role of Parents (Chapters 4 and 7)
(1) can parents be involved in the design of the language policy itself?
(2) can they be kept informed of the stages in its development?
(3) do they have a role in the school to supplement what teachers can offer in LAC? where? when?
(4) will LAC be promoted through parental involvement?
(5) would some brief introduction to LAC be valuable for parents who regularly mix with students in lesson time?
(6) how far will the school extend into the home in respect to language matters?

The Community Itself (Chapters 3 and 7)
(1)   what are the distinctive features of the school's community?
(2)   what ethnic minority communities does the school serve?
(3)   who are the leaders in these communities?
(4)   what are the communication networks within these communities?
(5)   what procedures are presently used to discover the educational hopes and wishes of the communities?
(6)   how does the school involve the communities in the school's management?
(7)   what areas of the school programme make use of community members' languages and skills?
(8)   what facilities are shared with the communities?
(9)   what extra-curricular involvement does the school have with the communities?
(10) is there a person on the staff responsible for home-school liaison?

(11) are parents and other community members welcome to observe and participate in classroom activities and in student social occasions?

(12) how are parents involved in assisting their children's learning, especially their reading, writing and oral work?

(13) how does the school communicate with parents about their children's language development?

School Attitudes to the Minority Culture (Chapter 7)

(1) does the school see the minority culture only as a deprived environment to be compensated for?

(2) does the school see the home culture as a topic of interest?

(3) does the school see the minority culture as an enduring need of the minority group children?

(4) does the school see an understanding of the minority culture as an enduring need of the majority group?

Participation of Minority Group Members in School Governance (Chapter 7)

(1) can minority group members participate in a direct decision-making capacity?

(2) can participation be through a consultative role?

(3) is there to be minority participation and visibility in the school's operations as teacher aids?

(4) is there to be participation and visibility in the school's operations through salaried posts?

(5) is there to be pupil grouping and separation from majority pupils for joint activities with community members?

Provisions for Community Language Support (Chapter 3)

(1) what does the school know about the languages represented among its student body?

(2) how is the use of community languages promoted in the school?

(3) what provisions are made for the formal learning of community languages?

(4) where formal language classes exist, how are they organised?

(5) how does the school support community efforts at language maintenance?

MINORITY STUDENTS

Teacher and School Attitudes to Minority Languages (Chapters 6 and 7)
(1) is there to be encouragement of the use of minority languages inside or outside the school?
(2) is there to be official encouragement without resource commitment?
(3) is the minority language to be used as a short-term transitional medium of instruction (i.e. less than two years)?
(4) is there to be teaching of the home language as a subject during school hours?
(5) is the minority language to be used as a transitional medium of instruction for long periods?
(6) is the minority language to be used as an official or quasi-official medium of instruction for much of schooling?
(7) does the school need to create a separate system of education in the minority language?

Avoiding Racial Discrimination (Chapter 9)
(1) will the school recruit and promote ethnic minority staff across all areas of employment in the school.
(2) will the school recognise the value of various cultures to the school and give space and finance to them within its programme?
(3) will the school give a high status to community languages and encourage bilingualism?
(4) how will the school demonstrate strong support to the learning of the majority language by all students?
(5) how will the school avoid methods of teaching and assessment that discriminate against minority group children?
(6) how will the school avoid methods for grouping students which disadvantage ethnic groups and reinforce stereotypes?

Approaches to the Cultural Characteristics of Minority Groups (Chapters 7 and 9)
(1) are pupils of the same or similar cultures to be grouped together?
(2) what can the school do to eliminate culturally negative elements in its curriculum?
(3) what can the school do to sensitise teaching staff to minority cultural characteristics and needs?
(4) can the school provide culturally relevant information to groups

other than the minorities?
(5) will the school give priority to appointing staff of the same culture?
(6) will the school introduce culture-related subjects into its teaching programmes?
(7) is there to be recognition of minority languages in instruction for minorities?
(8) is there to be recognition of minority languages in instruction for all students?

Withdrawal of Minority Groups (Chapter 7)
(1) is withdrawal necessary for any of these groups?
(2) how will the school ensure the provision of skilled teaching?
(3) how will the school ensure the provision of adequate well-ventilated accommodation?
(4) how will the school ensure the provision of a good supply of relevant books and audio-visual aids?
(5) how will the school ensure that wholehearted cooperation between teachers releasing pupils and those receiving them is demonstrated to show the pupils that their success is important to others?

Groupings of Minority Students for Instruction (Chapter 7)
(1) are minority group pupils to be dispersed into classes mixed with majority children, analogous to the 'mainstreaming' of special education pupils?
(2) is there to be a concentration of the minority into separate groups?
(3) is there to be episodic teaching of highly dispersed small groups by itinerant teachers?
(4) will the school recognise minority pupil preferences in grouping?

Bilingualism and Minority First Language Maintenance (Chapters 7 and 9)
(1) how and when does the school discover the languages represented across the school and in specific classes?
(2) what steps are needed to provide staffing arrangements that promote first language maintenance and development?
(3) how can bilingual speakers be used in the school's programme?
(4) how are minority languages used in school and class?

(5) what materials and resources representing the minority first language can be used?

(6) what in-service provisions are there to develop staff proficiency in language maintenance?

(7) how can each community language be used in contacts between the school and the wider community?

(8) what information can the school offer to parents to encourage them to maintain and develop their home languages?

(9) what procedures need to be introduced to implement bilingual programmes for those children who need them?

(10) how will levels of pupil language development, pupil ages, social background, ability levels and learning difficulties affect the bilingual provisions?

SECOND LANGUAGE TEACHING

Resources and Materials for Second Language Teaching (Chapter 7)
(1) is there a staff member with recognised responsibility for coordinating language learning among children with SL needs?

(2) can this person be better used than at present in providing staff development in SL learning pedagogy?

(3) how might resource people in the wider education system be used more fully?

(4) how might SL children themselves and community members be involved as resources for SL learning?

(5) are their culturally appropriate assessment procedures available for new students with SL needs?

(6) is there a role for an education support committee, involving ethnic groups, to liaise and work with the school?

(7) what large resource items for SL teaching should the school include as part of its long-term planning estimates?

(8) is the school's budget fairly allocated to meet the language learning needs of all children?

(9) does the community itself offer any sources of funding that might be directed towards the school's needs?

The Place of First and Second Languages (Chapters 7 and 9)
(1) in relation to the majority tongue which sequential treatments are preferred for which students:
(i)   immediate immersion;

(ii) short term teaching of some subjects in the minority tongue along with intensive majority language instruction;

(iii) long term teaching of most subjects in the minority tongue followed by entirely majority language instruction?

(2) which parallel or concurrent SL teaching is preferred for which students?

(i) additional or remedial language tuition after transfer to majority language tuition;

(ii) gradual transfer programmes with two languages used in the same class;

(iii) long-term study of the majority or the minority language as a subject?

Provisions for Second Language Support (Chapter 7)

(1) how are SL students to be identified?

(2) how are their needs to be assessed?

(3) what external support is needed to provide for them adequately?

(4) how can the students' first language be used in learning the second?

(5) what non-threatening environment can be provided for SL learning?

(6) what form of motivation to learn the SL would suit the needs of students?

(7) how might the school display a positive attitude towards the students' first language and towards the users themselves?

(8) what provisions for using language for listening, speaking, reading and writing would ensure a balanced approach to learning?

(9) how might students get feedback on their performance in the new language?

(10) what additional staffing is desirable and possible?

(11) is an SL coordinator necessary for the school?

(12) is an across the curriculum language support team needed?

(13) how might in-service training be provided for classroom teachers?

(14) how might in-service training be provided for SL teachers?

(15) what organisational arrangements best suit the needs of the students and the school?

(16) how will children with specific learning difficulties and other mainstreamed pupils be integrated into the programme?

(17) at what point and how are the provisions to be evaluated?

B Teacher Approaches to Language Use

ATTITUDES AND AWARENESS

Cultural Awareness (Chapters 3, 8 and 9)
 (1) do teachers know what different cultures are represented within their school?
 (2) how is this diversity reflected in the character of the school?
 (3) how do teachers give value to the special experiences that culturally different children can offer?
 (4) how do children and staff learn about important cultural practices of the cultures represented in the school?
 (5) what are the provisions for staff, children and community to work together?
 (6) do teachers know the different perceptions of success that are dominant in the cultures represented in the school?
 (7) how does the school presently respond to any overt racist behaviour among staff and children?

Teacher Attitudes to Language and Languages (Chapters 3, 5 and 7)
 (1) are all staff aware of the language and dialect repertoires of the pupils in the school?
 (2) do staff recognise that pupils' ability to use language effectively has an important impact on their view of themselves, and therefore on their confidence as learners?
 (3) do staff accept the validity of all pupils' spoken abilities, and use these as a basis for developing their skills in reading and writing?
 (4) are staff knowledgeable about what is meant by 'dialect' and 'variety' and do they have a positive approach to varieties other than the standard? How is this reflected in the way in which they assess pupils' written work?
 (5) are staff knowledgeable about the mother tongues which their pupils speak and do they see these as a potential or real strength in the school?
 (6) does the school acknowledge and support pupils' bilingualism and promote an interest in their language among all pupils?
 (7) is there a satisfactory system within the school for identifying pupils who need help with English as their second language, for providing this help and for monitoring their progress?
 (8) are the teaching resources for English as a second language

sufficient to meet the needs of the pupils in the school and organised so that pupils have access to them in a range of subject areas?

(9) do teachers make positive attempts to draw out the experience of pupils who as yet are not entirely confident in expressing themselves in English?

(10) Has progress been made in responding to the issue of language diversity through the language policy and practice of the whole school?

Gender, Language and the Curriculum (Chapter 9)

(1) what classroom strategies will guarantee boys and girls equal access to the teacher's time?

(2) are teachers familiar with research suggesting that boys and girls have different norms in some aspects of language behaviour?

(3) what steps can be taken to eliminate any undesirable gender stereotypes that might be reinforced across the curriculum?

(4) is there need for the school as a whole to rethink its policies in relation to gender and language issues?

C   The Curriculum

PEDAGOGY

LAC (Chapter 5)

(1) are staff familiar with the chief tenets of LAC?

(2) is there wide professional support for the development of an LPAC?

(3) is LAC in-service professional development desirable as part of the introduction of an LPAC?

(4) how will the following modes of language be addressed across the curriculum?
listening
speaking
reading
writing
moving
watching

shaping
viewing

The Development of Reading (Chapter 5)
(1) what teaching approaches might be developed to ensure a match between the child's language and the language of the text?
(2) what place does reading aloud have across the curriculum?
(3) is there regular curriculum space for free reading?
(4) are there desirable patterns that children can follow in receiving help from the teacher?
(5) how can children learn, through their reading, about using language to learn?
(6) what reading schemes are acceptable across the curriculum?
(7) how can the school gain access to the most recent research about the teaching of reading and how can that knowledge be applied across the curriculum?
(8) what resources for reading are there in the school and how can these be brought up to satisfactory levels?
(9) is the central library widely used?
(10) is there a class library system?
(11) do children and staff both understand the functions of central and class libraries?
(12) how are books recommended to the children?

Reading Across the Secondary Curriculum (Chapter 5)
(1) how will the school demonstrate its serious commitment to universal literacy among its pupils?
(2) how will reading be taught at all levels so that the children's level of reading mastery is continually extended?
(3) how can pupils be prepared in their early secondary years for the reading demands of later years?
(4) what opportunities for private reading, for reading aloud, for reading for pleasure, and for extension reading can be built into the curriculum?
(5) what is the most recent knowledge available about the teaching of reading and how can that knowledge be applied across the curriculum?
(6) what resources for reading are there in the school and how can these be brought up to satisfactory levels?
(7) is the central library widely used?

(8) is there a class library system?
(9) do children and staff both understand the functions of central and class libraries?
(10) how are books recommended to the children?
(11) is there a school bookshop?
(12) are books displayed?
(13) can the children read for pleasure or must they always write a review?
(14) do the teachers read outside school?
(15) are the teachers seen reading in school?
(16) can children take books home?
(17) are parents involved?
(18) are there opportunities to share responses to books?
(19) is a varied reading diet being offered: story, poem, novel, play, children's own writing?
(20) how are the poor readers to be identified and how are they to receive assistance that will lead to a planned upgrading of their skills?

Reading for Pleasure (Chapter 5)
(1) how can teachers ensure that all pupils use the school's library at least once a week for quiet reading and borrowing?
(2) can small collections of books be placed in class boxes so that quiet reading becomes the norm for children when other work is finished?
(3) can the time given to reading across the curriculum and to reporting back on the results of that reading be increased?
(4) do teachers agree that private voluntary reading for pleasure provides one good indicator of general competence in language matters?
(5) can attention be given to creating a book-club and a school bookshop.

Writing Across the Curriculum (Chapter 5)
(1) how can skill development in using the three functions of writing be guaranteed across the curriculum?
(2) how can real audiences for each child's writing in the three functions be provided across the curriculum?
(3) how can the approval and interest of parents in the children's writing be encouraged and sustained?

Handwriting (Chapter 5)
    (1) is agreement on the style of presentation of written work necessary?
    (2) do teachers accept any agreed pattern of presentation in their teaching or in their own written work?
    (3) is handwriting to be taught? by whom? how?
    (4) is there need for a fixed style of letter-shape (e.g. cursive, script etc.) across the school?
    (5) at what stage in the school's programme will formal handwriting classes end or begin?
    (6) is there a handwriting expert on the staff who could assume a consultancy role?
    (7) as an extension activity or option, can the techniques and scope of calligraphy be made available on a regular basis?

Marking Policy (Chapter 5)
    (1) what kinds of errors in class work are to be marked as children progress through the school?
    (2) is assessment of writing to be evaluative, summative or both?
    (3) can agreement be reached on the kinds of comments (positive or negative) that are to be appended to children's written work?
    (4) are conferences between individual teachers and children routinely provided to give feedback on writing?
    (5) what research about the assessment of children's writing can be used in the school to improve marking techniques?

Oral Language (Chapter 5)
    (1) what functions of oral language does the school feel responsible for developing?
    (2) what styles of oral language does the school feel responsible for developing?
    (3) what special experiences will the school provide to further the development of oral language?
    (4) what kinds of language are to be developed by teachers working with individuals, with groups, with whole classes or by children working with children?
    (5) where does small group discussion fit into the school's work?
    (6) where does role play fit into the school's work?
    (7) where does drama fit into the school's work?
    (8) where does pair work fit into the school's work?

(9)   where do public speaking or debates fit into the school's work?

(10)   what roles do adults other than teachers play in the language work of the school, in providing models of language in use and of language variety?

(11)   what emphasis is placed on listening skills and where can they be developed in the curriculum?

Watching and Moving: Improvisation and Role Play (Chapter 5)

(1)   where do improvisation and role play fit into the schools' work?

(2)   is the advice of an outside consultant needed to assist staff development in this area?

(3)   is there a staff member who is proficient in these areas who might take on a leadership role?

Shaping and Viewing: The Media and other Creative Arts (Chapter 5)

(1)   how can teachers give added weight to the place of visual effects in the language and learning work of their classrooms?

(2)   how can viewing and producing videotapes, newspapers, films, television programmes, photographs, paintings, comics, cartoons, signs, charts, collages, models, dioramas etc. enhance learning across the curriculum?

(3)   how can children be made more critically aware of the explicit and subtle effects of these modes of communication?

Approaches to Teaching a Second Language (Chapter 7)

(1)   what integration of approaches to SL teaching best suits the needs of students in the school:
'grammar translation'
'audio-lingual'
'structural/situational'
'functional/notional'
'language across the curriculum'
'communicative competence'?

(2)   are there policy decisions that can be taken in this area at whole school level?

(3)   should the SL coordinator develop guidelines for producing some consistency in methods used across the curriculum?

(4)   how can the latest research on teaching and learning in SL classrooms be located and applied within the school?

(5) are there aspects of communicative competence in the second language that are particular priorities for the school?

CURRICULUM CONTENT

Language Awareness (Chapter 5)
(1) how can the following areas of knowledge be included for children across the curriculum:
  (i) Knowledge of the structuring patterns of their own language;
  (ii) Knowledge that other languages may be very different from their own in the structures and in the meanings that they encode;
  (iii) Knowledge of varieties of their own language that exist in their own society;
  (iv) Knowledge that there are other varieties of their own language that are used in other societies;
  (v) Knowledge of the existence of other languages that are used in their own society;
  (vi) Knowledge of the lexical history of their own language, its etymology, its semantic fields, and the relationships between its words;
  (vii) Knowledge of values issues in judging 'appropriateness' in language use;
  (viii) Knowledge of conscious metacognitive skills that are valuable in certain styles of language use and for certain purposes;
  (ix) Knowledge that any sign system, including a language, depends for its communicative ability on a set of conventions between the users of the system about the system itself?

Foreign Language Teaching (Chapter 8)
(1) how many foreign languages should be taught in the school?
(2) which languages should be taught?
(3) to whom should they be taught?
(4) how much of the languages should be taught to each group?
(5) how should they be taught?
(6) how can cultural studies relevant to the FL be included across the curriculum?
(7) can the school undertake to provide students with access to the

full range of FL sub-competencies:

linguistic competence
sociolinguistic competence
discourse competence
strategic competence
sociocultural competence
social competence?

Critical Language Awareness (Chapter 9)
  (1) how can the school promote social awareness of discourse?
  (2) how can the school promote critical awareness of variety?
  (3) how can the school promote consciousness of change in language
      and practice in readiness for change?

EVALUATION AND ASSESSMENT

First Language Testing, Evaluation and Records (Chapter 5)
  (1) do staff consider testing to be useful?
  (2) how frequently should it be carried out?
  (3) for what reasons?
  (4) who should administer tests to students?
  (5) what use can be made of records from other schools?
  (6) whose responsibility is the updating of school achievement
      records?
  (7) whose responsibility is it to ensure uniformity and fairness in the
      use of records?
  (8) how is continuity in mother tongue development guaranteed for
      children moving between schools at the same or at different
      levels?

Mother Tongue Language Tests (Chapter 5)
  (1) what group tests of mother tongue proficiency are to be used?
  (2) what individual tests of mother tongue proficiency are to be used?

Approaches to Assessing Second Language Proficiency (Chapter 7)
  (1) is there a place for conventional testing methods?
  (2) is there a place for communicative proficiency assessment?

(3) how will the school assess the language of learning disabled and gifted minority language pupils?

Assessing Wider Developmental Outcomes (Chapter 5)
(1) can the LPAC refer specifically to and link into the development of broad 'prior' competencies?

acquiring information
conveying information
applying logical processes
undertaking practical tasks as an individual
undertaking practical tasks as a member of a group
making judgments and decisions
working creatively
(2) can the LPAC refer specifically to and link into the development of broad 'dependent' competencies?

act autonomously
act responsibly
show care and concern for other people
consider questions of beliefs and values

Bibliography

ADA, A. 1988, The Pajaro Valley experience: working with Spanish-speaking parents to develop children's reading and writing skills through the use of children's literature. In SKUTNABB KANGAS & CUMMINS. *op. cit.*

ADLER, M.J. 1983, *How to Speak: How to Listen*. New York: Macmillan.

AIRD, E. & LIPPMANN, D. 1983, *English is Their Right: Strategies for Teachers in the Multilingual Classroom*. Melbourne: Australasian Educational Press.

ALATIS, J. *et al.* (eds) 1981, *The Second Language Classroom*. Oxford University Press.

AMMON, U., DITTMAR, N. & MATTHEIER, K. 1987, *Sociolinguistics*. Berlin: Walter de Gruyter.

APPEL, R. 1988, The language education of immigrant workers' children in The Netherlands. In SKUTNABB KANGAS & CUMMINS. *op. cit.*

APPEL, R. & MUYSKEN, P. 1987, *Language Contact and Bilingualism*. London: Edward Arnold.

ARGYRIS, C. 1982, *Reasoning, Learning and Action*. San Francisco: Jossey Bass.

ASHWORTH, E. 1988, *Language Policy in the Primary School: Content and Management*. London: Croom Helm.

BAETENS BEARDSMORE, H. 1986, *Bilingualism: Basic Principles*. Clevedon, Avon: Multilingual Matters (second edition).

BAKER, C. 1988, *Key Issues in Bilingualism and Bilingual Education*. Clevedon, Avon: Multilingual Matters.

BARNES, D. 1976, *From Communication to Curriculum*. London : Penguin.

BARNES, D., BRITTON, J. & ROSEN, H. 1969, *Language, The Learner and the School*. London: Penguin.

BARNES, D., BRITTON, J. & TORBE, M. 1986, *Language, The Learner and the School*. London : Penguin.

BEEBY, C. 1966, *The Quality of Education in Developing Countries*. Cambridge Mass.: Harvard University Press.

BELL, H. 1988, *A Language Policy Across the Curriculum for 'Heatherton' Primary School*. Palmerston North: Massey University.

BELL, R. 1981, *An Introduction to Applied Linguistics: Approaches and Methods in Language Teaching*. London: Batsford Academic.

BENTAHILA, A. 1983, *Language Attitudes Among Arabic-French Bilinguals in Morocco*. Clevedon, Avon: Multilingual Matters.

BENTON, R. 1986, Schools as magnets for language revival in Ireland and New Zealand. In SPOLSKY *op. cit.*

BERNSTEIN, R. 1985, *Habermas and Modernity*. Cambridge: Polity Press.

BETTONI, C. 1985, *Tra Lingue Dialetto e Inglese*. Leichhardt: FILEF Italo-Australian Publications.

BHASKAR, A. 1978, *A Realist Theory of Science*. Brighton: Harvester Press.

BOLAM, R. 1982, *School Focused In-Service Training*. London: Heinemann.

BONSER, S. & GRUNDY, S. 1988, Reflective deliberation in the formulation of a school curriculum policy. *Journal of Curriculum Studies* 20, 35–45.

BOURDIEU, P. 1977a, *Reproduction in Society, Education and Culture* (with J. PASSERON). Los Angeles: Sage.

— 1977b, *Outline of Theory and Practice*. London: Cambridge University Press.

BOURNE, J. & CAMERON, D. 1988, No common ground: Kingman, grammar and the nation — A linguistic and historical perspective on 'The Kingman Report'. *Language and Education: An International Journal* 2, 3, 147–60.

BRANSON, J. 1988, Gender, education and work. In CORSON 1988d, *op. cit.*

BRAY, D.H. & HILL, C.G.N. 1973, *Polynesian and Pakeha in New Zealand Education: Volume 1, The Sharing of Cultures*. Palmerston North: Bennett.

BREARLEY, M. 1969, *Fundamentals in the First School*. London : Blackwell.

BRIDGES, E. 1967, A model for shared decision making in the school. *Educational Administration Quarterly* 3.

BRITTON, J. 1970, *Language and Learning*. London: Penguin.

— (ed.) 1975, *The Development of Writing Abilities* (pp. 11–18). London: Methuen.

BROPHY, J. 1985, Interactions of male and female students with male and female teachers. In L. WILKINSON & C. MARRETT (eds) *Gender Influences in Classroom Interaction* pp. (115–42). Orlando, Florida: Academic Press.

BROUGHTON, G., BRUMFIT, C., FLAVELL, R., HILL, P. & PINCAS, A. 1980, *Teaching English as a Foreign Language*. London: Routledge and

Kegan Paul (second edition).

BROWN, G. & ARMSTRONG, S. 1978, SAID: a system for analysing instructional discourse. In R. MCALEESE & D. HAMILTON (eds) *Understanding Classroom Life*. NFER: Slough.

BROWN, H. 1980, *Principles of Language Learning and Teaching*. New York: Prentice-Hall.

BROWN, R. & GILMAN, A. 1960, The pronouns of power and solidarity. In T. SEBEOK (ed.) *Style in Language*. Cambridge, Mass.: MIT Press.

BRUCK, M. 1984, The suitability of immersion education for children with special needs. In RIVERA (ed.) 1984a, *op. cit.*

— 1985, Consequences of transfer out of early French immersion programs. *Applied Psycholinguistics* 6, 39–61.

BRUMFIT, C. & JOHNSON, K. 1979, *The Communicative Approach to Language Teaching*. London: Oxford University Press.

BRUNER, J. 1966, *Towards a Theory of Instruction*. New York: Harvard University Press.

— 1975, Language as an instrument of thought. In A. DAVIES (ed.) *Problems of Language and Learning*. London: Heinemann.

— 1987, The transactional self. In J. BRUNER & H. HASTE (eds) *Making Sense: The Child's Construction of the World*. London: Methuen.

BULLIVANT, B. 1984, *Pluralism: Cultural Maintenance and Evolution*. Clevedon, Avon: Multilingual Matters.

BUTTON, G. & LEE, J. (eds) 1987, *Talk and Social Organisation*. Clevedon, Avon: Multilingual Matters.

BYRAM, M. 1988a, Foreign language education and cultural studies. *Language, Culture and Curriculum* 1, 15–31.

— 1988b, *Cultural Studies in Foreign Language Education*. Clevedon, Avon: Multilingual Matters.

CALDWELL, B. & SPINKS, J. 1986, *Policy-Making and Planning for School Effectiveness*. Hobart: Education Department of Tasmania.

— 1988, *The Self Managing School*. Taylor and Francis: London.

CAMPOS, S. & KEATINGE, H. 1988, The Carpinteria language minority student experience: from theory, to practice, to success. In SKUTNABB KANGAS & CUMMINS. *op. cit.*

CANALE, M. 1984, A communicative approach to language proficiency assessment in a minority setting. In RIVERA 1984a, *op. cit.*

CARR, W. & KEMMIS, S. 1983, *Becoming Critical: Knowing Through Action Research*. Geelong : Deakin University Press.

CARTWRIGHT, D. 1988, Language policy and internal geopolitics. In WILLIAMS *op. cit.*

CAZDEN, C.B. 1972, *Language in Early Childhood Education*. Washington: National Association for the Education of Young Children.

— 1987, Enhancing teacher interactions with Maori children in New Zealand. *Language and Education: An International Journal* 1, 69–70.

— 1988, *Classroom Discourse: The Language of Teaching and Learning*. Portsmouth, NH: Heinemann:.

CHAMOT, A. 1983, Towards a functional ESL curriculum in the elementary school. *TESOL Quarterly* 17, 459–472.

— 1988, Bilingualism in education and bilingual education: the state of the art in the United States. *Journal of Multilingual and Multicultural Development* 9, 11–35.

CHANDLER, P., ROBINSON, P. & NOYES, P. 1989, The treatment of children's writing by student teachers. *Language and Education: An International Journal* 3.

CHAUDRON, C. 1988, *Second Language Classrooms: Research on Teaching and Learning*. Cambridge University Press.

CHESHIRE, J., EDWARDS, V. & WHITTLE, P. 1988, Survey of British Dialect Grammar: An unpublished report. ESRC Project: Birkbeck College University of London.

CHILCOTT, J. 1987, Where are you coming from and where are you going? The reporting of ethnographic research. *American Educational Research Journal* 24, 199–218.

CHILVER, P. & GOULD, G. 1983, *Learning and Language in the Classroom: Discursive Talking and Writing Across the Curriculum*. Oxford: Pergamon.

CHOMSKY, N. 1979, *Language and Responsibility*. Harvester: London.

CHRISTIE, F. 1987, Young children's writing: from spoken to written genre. *Language and Education: An International Journal* 1, 3–13.

CHURCHILL, S. 1986, *The Education of Linguistic and Cultural Minorities in OECD Countries*. Clevedon, Avon: Multilingual Matters.

CLAYDON, L., KNIGHT, T. & RADO, M. 1977, *Curriculum and Culture: Schooling in a Pluralist Society*. Sydney: Allen and Unwin.

CLSL (Centre for Language in Social Life), 1987, *Critical Language Awareness*. CLSL Working Paper Series 1, Language-Ideology-Power Research Group: University of Lancaster.

CLYNE, M. (ed.) 1976, *Australia Talks: Essays on the Sociology of Australian Immigrant and Aboriginal Languages*. Canberra: Australian National University Press.

— 1982, *Multilingual Australia: Resources, Needs, Policies*. Melbourne: River Seine.

— 1984, Some thoughts on language contact research, *International Journal of the Sociology of Language* 45, 9–20.

— 1984b, *Language and Society in the German-Speaking Countries*. Cambridge University Press.

— 1988, Community language in the home: a first progress report. *Vox* (The Journal of the Australian Advisory Council on Languages and Multicultural Education) 1, 22–27.

COATES, J. 1986, *Women, Men and Language*. Harlow, Essex: Longman.

COBARRUBIAS, J. & FISHMAN J. A. (eds) 1983, *Progress in Language Planning: International Perspectives*. Berlin: Mouton.

COCKBURN, J. 1988, *A Language Policy for St Jude's School*. Palmerston North: Massey University.

COHEN, A. 1976, The case for partial or total immersion education. In A. SIMOES (ed.) *The Bilingual Child*. New York: Academic Press.

COLLIER, V. 1987, Age and rate of acquisition of second language for academic purposes. *TESOL Quarterly* 21, 617–641.

Commonwealth Department of Education 1982, *Towards a National Language Policy*. Canberra: AGPS.

CONDRY, J. & CONDRY, S. 1976, Sex differences: a study in the eye of the beholder. *Child Development* 47, 812–819.

CONNORS, B. 1984, A multicultural curriculum as action for social justice. In SHAPSON & D'OYLEY, *op. cit.*

CORDER, S.P. 1981, *Error Analysis and Interlanguage*. London: Oxford University Press.

CORSON, D.J. 1972, Teaching spelling through etymology and word relationships. *Tasmanian Journal of Education* 6, 69–71.

— 1977, 50,000 Tasmanians? The Adult Literacy Program. *Australian Council for Adult Literacy Occasional Papers*. Canberra: ACAL 1, 3–6.

— 1978a, Profile of the adult literacy student. *Literacy Work*. UNESCO International Institute for Adult Literacy Methods, Teheran, 8, 65–68.

— 1978b, Profile of the adult literacy student: Tasmania. *Australian Council for Adult Literacy Occasional Papers*. Canberra: ACAL 2, 7–24.

— 1980, Chomsky on education. *Australian Journal of Education* 24, 164–185.

— 1981, Literacy and world view. In A. J. A. NELSON (ed.) *On the Importance of Being Literate*. Australian Council for Adult Literacy, Canberra: University of New England Press.

— 1985a, Language, education and polity: a National Language Policy for Australia?. In P. HUGHES, D. CORSON & B. CALDWELL, (eds) *Education and Polity: Interface Between Education and State Policy: Australia*. UNESCO Office for Education in Asia and the Pacific: Bangkok.

— 1985b, *The Lexical Bar*. Pergamon Press: Oxford.

— 1985c, Educational research and Popper's theory of knowledge. *The Universities' Quarterly (Culture, Education and Society)* 40, 73–89.

— 1985d, Quality of judgment and deciding rightness: ethics and educational administration. *Journal of Educational Administration* 23, 122–130.

— 1986a, Policy in social context: a collapse of holistic planning in education. *Journal of Education Policy* 1, 5–22.

— 1986b, Primitive semantic notions about hierarchical structures: implications for educational organisations and educational knowledge. *Journal of Educational Administration* 24, 173–186.

— 1988a, *Oral Language Across the Curriculum.* Clevedon, Avon: Multilingual Matters.

— 1988b, Making the language of education policies more user friendly. *Journal of Education Policy* 3, 249–260.

— 1988c, The social epistemologies of education. *Social Epistemology: A Journal of Knowledge, Culture and Policy* 3, 19–37.

— 1988d, *Education for Work: Background to Policy and Curriculum.* Palmerston North: The Dunmore Press.

— 1989a, FLT school level policies and cultural studies across the curriculum. *Foreign Language Annals* 22, 4.

— 1989b, Adolescent lexical differences in Australia and England by social group. *Journal of Educational Research* 82, 146–157.

CRYSTAL, D. 1987, *The Cambridge Encyclopedia of Language.* Cambridge University Press.

CSC (Commonwealth Schools Commission), 1984, *A Review of the Commonwealth English as a Second Language ESL, Program.* Canberra.

CUMMINS, J. 1981, *Bilingualism and Minority Language Children.* Toronto: OISE Press.

— 1983, Linguistic minorities and multicultural policies in Canada. In J. EDWARDS (ed.) *Bilingualism, Pluralism and Language Planning Policies.* London: Academic Press.

— 1984, Wanted: a theoretical framework for relating language proficiency to academic achievement among bilingual students. In RIVERA 1984c, *op. cit.*

— 1984a, The minority language child. In SHAPSON & D'OYLEY, *op. cit.*

— 1984b, *Bilingualism and Special Education: Issues in Assessment and Pedagogy.* Clevedon, Avon: Multilingual Matters.

— 1988, From multicultural to anti-racist education: an analysis of programmes and policies in Ontario. In SKUTNABB KANGAS & CUMMINS, *op. cit.*

CUMMINS, J. *et al.* 1984, Linguistic interdependence among Japanese and

Vietnamese immigrant students. In RIVERA (ed), 1984a, *op. cit.*

CUMMINS, J. & SWAIN, M. 1986, *Bilingualism in Education: Aspects of Theory, Research and Practice.* London: Longman.

DAHRENDORF, R. 1978, *Life Chances.* Chicago: University of Chicago Press.

DANNEQUIN, C. 1987, Les enfants baillonnés: the teaching of French as mother tongue in elementary school. *Language and Education: An International Journal* 1, 15–31.

DAVIE, R., BUTLER, N. & GOLDSTEIN, H. 1972, *From Birth to Seven.* London: Longmans.

DEPARTMENT OF EDUCATION 1987, *The Curriculum Review: Report of the Committee to Review the Curriculum for Schools.* Wellington.

— 1988a, *Towards a Primary School Language Policy: Immigrant Minority Needs.* Wellington (unpublished draft).

— 1988b, *Towards a Language Policy in Secondary Schools: Immigrant Minority Needs.* Wellington (unpublished draft).

DES (Department of Education and Science) 1975, *A Language for Life* (The Bullock Report). HMSO: London.

— 1985, *Education for All: Report of the Committee of Inquiry into the Education of Children from Ethnic Minority Groups* (The Swann Report). HMSO: London.

— 1988, *Report of the Committee of Inquiry into the Teaching of English Language* (The Kingman Report). HMSO: London.

— 1988a, *English for Ages 5–11: Proposals of the Secretary of State for Education and Science and the Secretary of State for Wales* (The Cox Report). HMSO: London.

DODSON, C. (ed.) 1985, *Bilingual Education: Evaluation, Assessment and Methodology.* Cardiff: University of Wales Press.

D'OYLEY, V. 1984, Beyond the English and French realities in Canada: the politics of empowerment of minorities. In SHAPSON and D'OYLEY *op. cit.*

DURKHEIM, EMILE 1893, *The Division of Labour in Society.* London: Free Press of Glencoe. (1964 edition).

EAGLESON, R.D. 1976, The evidence for social dialects in Australian English. In M. CLYNE (ed.) *op. cit.*

EDWARDS, A.D. 1976, *Language in Culture and Class: The Sociology of Language and Education.* London: Heinemann.

EDWARDS, A.D. & FURLONG, V.J. 1978, *The Language of Teaching.* London: Heinemann.

EDWARDS, J. 1988, Bilingualism, education and identity. *Journal of Multilingual and Multicultural Development* 9, 203–210.

EDWARDS, V. 1983, *Language in Multicultural Classrooms.* Batsford: London.

BIBLIOGRAPHY

— 1986, *Language in a Black Community*. Clevedon, Avon: Multili Matters.

ENTWISTLE, HAROLD 1978, *Class, Culture and Education*. London: Methuen.

ERICKSON, F. 1987, Ethnicity. In AMMON, DITTMAR & MATTHEIER, *op. cit.*

ERICKSON, F. & SCHULTZ, J. 1982, *The Counsellor as Gatekeeper: Social Interaction in Interviews*. New York: Academic Press.

ERVIN-TRIPP, S. 1964, An analysis of the interaction of language, topic and listener. In J. GUMPERZ & D. HYMES (eds) *The Ethnography of Communication: American Anthropologist* 66, 86–102.

FARGHER, R. & ZIERSCH, R. 1981, What happened at Hermansburg? *Set No. 2*. NZCER: Wellington.

FEAGANS, L. & FARRAN, D. 1982, *The Language of Children Reared in Poverty*. New York: Academic Press.

FENNEMA, E. & PETERSON, P. 1985, Autonomous learning behaviour: a possible explanation of gender-related differences in mathematics. In L. WILKINSON & C. MARRETT, (eds) *Gender Influences In Classroom Interaction* (pp. 17–36). Orlando, Florida: Academic Press.

FERGUSON, C.A. 1959, Diglossia. *Word* 15, 325–340.

FILLION, B. 1983, Let me see you learn. *Language Arts* (September) 702–703.

FILLMORE, C. & KAY, P. (1980), Progress report: Test semantic analysis of reading comprehension tests. Unpublished Report. University of California at Berkeley.

FINOCCHIARO, M. 1983, *Teaching English as a Second Language: From Theory to Practice*. New York: Harper and Row.

FINOCCHIARO, M. & BRUMFIT, C. 1983, *The Functional-Notional Approach: From Theory to Practice*. New York: Oxford University Press.

FISHMAN, J. (ed.) 1972, *The Sociology of Language*. Rowley Mass.: Newbury House.

— 1973, Language modernization and planning in comparison with other types of national modernization and planning. *Language in Society* 2, 23–42.

— (ed.) 1978, *Advances in the Study of Societal Multilingualism*. The Hague: Mouton.

— 1980, Minority language maintenance and the ethnic mother tongue school. *Modern Language Journal* 64, 167–172.

FISHMAN, P. 1983, Interaction: the work women do. In B. THORNE, C. KRAMARAE & N. HENLEY, *op. cit.*

FITZPATRICK, F. 1987, *The Open Door*. Clevedon, Avon: Multilingual Matters.

FLORIO-RUANE, S. 1987, Sociolinguistics for educational researchers.

American Educational Research Journal 24, 185–197.

FORD, A. 1988, *A Language Across the Curriculum Policy for St John the Evangelist School*. Palmerston North: Massey University.

FOSTER, L. & STOCKLEY, D. 1988, *Australian Multiculturalism: A Documentary History and Critique*. Clevedon, Avon: Multilingual Matters.

FREIRE, P. 1972, *Pedagogy of the Oppressed*. London: Penguin.

FRENCH, J. 1985, Whatever happened to language across the curriculum? *Education Canada* (Winter) 38–43.

FULLER, S. (1987), Towards objectivism and relativism. *Social Epistemology: A Journal of Knowledge, Culture and Policy* 1, 351–361.

GARCIA, O. & OTHEGUY, R. 1987, The bilingual education of Cuban–American children in Dade County's ethnic schools. *Language and Education: An International Journal* 1, 83–95.

GARNER, M. (ed.) 1981, *Community Languages: Their Role in Education*. Melbourne: River Seine.

GENESEE, F. 1984, French immersion programs. In SHAPSON & D'OYLEY, *op. cit.*

GIDDENS, A. 1985, Jurgen Habermas. In Q. SKINNER (ed.) *The Return of Grand Theory in the Human Sciences*. London: Cambridge University Press.

GILES, H. *et al.* 1987, Research on language attitudes. In AMMON, DITTMAR & MATTHEIER, *op. cit.*

GILES, H., TAYLOR, D. & BOURHIS, R. 1987, Toward a theory of interpersonal accommodation through speech: some Canadian data. *Language in Society* 2, 177–192.

GLASER, R. & CHI, M. 1988, Overview. In M. CHI, R. GLASER & M. FARR (eds) *The Nature of Expertise*. Hillsdale, NJ: Erlbaum Associates.

GLENNY, M. 1988, *A Language Policy Across the Curriculum for Selwyn College*. Palmerston North: Massey University.

GOODHAND, L. 1986, Planning discussion. In MARLAND (1986) *op. cit.*

GOODMAN, K. 1987, Whole language: what's new? *The Reading Teacher*. New York: International Reading Association.

GRAHAM, A. 1973, The making of a nonsexist dictionary. *Ms.*, 2, 12–16.

GRAMBS, J.D. & CARR, J.C. 1979, *Modern Methods in Secondary Education*. New York: Holt, Rinehart and Winston.

GRAMSCI, A. (1948), *Opere di Antonio Gramsci (Quaderni Del Carcere)*. Turin: Einaudi.

GRAVES, D. 1978, *Balance the Basics: Let Them Write*. New York: Ford Foundation.

GRAVES, D. 1983, *Writing: Children and Teachers at Work*. Exeter, NH: Heinemann.

GRIMSHAW, A. 1987a, Sociolinguistics versus sociology of language:

tempest in a teapot or profound academic conundrum? In AMMON, DITTMAR & MATTHEIER, op. cit.

— 1987b, Micro/Macrolevels. In AMMON, DITTMAR & MATTHEIER, op. cit.

GUBOGLO, M. 1986, Factors affecting bilingualism in national languages and Russian in a developed socialist society. In SPOLSKY op. cit.

GUDYKUNST, W. & SCHMIDT, K. 1987, Language and ethnic identity: an overview and prologue. Journal of Language and Social Psychology 6, 157–170.

HABERMAS, J. 1970, Towards a theory of communicative competence. Inquiry 13.

— 1985, The Theory of Communicative Action : Volume 1, Reasoning and the Rationalisation of Society (translated by T. MCCARTHY) London: Heinemann.

HAGMAN, T. & LAHDENPERÄ, J. 1988, Nine years of Finnish-medium education in Sweden: What happens afterwards? The education of minority children in Botkyrka. In SKUTNABB-KANGAS & CUMMINS op. cit.

HALL, E. 1976, Beyond Culture. New York: Garden City Press.

HALLIDAY, M. 1975, Learning How to Mean. London: Arnold.

HARE-MUSTIN, R. & MARACEK, J. 1988, The meaning of difference: gender theory, postmodernism, and psychology. American Psychologist 43, 6, 455–464.

HARRÉ, R. 1974, Blueprint for a new science. In N. ARMISTEAD (ed.) Reconstructing Social Psychology. London: Penguin.

HARRISON, S. 1988, Language Policy of the Science Department: Rotorua Boys' High School. Palmerston North: Massey University.

HAUGEN, E. 1983, The implementation of corpus planning: theory and practice. In J. COBARRUBIAS & J.A. FISHMAN (eds) Progress in Language Planning: International Perspectives. Berlin: Mouton.

HAUGEN, E. 1987, Language planning. In AMMON, DITTMAR & MATTHEIER, op. cit.

HAWKINS, E. 1984, Awareness of Language: An Introduction. London: Cambridge University Press.

HEATH, S. 1972, Telling Tongues: Language Policy in Mexico — Colony to Nation. New York: Teachers College Press.

— 1983, Ways with Words: Language, Life and Work in Communities and Classrooms. London: Cambridge University Press.

HEINICH, J. (ed.) 1982, Instructional Media. New York: Wiley and Sons.

HEWSTONE, M. & GILES, H. 1986, Social groups and social stereotypes in intergroup communication. In W. GUDYKUNST (ed.) Intergroup Communication. London: Edward Arnold.

HIRSH, WALTER 1987, *Living Languages*. Auckland: Heinemann.

HONIG, A.S. 1982, Language environments for young children. *Young Children* 38, 1, 56–67.

HORVATH, B. 1980, *The Education of Migrant Children: A Language Planning Perspective*. ERDC Report No. 24, Canberra: AGPS.

HOULTON, D. 1986, *Cultural Diversity in the Primary School*. London: Batsford.

HUGHES, J. 1983, *The Philosophy of Social Research*. London: Longmans.

HYLTENSTAM, K. & PIENEMANN, M. (eds) 1985, *Modelling and Assessing Second Language Acquisition*. Clevedon, Avon: Multilingual Matters.

HYMES, D. 1972, On communicative competence. In J. PRIDE & J. HOLMES (eds) *Sociolinguistics*. London: Penguin.

HYMES, D. 1987, Communicative competence. In AMMON, DITTMAR & MATTHEIER, *op. cit.*

INGRAM, D. 1985, Assessing proficiency: an overview of some aspects of testing. In HYLTENSTAM & PIENEMANN (1985) *op. cit.*

INNER LONDON EDUCATION AUTHORITY 1980, *Language Policy Statements in the Inner London Education Authority: A Consideration of Responses from Secondary Schools*.

JACKSON, W. 1988, Talking through writing. *Language and Education: An International Journal* 2, 1–14.

JAKOBSON, R. 1980, *The Framework of Language*. Michigan University: Michigan Studies in the Humanities.

JESPERSEN, O. 1922, *Language: Its Nature, Development and Origin*. London: Allen and Unwin.

JICK, T. 1979, Mixing qualitative and quantitative methods: triangulation in action. *Administrative Science Quarterly* 24, 602–611.

JONES, A. 1987, Which girls are 'learning to lose'? In S. MIDDLETON (ed.) *Women and Education in Aotearoa* (pp. 143–152) Wellington: Allen and Unwin.

JORDAN, D. 1988, Rights and claims of indigenous people: education and the reclaiming of identity. The case of the Canadian Natives, the Sami and Australian Aborigines. In SKUTNABB KANGAS & CUMMINS, *op. cit.*

KASPER, G. 1988, Bilingual education and bilingualism in education: a comment. *Journal of Multilingual and Multicultural Development* 9, 37–42.

KEHOE, J. & ECHOLS, F. 1984, Educational approaches for combatting prejudice and racism. In SHAPSON & D'OYLEY, *op. cit.*

KELLY, A 1988, Gender differences in teacher-pupil interactions: a meta-analytic review. *Research in Education* no 39.

KELSEY, J. 1984, Legal imperialism and the colonisation of Aotearoa. In SPOONLEY *et al.*, *op. cit.*

KENNEDY, C. (ed.) 1983, *Language Planning and Language Education*. London: Allen and Unwin.

KERR, A. 1983, A National Language Policy. In B. FALK & J. HARRIS (eds) *Unity in Diversity: Multicultural Education in Australia*. Melbourne: Australian College of Education.

KNOTT, R. 1985, *The English Department in a Changing World*. Open University Press: Milton Keynes.

KRASHEN, S. 1982, *Principles and Practice in Second Language Acquisition*. Oxford: Pergamon Press.

LABOV, W., COHEN, P., ROBINS, C. & LEWIS, J. 1968, *A Study of the Non-Standard English of Negro and Puerto Rican Speakers in New York City, I and II*. Washington D.C.: US Office of Health, Education and Welfare.

LABOV, W. 1972, *Sociolinguistic Patterns*. Philadelphia: University of Pennsylvania Press.

LAFONTAINE, H. *et al.* (eds) 1978, *Bilingual Education*. New York: Avery Publishers.

LAKOFF, R. 1975, *Language and Women's Place*. New York: Harper and Row.

LAMBERT, W. & TUCKER, G. 1972, *Bilingual Education of Children*. Rowley, Mass.: Newbury House.

LAMBERT, W. 1975, Culture and language as factors in learning and education. In A. WOLFGANG (ed.) *Education of Immigrant Students: Issues and Answers*. Toronto: Ontario Institute for Studies in Education.

LEICESTER BILINGUAL SUPPORT GROUP 1982, *Languages in Leicestershire*. Rushey Mead Centre, Leicester: NAME.

LEVINE, R. & WHITE, M. 1986, *Human Conditions: The Cultural Basis of Educational Development*. New York: Routledge and Kegan Paul.

LEVINE, S. & VASIL, R. 1985, *Maori Political Perspectives*. Auckland: Hutchinson.

LEWIS, E. 1972, *Multilingualism in the Soviet Union*. The Hague: Mouton.

— 1981, *Bilingualism and Bilingual Education*. Oxford: Pergamon Press.

LIEBERSON, S. 1970, *Language and Ethnic Relations in Canada*. New York: Wiley and Sons.

LITTLEWOOD, W. 1981, *Communicative Language Teaching: An Introduction*. Cambridge University Press.

LO BIANCO, J. 1987, *National Policy on Languages*. Canberra: Australian Government Printing Service.

LYONS, H. 1988, Needing to know about language: a case study of a nine year old's usage. *Language and Education: An International Journal* 2, 3, 175–88.

MACKEY, W. 1987, Bilingualism and multilingualism. In AMMON, DITTMAR & MATTHEIER, *op. cit.*

MACAULAY, R. 1977, *Language, Social Class and Education: A Glasgow Study.* Edinburgh: University of Edinburgh Press.

MALLETT, M. & NEWSOME, B. 1977, *Talking, Writing and Learning.* London: Methuen.

MALTZ, D. & BORKER, R. 1982, A cultural approach to male–female miscommunication. In J. GUMPERZ (ed.) *Language and Social Identity* (pp. 195–217). Cambridge: Cambridge University Press.

MARCELLESI, J. & ELIMAM, A. 1987, Language and society from a Marxist point of view. In AMMON, DITTMAR & MATTHEIER, *op. cit.*

MARLAND, M. 1977, *Language Across the Curriculum.* London: Heinemann.

— 1986, *School Management Skills.* London: Heinemann.

MARTIN, N. *et al.* 1979, *Writing and Learning Across the Curriculum.* London: Ward Lock.

MARTYNA, W. 1978, What does 'he' mean? Use of the generic masculine. *Journal of Communication* 28, 131–138.

— 1983, Beyond the he/man approach: The case for nonsexist language. In B. THORNE, C. KRAMARAE & N. HENLEY (eds) *op. cit.*

MAYBIN, J. 1985, Working towards a school language policy. In *Every Child's Language: An In-Service Pack for Primary Teachers.* Bristol: Open University and Multilingual Matters.

— 1988, A critical review of the DES Assessment of Performance Unit's Oracy Surveys. *English in Education* 22, 3–18.

MCCARTHY, T. 1984, *The Critical Theory of Jurgen Habermas.* Cambridge: Polity Press.

MC CONNELL-GINET, S. 1983, Intonation in a Man's World. In B. THORNE, C. KRAMARAE & N. HENLEY (eds) *op. cit.*

MCDONALD, D. 1988, *A Draft Language Policy for Otahuhu Primary School.* Palmerston North: Massey University.

MCEWEN, E. *et al.* 1975, *Language Proficiency in the Multiracial Junior School.* NFER: London.

MCLAUGHLIN, B. 1986, Multilingual education: theory east and west. In SPOLSKY, *op. cit.*

MCLEAN, B. 1982, *Languages Other than English in the Primary School.* Schools Commission: Canberra.

MCNAMARA, T. 1987, Language and social identity: Israelis abroad. *Journal of Language and Social Psychology* 6, 215–228.

MCPHERSON, J. & CORSON, D. 1989, *Language Policy Across the Curriculum: Eight Case Studies of School-Based Policy Development.* New Zealand Education Department: Wellington.

MEGARRY, J. 1981, *Sex, Gender and Education*. Glasgow: Jordanhill College of Education.

MEHAN, H. 1979, The competent student. *Working Papers in Sociolinguistics* 61. Austin: University of Texas.

MOFFETT, J. 1968, *Teaching the Universe of Discourse*. London: Houghton Mifflin, 1968.

MORSE, L. & HANDLEY, H. 1985, Listening to adolescents: gender differences in science class interaction. In L. WILKINSON & C. MARRETT (eds) *Gender Influences In Classroom Interaction*. Orlando, Florida: Academic Press.

MOORFIELD, J. 1987, Implications for schools of research findings in bilingual education. In HIRSH (1987), *op. cit.*

MULTICULTURALISM ACT 1988, *Canadian Multiculturalism Act, July 1988*. Ottawa: Canadian Government Publishing Centre.

MURPHY, J. 1980, School administrators besieged: a look at Australian and American education. *American Journal of Education* 1–26.

NASH, R. 1988, IQ and class differences in education: what about genetics? *British Journal of Sociology of Education* 9, 237–243.

NATIONAL ASSOCIATION FOR THE TEACHING OF ENGLISH. 1976, *Language Across the Curriculum: Guidelines for Schools*. Birmingham: Ward Lock.

NEMETZ ROBINSON, G. 1978, *Language and Multicultural Education: An Australian Perspective*. Sydney: ANZ Book Co.

— 1985, *Crosscultural Understanding: Processes and Approaches for Foreign Language, English as a Second Language and Bilingual Educators*. Oxford: Pergamon Press.

NEWMAN, C. 1988, *A Language Policy Across the Curriculum for Christchurch Girls' High School*. Palmerston North: Massey University.

NICHOLAS, J. 1988, British language diversity surveys (1977–87): A critical examination. *Language and Education: An International Journal* 2, 15–33.

NIXON, J. 1985, *A Teacher's Guide to Multicultural Education*. London: Blackwell.

ONTARIO MINISTRY OF EDUCATION. 1984, *Ontario Schools: Intermediate and Senior Divisions*. Toronto: Ministry of Education.

OUTHWAITE, W. 1988, *New Philosophies of Social Science: Realism, Hermeneutics and Critical Theory*. London: Macmillan Education.

PASCAL, C. 1987, Democratised primary school government: relevant theoretical constructs. *Oxford Review of Education* 13, 321–330.

PATTANAYAK, D. 1988, Monolingual myopia and the petals of the Indian lotus: do many languages divide or unite a nation? In SKUTNABB

KANGAS & CUMMINS, op. cit.

PAULSTON, C. 1978, Education in a bi-multilingual setting. *International Review of Education* 24, 309–328.

PENETITO, W. 1988, Maori education for a just society. *Royal Commission on Social Policy*. Wellington.

PHILIPS, S. 1983, An ethnographic approach to bilingual language proficiency assessment. In C. RIVERA (1983), op. cit.

PIAGET, J. 1978, *The Development of Thought: Equilibration and Cognitive Structures*. London: Blackwell.

PIAGET, J. & INHELDER, B. 1958, *The Growth of Logical Thinking: From Childhood to Adolescence*. London: Routledge and Kegan Paul.

PIPER, D. 1986, Language growth in the multi-ethnic classroom. *Language Arts* (January) 23–36.

— 1988, Language awareness for student teachers. *Journal of Education for Teaching* 14, 5–22.

POLLNER, M. 1987, *Mundane Reason: Reality in Everyday and Sociological Discourse*. London: Cambridge University Press.

POPPER, K. 1972, *Objective Knowledge: An Evolutionary Approach*. Oxford: Clarendon.

POTTER, J. & WETHERELL, M. 1987, *Discourse and Social Psychology*. London: Sage.

PREBBLE, T. & STEWART, D. 1981, *School Development: Strategies for Effective Management*. Palmerston North: The Dunmore Press.

PRESTHUS, R. 1962, *The Organisational Society*. New York: Random House.

PRICE, E. 1985, Schools Council Bilingual Education Project (Primary Schools), 1968–1977: An Assessment, In DODSON (1985), op. cit.

PRICE, E. & DODSON, C. 1978, *Bilingual Education in Wales 5-11*. London: Methuen.

PUNETHA, D., GILES, H. & YOUNG, L. 1987, Ethnicity and immigrant values: religion and language choice. *Journal of Language and Social Psychology* 6, 229–241.

RABAN, B. 1988, Reviews. *Language and Education: An International Journal* 2, 71–72.

RATSOY, F. 1976, Policy making in educational organisations. *The Canadian Administrator* (December).

REHBEIN, J. 1984, *Diskurs und Verstehen: Zur Role der Muttersprache bei der Textverarbeitung in der Zweitsprache*. University of Hamburg.

REID, E. 1988, Linguistic minorities and language education: the English experience. *Journal of Multilingual and Multicultural Development* 9, 181–191; 220–223.

RINGBOM, H. 1987, *The Role of the First Language in Foreign Language*

Learning. Philadelphia: Multilingual Matters.

RIVERA, C. (ed.) 1983, *An Ethnographic/Sociolinguistic Approach to Language Proficiency Assessment.* Clevedon, Avon: Multilingual Matters.

RIVERA, C. (ed.) 1984a, *Communicative Competence Approaches to Language Proficiency Assessment: Research and Application.* Philadelphia: Multilingual Matters.

— 1984b, *Placement Procedures in Bilingual Education: Education and Policy Issues.* Philadelphia: Multilingual Matters.

— 1984c, *Language Proficiency and Academic Achievement.* Philadelphia: Multilingual Matters.

RIVERS, W.M. & TEMPERLEY, M.S. 1978, *A Practical Guide to the Teaching of English as a Second or Foreign Language.* New York: Oxford University Press.

RIZVI, F. & KEMMIS, S. 1987, *Dilemmas of Reform.* Geelong: Deakin University Press.

ROBINSON, W.P. 1978, *Language Management in Education — The Australian Context.* London: Allen and Unwin.

ROMAINE, S. 1978, Postvocalic /r/ in Scottish English: sound change in progress?. In P. TRUDGILL (ed.) *Sociolinguistic Patterns in British English.* London: Edward Arnold.

— 1984, *The Language of Children and Adolescents: The Acquisition of Communicative Competence.* Oxford: Blackwell.

ROSEN, C. & ROSEN, H. 1973, *The Language of Primary School Children.* London: Penguin.

ROSENTHAL, R. & JACOBSON, L. 1968, *Pygmalion in the Classroom.* New York: Holt, Rinehart and Winston.

RUBIN, J. 1968, *National Bilingualism in Paraguay.* The Hague: Mouton.

— 1977, Bilingual education and language planning. In B. SPOLSKY & R.L. COOPER (eds) *Frontiers of Bilingual Education.* Rowley Mass.: Newbury House.

RUSSELL, N. 1987, Breakthrough for the bloody-minded. *Times Higher Education Supplement* 25 September.

SAUNDERS, G. 1982, *Bilingual Children: Guidance for the Family.* Philadelphia: Multilingual Matters.

SAVIGNON, S. 1972, *Communicative Competence: An Experiment in Foreign Language Teaching.* Philadelphia: Center for Curriculum Development.

SAVIGNON, S. 1983, *Communicative Competence: Theory and Classroom Practice. Texts and Contexts in Second Language Learning.* New York: Addison Wesley.

SAVILLE-TROIKE, M. 1983, An anthropological linguistic perspective on uses of ethnography in bilingual language proficiency assessment. In RIVERA (1983), *op. cit.*

— 1987, The ethnography of speaking. In AMMON, DITTMAR & MATTHEIER, *op. cit.*

SCHOOLS BOARD OF TASMANIA 1986, *Handbook for Syllabus Development*. Hobart: Schools Board.

SCDC (School Curriculum Development Committee) 1982, *Cambridge Latin Course (Second Edition)*. London: Cambridge University Press.

SCHOOLS COUNCIL WORKING PAPER No. 64. 1979, *Learning through Talking 11–16*. London: Methuen.

SCHOOLS COUNCIL WORKING PAPER No. 67. 1980, *Language Across the Curriculum*. London: Methuen.

SCOLA (Scottish Committee on Language Arts in the Primary School) 1986, *Responding to Children's Writing*. Edinburgh: Scottish Curriculum Development Service, Moray House.

SENATE STANDING COMMITTEE ON EDUCATION AND THE ARTS 1984, *A National Language Policy*. Canberra: AGPS.

SHAPSON, S. & D'OYLEY, V. (eds) 1984, *Bilingual and Multicultural Education: Canadian Perspectives*. Clevedon, Avon: Multilingual Matters.

SHARWOOD SMITH, J. 1977, *On Teaching Classics*. London: Routledge and Kegan Paul.

SIMICH-DUDGEON, C. & RIVERA, C. 1983, Teacher training and ethnographic/sociolinguistic issues in the assessment of bilingual students language proficiency. In RIVERA (1983), *op.cit.*

SKUTNABB KANGAS, T. 1981, *Bilingualism or Not: The Education of Minorities*. Philadelphia: Multilingual Matters.

— 1988, Multilingualism and the education of minority children. In SKUTNABB KANGAS & CUMMINS, *op. cit.*

SKUTNABB KANGAS, T. & CUMMINS, J. 1988, *Minority Education: From Shame to Struggle*. Clevedon, Avon: Multilingual Matters.

SMITH, F. 1983, *Essays into Literacy*. Exeter, NH: Heinemann.

SMOLICZ, J. 1979, *Culture and Education in a Plural Society*. Canberra: Curriculum Development Centre.

SPENDER, D. 1980, *Man Made Language*. London: Routledge and Kegan Paul.

— 1984, Defining reality: a powerful tool. In C. KRAMARAE, M. SCHULTZ & W. O'BARR (eds) *Language and Power*. Beverly Hills, California: Sage.

SPINDLER, G. (ed.) 1982, *Doing the Ethnography of Schooling*. New York: CBS Publishing.

SPOLSKY, B. 1986, *Language and Education in Multilingual Settings*. Clevedon, Avon: Multilingual Matters.

SPOONER, A. 1988, *Lingo: A Course on Words and How to Use Them*. Bristol: Bristol Classical Press.

SPOONLEY, P., MACPHERSON, C., PEARSON, D. & SEDGWICK, C. (eds) 1984, *Tauiwi: Racism and Ethnicity in New Zealand*. Palmerston North: The Dunmore Press.

STANLEY, J. 1977, Paradigmatic women: the prostitute. In D. SHORES, (ed.) *Papers in Language Variation*. Birmingham: University of Alabama Press.

STEINER, G. 1978, *On Difficulty and Other Essays*. London: Oxford University Press.

STERN, H.H. 1976, Optimal age: myth or reality? *Canadian Modern Language Review* 32, 283–294.

— 1983, *Fundamental Concepts of Language Teaching*. London: Oxford University Press.

SIGUAN, M. & MACKEY, W. F. 1987, *Education and Bilingualism*. London: Kogan Page/UNESCO.

SWAIN, M. & LAPKIN, S. 1982, *Evaluating Bilingual Education: A Canadian Case Study*. Clevedon, Avon: Multilingual Matters.

SWANN, J. & GRADDOL, D. 1988, Gender inequalities in classroom talk. *English in Education* 22, 1.

TARONE, E. 1984, Teaching strategic competence in the foreign language classroom. In SAVIGNON, S. (ed.), *op. cit.*

THOMAS, J. 1988, The role played by metalinguistic awareness in second and third language learning. *Journal of Multilingual and Multicultural Development* 9, 235–246.

THOMPSON, J. 1984, *Studies in the Theory of Ideology*. Cambridge: Polity Press.

THORNE, B., KRAMARAE, C. & HENLEY, N. (eds.) 1983, *Language, Gender and Society*. Cambridge, Mass.: Newbury House.

THREADGOLD, T. 1988, Language and gender. *Australian Feminist Studies* 6, (Autumn).

TITONE, R. 1987, *Second Language Learning and Bilingualism: Psychological Studies*. Milano: I.S.F.A.P.

TIZARD, B. & HUGHES, M. 1984, *Young Children Learning: Talking and Thinking at Home and at School*. London: Fontana.

TIZARD, J., SCHOFIELD, W. & HEWISON, J. 1982, Collaboration between teachers and parents in assisting children's reading. *British Journal of Educational Psychology* 52, 1–15.

TOLLEFSON, J.W. 1981, Alternative paradigms in the sociology of language. *Word* 32, 1–13.

TORBE, M. (ed.) 1980, *Language Policies in Action: Language Across the Curriculum in Some Secondary Schools*. London: Ward Lock.

TORBE, M. & MEDWAY, P. 1981, *Language and the Climate for Learning*. London: Ward Lock.

TOSI, A. 1984, *Immigration and Bilingual Education*. Oxford: Pergamon.

TOSI, A. 1988, The jewel in the crown of the modern prince: the new approach to bilingualism in multicultural education in England. In SKUTNABB KANGAS & CUMMINS, *op. cit.*

TOUGH, J. 1977, *Talking and Learning*. London: Ward Lock.

— 1979, *Talk for Teaching and Learning*. London: Ward Lock.

TROIKE, R. 1981, A synthesis of research on bilingual education. *Educational Leadership* 14, 498–504.

— 1984, SCALP: social and cultural aspects of language proficiency. In RIVERA (1984c), *op. cit.*

TRUDGILL, P. 1974, *The Social Differentiation of English in Norwich*. Cambridge: Cambridge University Press.

— 1983, *On Dialect: Social and Geographical Perspectives*. New York: New York University Press.

TWITCHIN, J. & DEMUTH, C. 1985, *Multicultural Education*. BBC Books: London.

VALDES, G., LOZANO, A. & GARCIA-MOYA, R. (eds) 1981, *Teaching Spanish to the Hispanic Bilingual: Issues, Aims and Methods*. New York: Teachers College Press.

VALLEN, T. & STIJNEN, S. 1987, Language and educational success of indigenous and non-indigenous minority students in the Netherlands. *Language and Education: An International Journal* 1, 109–124.

VAN ELS, T. 1988, Towards a foreign language teaching policy for the European community: a Dutch perspective. *Language, Culture and Curriculum* 1, 53–65.

VAN EK, J. 1986, *Objectives for Foreign Language Learning (Volume I: Scope)*. Council of Europe, Strasbourg.

VERHALLEN, M., APPEL, R. & SCHOONEN, R. 1988, Language functions in nursery classes: the cognitive/linguistic experiences of bilingual and monolingual children. *Language and Education: An International Journal*.

VERMA, G. & BAGLEY, C. *Race and Education Across Cultures*. London: Heinemann.

VYGOTSKY, L. 1962, *Thought and Language*. Cambridge, Mass.: MIT Press.

WALD, B. 1984, A sociolinguistic perspective on Cummins' current framework for relating language proficiency to academic achievement. In RIVERA (1984c).

WALKER, J.C. 1988, Building on youth cultures in the secondary curriculum. In CORSON (1988d), *op. cit.*

WARDHAUGH, R. 1985, *How Conversation Works*. Oxford: Blackwell.

WEDDERBURN, D. 1970, Workplace inequality. *New Society*. 9 April.

WELLS, C.G. 1979, Describing children's linguistic development at home and at school. *British Educational Research Journal* 5, 75–89.

— 1984, *Language Development in the Pre-School Years*. London: Cambridge University Press.

WHYLD, J. (ed.) 1983, *Sexism in the Secondary Curriculum*. London: Harper and Row.

WIDDOWSON, H. & BRUMFIT, C. 1981, Issues in second language syllabus design. In J. ALATIS *et al.* (eds), *op. cit.*

WILKINS, D. 1974, *Second Language Learning and Teaching*. London: Edward Arnold.

WILKINSON, A. 1975, *Language and Education*. London: Oxford University Press.

WILLIAMS, C. (ed.) 1988, *Language in Geographic Context*. Philadelphia: Multilingual Matters.

WILLIG, A. & GREENBERG, H. (eds) 1986, *Bilingualism and Learning Disabilities*. New York: American Library Publishing.

WITTGENSTEIN, L. 1967, *Philosophical Investigations*. Oxford: Blackwell.

WOOD, D., MCMAHON, L. & CRANSTOUN, Y. 1980, *Working with Under Fives*. London: Grant McIntyre.

WONG FILLMORE, L. 1983, The language learner as an individual. In M. CLARKE & J. HANDSCOMBE (eds) *On TESOL 82: Pacific Perspectives on Language Learning and Teaching* (pp. 157–173). Washington D.C.: TESOL.

WRIGHT, C. 1987, The relations between teachers and Afro-Caribbean pupils: observing multiracial classrooms. In G. WEINER, & M. ARNOT (eds) *Gender Under Scrutiny* (pp. 173–186). London: Hutchinson.

WRIGHT, I. & LABAR, C. 1984, Multiculturalism and morality. In SHAPSON & D'OYLEY, *op. cit.*

YOUNG, M. (ed.) 1971, *Knowledge and Control: New Directions for the Sociology of Education*. London: Collier-MacMillan.

YOUNG, R.E. 1983, A school communication deficit hypothesis of educational disadvantage. *Australian Journal of Education* 27, 3–16.

— 1987, Critical theory and classroom talk. *Language and Education: An International Journal* 1, 125–134.

— 1989, *Critical Theory and School Communication*. Clevedon, Avon: Multilingual Matters.

YU, V. & ATKINSON, P. 1988, An investigation of the language difficulties experienced by Hong Kong secondary school students in English-medium schools. *Journal of Multilingual and Multicultural Development* 9, 267–84.

Index